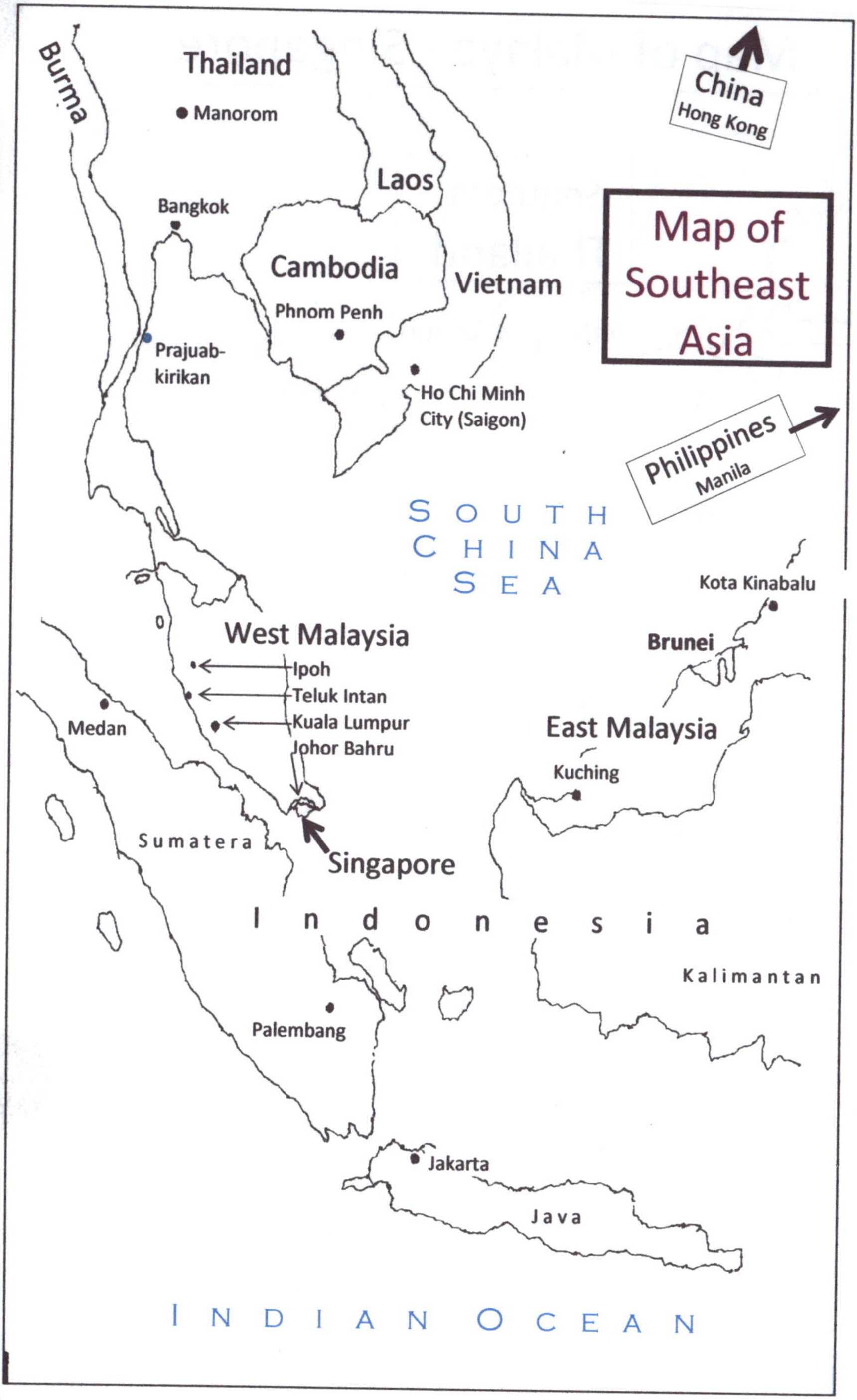
Map of Southeast Asia
Burma
Thailand
Manorom
Bangkok
Prajuab-kirikan
Laos
Cambodia
Phnom Penh
Vietnam
Ho Chi Minh City (Saigon)
China
Hong Kong
Philippines
Manila
SOUTH CHINA SEA
Kota Kinabalu
Brunei
West Malaysia
Ipoh
Teluk Intan
Kuala Lumpur
Johor Bahru
Medan
East Malaysia
Kuching
Sumatera
Singapore
Indonesia
Kalimantan
Palembang
Jakarta
Java
INDIAN OCEAN

David Huntley's book is a lively and personal account of Christian mission in Asia in the era after World War II. It paints a vivid and engaging picture of the backdrop to Christian activity in our contemporary world. David's experiences will also be a great encouragement to readers as to how God can use and develop our gifts right through our lives! I warmly commend it to the Christian community.

Dr Warren Beattie
OMF Singapore and Scotland

I shared a room with David at London Bible College in 1957-59. David is a delightful guy, friendly and helpful. Since our College days, we have met again several times around the world where the Lord has used him. He has been a great blessing to countless numbers of people. He has an elephant's memory of people and events. You will be fascinated and captivated by this readable book.

Revd Dr Alfred C H Yeo
Chairman, Scripture Union Council, Singapore

No Moss

NO MOSS

A Mission Journey Around the Globe

DAVID HUNTLEY

Copyright © 2012 by David Huntley

Published by Genesis Books
An imprint of ARMOUR Publishing Pte Ltd
Kent Ridge Post Office
P. O. Box 1193
Singapore 911107
Email   : sales@armourpublishing.com
              enquiries@armourpublishing.com
Website : www.armourpublishing.com

21   20   19   18   17   16   15   14   13   12
10   9   8   7   6   5   4   3   2   1

Printed in Singapore

ISBN 13:   978-981-4305-88-4
ISBN 10:   981-4305-88-X

National Library Board, Singapore Cataloguing-in-Publication Data

Huntley, David Anthony, 1932-
     No moss : a mission journey around the globe / David Huntley. –
Singapore : Armour Publishing, 2012.
     p. cm.
     ISBN : 978-981-4305-88-4 (pbk.)

     1. Missions. 2. Missionaries – Great Britain. I. Title.

BX9.5.M5
266.0092 -- dc23   OCN794135560

Contents

Preface

A rolling stone gathers no moss.
Ancient proverb

David, why don't you write a book?

During our overseas years many people have asked this question. When we joined the China Inland Mission – Ruth in Melbourne and me in London, the expectation was that we would serve in one particular Asian country for the rest of our working lives, even though we would move from town to town as churches were planted and taken on by nationals.

But the world was changing and Christian missions were adapting to the new situations. Firstly, many countries would no longer give visas to missionaries, or they terminated them after a few years. Secondly, completely new spheres of missionary service were opening up in, for example, communications, where no single geographical location contains the task. Then thirdly, emerging church leaders were requesting missionary help in such realms as training their own people, working among minorities, or just affording administrative assistance in an increasingly complex world.

A combination of these three has privileged us to serve full time in seven different Asian countries, plus two more – and once in Africa – in short terms after retirement.

During the 1980s and 1990s we were urged to sell OMF's books – then over 100 titles – as we travelled around speaking at meetings in the UK, North America and Australasia; the wide range of books sold fast if properly promoted. Thus we realised the value and impact of the printed volume.

I would like to thank the many friends who have encouraged me, and also specially appreciate Ruth's putting up with my sitting glued to the computer for hours – and then her reading the text. Mrs Marven

Harkness has been the 'second pair of eyes' and has motivated a large number of useful changes and improvements to my manuscript. Others like Mr Chua Hong Koon, Fern Chua and Christina Lim at Armour Publishing have warmly encouraged me from my first encounter with them.

Ruth and I hope that this volume will bear witness to God's leadings and provision from small beginnings in the faith, leading across the seas to service, and to our marriage, our family and beyond.

In the many tasks entrusted to us, to be where God wants us to be and to do what he wants us to do has sometimes been puzzling but always the most satisfying!

David Huntley
2012

Early Adventures

Like most children, I have few memories of my earliest years. I can recall my mother rocking me to sleep in our modest end-of-terrace house, 36 Ashley Road, in Thornton Heath, South of London. My parents had met while vacationing at Rye in Sussex. My father Horace Frederick Huntley was a mechanical engineer, son of Horace Alfred Huntley, a hotelier, and Eliza Louisa née Cates, and they ran a hotel near Richmond Park. Before my arrival my mother, Phyllis Mary Williams, worked in a department store in west London.

Horace Alfred and Eliza were not astute businesspersons. In their early married years most of their patrimony was used up on extensive tours in Europe, bringing back numerous Alpine oil paintings to decorate their home. But after a couple of disastrous property deals, compounded by dishonest hotel staff, he took his Eliza – he called her 'Liley' – to live in the Licensed Victuallers' Benevolent Institution (LVBI) in Peckham. He had earlier purchased an apprenticeship for my father, with Vickers, an engineering conglomerate, in their shipyard in northeast England. Apprentices were supposed to be trained

Horace Alfred and Eliza.

to become what would be considered today as a 'qualified engineer'; meanwhile they received a derisory 'pocket money' salary. But my father ran a motor bike and got to love the nearby English Lake District. Moreover he did attain membership of the Institution of Mechanical Engineers, and could put A.M.I.Mech.E after his name, which was well on the way to degree – and indeed is still preferred by many employers today.

My parents often took me in our Lea Francis touring car to meet Horace Alfred and Eliza at LVBI, a large garden-estate with self-contained one-up, one-down terrace houses arranged around flower beds, immaculate gravel roads, spacious lawns, bowling greens and a sizeable chapel. There were no bathrooms, nor any electricity so all lighting and cooking was done with gas, and residents needed battery radios which required a rechargeable 'accumulator' to light the valves and also a large dry battery. My father built single-valve headphone receivers for his parents so as to reduce the cost of batteries. The only telephone on the estate appeared to be in the Matron's apartment.

My Grandfather had been the 'Master' of the LVBI – which had a strong flavour of Freemasonry; so he and Eliza occupied a privileged, rather larger unit, No. 79. But as age progressed they retired from those responsibilities and moved to an ordinary unit, No. 6. As I grew older, I made evening visits to them after school, travelling alone by train and tram. They in turn took me out to such places as Greenwich Park to see the enormous flowers.

My grandparents belonged to a quasi-Christian sect called the Muggletonians, which appears in the Oxford Dictionary of Religion. They followed the teaching of Messrs Reeve and Muggleton who embodied a mixture of biblical strictness combined with a dismissiveness toward some of the biblical books. They did not believe in any form of evangelism – that was for St Paul to do, not for his successors. They did not even tell their children about their faith unless they actually asked. Only much later did my second cousin Vera tell me a little more about the Muggletonians; as an ageing spinster she evidently practiced the faith alone, together with a more distant family named Noakes whom I never met.

Horace Alfred passed away during World War II while I was evacuated, but Eliza lived on until the war was almost over. She passed away just before the horrors of the German extermination camps hit the newspapers; my kindly Grandma would have found that unbearably distressing. Wartime blackout of the LVBI units was no problem – each window had a lift-up sill to access weight-balanced shutters which slid up to completely close-off the window. Some of the older people feared that if they did not close the shutters, German pilots could see them through the windows!

Both Horace and Eliza are buried in Honor Oak Cemetery. I have visited it recently and am registered as a 'contact' for the grave. There is no stone, so the space will probably be re-used as it has already been 67 years since Eliza was buried.

After World War II, LVBI moved to an out-of-town setting and the Peckham property became an older peoples' home, named Caroline Gardens. The estate is now much as it was; the units are modernised, but nowadays the gardens are neglected. Anyone is still free to stroll around; I knocked at the door of No. 6, but the present incumbent spoke no English.

My mother grew up in Pontypridd, South Wales where her father was Senior Goods Agent of the lucrative Taff Vale Railway; lucrative because its main business was hauling coal downhill from the mines to Cardiff docks, needing very little motive power, and the same locomotives could haul the empty trucks back up to the mines.

Once married, my parents had embarked on the adventure of a mortgage to buy the house before it was built; thus my first memories of home were there in Thornton Heath – part of the Borough of Croydon.

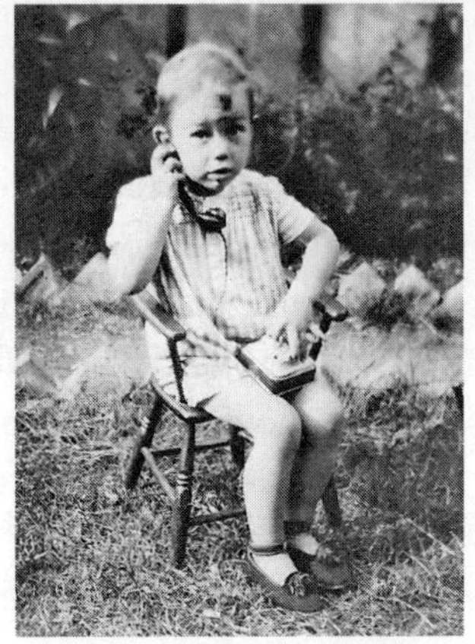

Age three – with toy phone in our garden at Thornton Heath.

Rather more vivid are my recollections of the illuminations for the 1937 Coronation of King George VI: lit-up plastic ducks floated on Thornton Heath Pond[1] while neon owls perched on trees in nearby Grange Wood Park. Croydon's seven-mile section of the London to Brighton main road was lined both sides with fairy-lights strung from lamp posts.

In fact the Coronation celebrated not only the accession of King George VI, but also Britain's emergence from the economic recession suffered by most of the industrialised world in the later 1920s and early 30s.

---

1   As part of traffic improvements the pond was replaced by a small ornamental pool, now removed due to vandalism.

The 1930s saw a huge housing boom in Britain. Our home was among the fruit of the boom – there was even a garage where my father kept our Lea Francis open-top four-door touring car. (As far as I can make out, since World War II, not a single four-door open-top tourer has been produced.)

My schooling was a somewhat 'mixed grill'. First came Brendon House School in Thornton Heath, 1005 London Road. Brendon House belonged to a Miss Isobel Jones who held no degree, and lived by running a typical latter-day 'dame's school'. For a modest fee she, and one or two assistants, 'started' small children with the 'Three R's'[2] and general knowledge, incidentally putting them far, far ahead of the state system. By the age of six we were well able to read, write, and do simple sums.

The road outside the school was an education in itself. All day passed a parade of red double-deck trams and buses as well as cars, vintage and modern, and horse-drawn vehicles of all types. The last remaining traction engines (coal-fired steam lorries) puffed past, with their glowing fire clearly visible in their nether regions. (The Town Hall decided to test out its first push-button pedestrian crossing on the busy main road outside our school.)

By that time I had experienced a few railway journeys, and our local trains were electric, lacking the puffing steam locomotives so common on our visits to Wales. I asked our teacher if these electric trains could run on the tram tracks. She did not think they could[3]! To give us a well-rounded education beyond the Three R's, Miss Jones organised excursions to London Zoo and to Kew Gardens, and even introduced us to a basic form of junior cricket.

Miss Jones lived in one room of her simple terrace house, the rest of the interior was adapted into classrooms, and she had most of the garden cemented over as a playground and sand-pit. Her great gift was imparting knowledge, so that by age seven I was ferociously devouring books from the Public Library. Sadly, modern bureaucracy has strangled such basic but excellent schools out of existence.

---

2   Three R's entered English slang from a story about a boy who, when questioned at home, told his parents that he had 'done the Three R's – reading 'riting and 'rithmetic...'

3   They can't – needing, of course, platforms and live power rails.

Brendon House School in Thornton Heath, Croydon. I am the tie-less little fellow fourth in the front (seated row). The Chinese children in the left of the same row were in the UK with a circus troupe. Miss Jones (centre) was the owner and principal of the school.

My friend at Brendon House was a fellow six-year-old, Ralph Smith, who sat next to me. One day when I was – in my parents' imagination – riding my tricycle around our block, I decided that I would 'go and see Ralph'. I asked grown-ups to see me across two busy roads – and they kindly obliged! I was well received at the Smith household, played with Ralph for a little and then started home. It was not a long excursion, but no doubt helped me to get confidence in the life skill of finding my own way round. As I write, a newspaper reports a three-year-old finding his own way out of his house in the small hours of the morning to a supermarket where he knew sweets were available. It was closed, but a van driver spotted him and took him to the police, who had difficulty in waking up his parents when the child conducted them to his home! This illustrates that small children can easily place themselves in danger. We should not underestimate their ability to remember routes and places – and then to set out along them!

Our annual family vacations were taken at Studland Bay, in Dorset. A wide sandy sweep with clear water was ideal for a small boy to paddle, or be rowed by his parents across the bay. Small motor ferries ran to Poole and Sandbanks, where one day my parents took me into an amusement arcade and gave me a penny to try a simple machine. The penny was placed on a sprung shelf, and when released the penny shot across to a 'prize' (or more likely onto nothing). However, my sole attempt won a packet of cigarettes which no doubt my parents enjoyed!

I recall three summers at Studland Bay – now crowded because it is so accessible by motorway – and also one white Christmas, very rare in the south. My father decided the roads were too icy to take the long (by UK standards) 120-mile drive in our unheated Lea Francis Tourer; thus we went by train, arriving in the dark. I can recall my father pointing out the three illuminated funnels of the RMS *Queen Mary* as we passed Southampton. His Christmas present to me was a couple of batteries, some wire and some small bulbs to learn how electric circuits were made. (Decades later, I built a similar assemblage for my son Andrew.)

When my parents moved to a larger house in South Croydon, they placed me pro-tem in the Howard School, a state-system primary institution, and there the excellence of Miss Jones' school was thrown into sharp relief. I was far ahead of my age group in a class of over 40 kids, and was soon moved to the next class up. Only the 'tinies' were brought and collected by their parents; those of us aged six or above were considered big enough to walk alone, or even to take a bus.

At the Junior Public Library I met Thornton W. Burgess, the author of nature tales in a Canadian setting, and had soon read though all of his prolific output. When I was seven, my mother worked out a way for me to go alone to the public library by bus without crossing the main road – except at one point where there was a policeman directing traffic and ensuring that pedestrians got a safe crossing.

Sometimes my mother arranged with mothers of other children she knew to all visit London together. So at a young age I knew about the Changing of the Guard, the Crown Jewels, Tower Bridge, ascending St Paul's Cathedral, the Opening of Parliament by the King, and – most exciting of all – the Science Museum. One of my most vivid memories of the exhibits was attempting to pass between two pillars a few feet apart; an invisible light-beam crossed the space, which when broken sounded an alarm and lit a 'Burglar' sign!

Yet another visit was to see a fireman's exercise at Lambeth Fire Station. Various equipment was demonstrated including setting alight a large metal tray of petrol and oil – and quenching it with foam. One doubts if Health and Safety rules would allow the public so close to such demonstrations today.

All these various trips and visits were a part of my education which nothing in formal schooling could replace. In fact, travel and moving around were to become a major part of my life, and it started sooner than I could have expected.

Going Away

Like many children of that era I had my tonsils out, and then my adenoids; no one knew quite why, but the doctor advised it because I was occasionally asthmatic. I remained a tall, but somewhat thin and pale-faced child. The surgery didn't seem to bring much – if any – improvement but my parents arranged for me to convalesce after the two operations – in a properly organised way.

A week or two later my parents took this barely seven-year-old to London's Victoria Station where several other kids around my age gathered, all with suitcases labelled to the Alfred Yarrow Children's Convalescent Home at Broadstairs. I was assured Broadstairs was a lovely place near the sea where I would enjoy everything and quickly recover – though I was not quite sure *what* I was supposed to be recovering from and I felt I was quite energetic anyway!

Sir Alfred Yarrow[1] was a self-made, no-nonsense shipbuilding magnate and the Convalescent Home was planned in the 1890s. He had visited other convalescent homes, most of which seemed to him to be overcrowded and airless – more likely to spread sickness than to cure it! He resolved to build the best, and if possible a perfect home – and to endow it. After extensive searching he found an ideal piece of property, on high ground overlooking the sea at Broadstairs, Kent, the most easterly part of Britain and noted for bracing breezes and – by British standards – clear skies. The Victorians laid great store on the curative properties of fresh sea air and sunshine. Thus the Broadstairs convalescent home became another of Yarrow's several charities. Most of them ministered

---

1   *Alfred Yarrow, His Life and Work* by Eleanor Barnes. A photo below depicts the four-to five-floor Convalescent Home from the spacious grounds at the rear. The Google summary omits the story of the Home's completion. Yarrow died the year that I was born – 1932. His shipbuilding company was bought by GEC and currently is part of British Aerospace Marine.

to the very poor, especially in industrial cities, but this one was pitched for parents 'of the better classes who were unable to pay the full cost of their children's convalescence.' In retrospect I can certainly recall that the home was pervaded by an overwhelmingly British middle-class ethic!

Pre-war trains were quite good and a lady from the Home conducted our juvenile party to a reserved coach, and we duly drew into Broadstairs station where a hired bus drove us to the Home. The children in residence were waving a welcome to us from the first floor corridor windows – I never recall being invited to take part in any later such welcome, nor can I recall the arrival of new inmates. Later we shall see the probable reason for this.

My bed was one of several on a long, covered, open-sided balcony overlooking the vast back garden. The balcony was really an extension of the 'Alfred Ward' through which we walked to the toilets – we were told to call them the 'lah'. During those summer evenings darkness came late, it seemed very early to go to bed, and before I dropped off to sleep, a nurse came along to slide closed the long glazed panels which closed-off the balcony. The building was vast and ornate – late Victorian in all its glory. A large central entrance hall with models of steamships (probably built by Alfred Yarrow) appeared to be the only carpeted and soft-furnished place, and parents were entertained there. Elsewhere floor-areas and bare corridors provided play space as well as wards for the children. There were nurses everywhere – the entire staff were in hospital-style dress. In the mornings we were free to explore and play in the huge garden, a wall enclosed the property and a small copse, so there was not much chance of getting lost. Beyond this, though not visible from the boys' quarters, were the cliffs and the sea.

There were few organised activities and one day seemed much like another; I cannot even recall Sundays being marked by a Sunday School or the like – virtually a Sunday fixture for institutional life in those days. I don't even recall saying grace before meals – the universal practice then in children's boarding establishments. Sometimes it rained and we stayed in the indoor play areas, and quite often we were taken on 'crocodile walks' around the cliff-top gardens, or even down to the beach. I barely recalled those seaside scenes of Broadstairs bay in the opening shots of the film *Chariots of Fire*, because we were usually taken down to a much narrower beach below the cliffs. I did not find any particular friend of my own.

Modern view of the former Yarrow Convalescent Home over the trees which have grown up in the grounds. The balcony where I initially slept is just visible (arrowed). The roof exemplifies the glory of a Victorian architect commissioned to embody 'all that is best' in the Home for 100 children. The right hand wing – mirror image of that on the left-is out of the view.

The Home was designed for 50 boys and 50 girls. Each end of the shallow-U shaped building was a mirror image of the other, divided in the centre by stairways so the boys were completely independent from the girls.

We washed our hands in the 'lah' and waited for meals seated on long benches in the broad bare corridor at the front of the house. This part of the corridor contained a bay window with a rocking horse and a piano. On one occasion the nurses entertained us with a rendering of *Doing the Lambeth Walk*!

In due time we were shepherded downstairs and allotted to cast-iron-framed tables for four. At one end of the hall the Matron doled out platefuls which the nurses served to us. The food was neither good nor bad, just good old English plain cooking. Courses were usually meat and two veg. Second helpings especially of the sweet course ('pudding') were offered to any who wanted more. With lunch over, I assumed there would be more outdoor freedom, but no. We were supposed to be convalescing and were sent back to the beds on the balcony; there we remained until evening meal was brought to us. Some of us were lucky enough to have a book or magazine or two to pass the time – otherwise we were supposed to be just in need of rest!

Daily the nurses appeared with a tray of medicines and dosed each child from a selection of bottles. Most us were given 'Angiers Emulsion', a sickly whitish syrup, then a well-known cure-all for sickening children.

Other potions were specific for sundry juvenile conditions. There was a large cupboard in the 'Day Room' (or 'play room') full of games and one day I caught my finger in its sliding door. I needed minor first aid from a nurse. It did not heal at first, but formed a nasty black scab. One of the nurses picked the scab off with a sewing needle and re-bandaged it, but it was still a long time before it healed.

The nurses were not particularly strict; we were told that if we misbehaved we would be put in a side-ward. (I thought they said a side-*board*.) This evidently meant an hour or two in a small room alone.

So I was filled with apprehension when one of the nurses told me – to the merriment of the other boys – that I was to be transferred to a side-ward. I could not think of anything I had done wrong but the kindly Matron led me up one floor to a small single-bed room with a washbasin and with a door onto an upper, open-air balcony. It was next door to the operating theatre, and was probably designed as a post-op recovery room.

"See," said the Matron, "this is a lovely little bedroom for you." Evidently they had decided that my asthma – more likely the pale face and poor stature – justified this 'privilege' or else my parents had been advised to ask for it. They forgot to bring my evening meal that day, till a kindly domestic staff member found out and contrived a fried egg on toast for me!

In one sense I felt even more imprisoned because although I was free to get out of bed, I was expected to sunbathe most of the day on a divan on the open balcony and clad only in a pair of brief shorts. My parents visited me once and brought me a painting set and toy field glasses. They wrote to me regularly and sent me stamped addressed envelopes to write to them and to Aunt Doily in Wales. One hesitates to think that children would have slept on the unheated semi-open balconies in winter, although evidently TB patients in some institutions did just that. One also gasps at the amount of coal-carrying that would have been necessary in winter to feed the 50 or so fireplaces.

The staff must have been very concerned at the world situation because it was the early summer of 1939, and Broadstairs is right opposite France. But we kids knew nothing of this; we did not see newspapers, nor did we grasp the serious overtones of 'Munich' though there was a 'radio relay' – a kind of wired radio system in the Day Room. But even before going away to Broadstairs my mother's lady-help had told me of the threats by one Herr Hitler in Germany which, she warned, could well lead to war.

Now it was becoming clear that 'something big' was up. Activities and beach walks were curtailed and the nurses improvised games and activities indoors. Workmen appeared everywhere, upper windows were blacked out with brown paper, and I was moved into a large ward again (the Eric Ward) with several other boys mostly a little older than me. I then regained freedom of access to the Day Room and gardens. Again we were told nothing, but in a day or two our suitcases were being packed by the nurses and we all had address cards strung round our necks inside our shirts. We were told that if we got lost we were to show our card to someone! Would we give that instruction to a child today?

It was clear that the Convalescent Home was being emptied, and the blacking out of the windows probably indicated the arrival of an advance party for a military take-over. Apparently, some months beforehand a preliminary warning had been issued by the government, stating explicitly that if the political situation demanded requisitioning, the children would have to leave. In fact there proved to be over two months' grace before war was actually declared.

I cannot recall any more children arriving during my stay there, nor were we asked to wave to any newcomers from the upstairs windows, as we had been so welcomed. Thus my cohort of children must have been the last to convalesce at Yarrow until after the war.

We were bussed to the station; our parents had been alerted by telegram to collect us from the train at Victoria. My few weeks' stay in Broadstairs was over. I imagine that a high proportion of the children, especially the boys, would have moved on to boarding school, for which life at Yarrow would have been excellent preparation.

Medically I doubt if I gained anything from my parents' expenditure (if any) on the Yarrow Home. As it was, living away from home at Yarrow proved to be a preparation for very different changes that neither I nor my parents could have foreseen!

Postscript

The Yarrow Home was indeed used for military purposes during the war, including some time as a hospital. It reverted to the Yarrow

Foundation afterwards, serving children's convalescence for a few more years. But by the late 1950s modern medication was found to be more effective than long (and expensive) seaside convalescence. With various clean air acts, the need to give sick children a country break from smog and pollution was less pressing.

The building passed to Thanet College but became 'listed' for its historic and architectural value, and a number of sizeable modern buildings have been added in the extensive grounds.

Ruth and I were welcomed by the College to visit the Yarrow building in the spring of 2009, and I was easily able to recognise the main areas where I had 'convalesced.' The balcony's wooden shutters were flaking and loose, but most of the building appears to be much as I knew it.

The College specialises in catering, hospitality and engineering, and as visitors we enjoyed lunch in the College Refectory on an upper floor with a sea view. The hairdressing workshop occupies the former boys' Day Room. The dining hall is now the College gymnasium, and the 'Central Hall', minus the model ships is now a welcoming reception desk for visitors, enquirers and prospective students.

At present it seems that since the Yarrow Building is located in a prime residential area, a property developer will convert it into high-class flats, some with a sea view. It is good that the building will be preserved, but sad that it cannot continue as a home for some educational or humanitarian institution.

War!

Change was in the air – World War II was imminent and everyone now knew it. It was anticipated that bombing, and even invasion would occur *immediately* on declaration. So in August 1939 the government advised all families who could do so, to leave London and other large cities and move at least to the outer suburbs or to the countryside beyond[1]. Mr Tudor Jackson was a partner in the firm my father worked for, and offered to take my mother and me into their household near Beaconsfield, Buckinghamshire. One weekend when he had home leave, we all helped the son of the house to polish his brasses; even under war conditions the army wasted valuable man-hours on polishing shoes and leather, not to mention blanco-ing webbing equipment.

The Jackson household enjoyed an acre of garden, and woodland surrounded the property. This was really my first introduction to the delights of wandering in the country. While Mr Jackson was not a particularly welcoming host, Mrs Jackson was motherly and kind. She often took me to nearby Sandels Wood when she exercised her dogs. Sometimes she took me hiking or blackberrying. She was an excellent cook and occasionally made my favourite jam sponge in custard. My father remained in Croydon, and like Mr Jackson, commuted daily to the office in London.

My mother and I were at Beaconsfield just before war actually started. On the eve of declaration, the ladies were all busy sewing black-out curtains, but the evenings were still quite long. On the first night of blackout we ate a salad evening meal at dusk under a dim, blue-coloured

---

1   I still read books and watch modern films of children being evacuated to the countryside. The biographical experience most similar to mine was that of Ray Evans in *Before the Last All-clear* (Lewes, Book Guild, 2005) though Ray had both better and much worse experiences than mine. *Growing Up in a War* by Bryan Magee also resonates well.

'blackout bulb.' The next morning I woke to the sound of what sounded like a car engine starting up and then slowing down – it was our first rising-falling-rising-falling air-raid warning siren. Fortunately it was a false alarm.

School at Beaconsfield was a lot better than in Croydon. My mother enrolled me in another 'dame's school' of the same type as Miss Jones'. Miss LePla and Miss Wills presided over our education and we picked up quite a bit of general knowledge and penmanship. In those days, we used steel nibs dipped into inkwells, and Miss Wills provided a flower-shaped nib-wiper made of coloured flannel. It seemed to me far too beautiful a thing to use for such a purpose! My principal memory of her lessons was how to distinguish *there* from *their*. At an age of barely seven, I found my way to school and back – about a mile – by bus. The bus stop was not far beyond the entrance to our house and I had been told to ask the driver to drop me off right at the house. His jocular response was "I'll put you to bed if you like!" I didn't ask again but just walked back from the proper stop.

It became clear by the late autumn that Hitler was still a long way off – on the far side of France, in fact. Not a single air raid had occurred; many things were much as they were in peacetime. Nevertheless all the signs of preparation were there: conscription, black-out, deep-shaded street lamps and car headlights, barrage balloons, air raid shelter signs and ration-books; the military were everywhere. Meanwhile Hitler bided his time behind the German Siegfried Line of land defences and parallel to it, the French Maginot Line. A popular song of the time was:

We're going to hang out the washing on the Siegfried Line.
Have you any dirty washing Mother dear?

As Christmas drew close, and with no immediate threat from Germany, my parents returned to our own Croydon home. Crossing London, we found the sky full of barrage balloons and lights shaded, but otherwise it was the same busy, familiar city. Corned beef appeared on the menu – I thought it tasted good! The street lamps in Croydon were still operational, though only with a small shrouded bulb hung below each ornamental lamp.

Back in the Howard School, which was in disarray, we younger ones were squeezed into the side of a large classroom of older children, so we learnt very little indeed. I was in trouble for not calling Mr Maynard, the class-master 'sir' but I had never had a male teacher before. The only thing I can recall learning was the word *insectivorous* – a plant which eats insects! Being among older children I felt somewhat subject to mild bullying. I still made my own friends without difficulty, but fewer than before.

My mother started to correspond with her sister, my Aunt Doily, in South Wales about possible evacuation to the remote village of Pentyrch, tucked away in the mountains above the coal-mining valleys. It would probably have been safe enough from air raids, though the industrialised valleys were to receive occasional bombs from Hitler to remind the inhabitants that he *could* reach that far! Nowadays we find it hard to realise how dependent the country was on coal: it fired almost all electrical generation, all heavy industry, most railway locomotion and almost all home and office heating.

Correspondence on Pentyrch did not seem to reach any conclusion. But back in South Croydon we children realised that there was something much more serious afoot about the war, and for a day or two my mother did not want to miss a single BBC newscast. It was the fall of France and Benelux that challenged the sense of security in Britain. Ignoring the Maginot line German forces swept through Belgium, the Netherlands and Luxembourg and advanced into northern France. A huge contingent of British forces was caught behind the German advances leaving only the small port of Dunkirk available to them. Hitler's guns were within sight of the White Cliffs of Dover, so now the Nazis enjoyed freedom to bring U-boats through the English Channel.

After the famous evacuation of British forces from Dunkirk, all of Britain's southern and eastern beaches were mined, and the immediate hinterlands for a mile or two were restricted to authorised personnel. Apart from those zones anyone was free to go anywhere in the UK without paperwork. How different from the Continent where even in Germany, loyal citizens were subject to endless checks by the Gestapo, and needed papers to travel at all. Soon petrol became restricted and later ordinary motorists could get none at all.

The Germans were forbidden to listen to any radio broadcasts – under pain of death if they repeated anything they had heard outside the newscasts of the Hitler regime. On the other hand we were free to tune-in to any station, including German broadcasts by the traitorous William Joyce – better known as Lord Haw-Haw. None of us found Joyce very convincing. The Germans did not let him broadcast 'live' and a faint pre-echo of his words (from the early methods of recording) gave this away.

With the fall of France, evacuation of those still remaining in towns assumed an urgency not felt while the enemy was so far away. All the transport and complexities were managed by mail or messenger so that the complex, logistics-consuming operation would not be advertised to the enemy.

The first Government evacuation, on the outbreak of war in 1939, had been quite chaotic; some of the urban children were dumped in rural villages that had not been properly prepared for them. But this time (summer 1940) the operation went unexpectedly smoothly.

It was 7.30 am on 6 June 1940. I was almost eight years old. We assembled at Howard School alongside red double-deck buses which were to take us to West Croydon railway station. I recall seeing – between the coaches of another train – my mother's white-dotted blue dress. Against official advice, my parents were standing on the opposite platform trying to see us off. It was policy also not to be told about our destination lest it generate a rush of parents to their children's foster homes; that could further overload the railways which were increasingly occupied with war traffic. Each of us carried a small bag or rucksack, our gas-mask, and a packed lunch or some fruit. To minimise toilet problems, no child was to bring drink.

A few minutes' local train ride from West Croydon[2] took us to Wimbledon Station where we were allotted seats for the long journey ahead. We sped along the former Southern Railway main line to Devon at high speed. It was a sweltering hot day, and at the few stops we hung out of the window calling for water to drink. Nothing was provided but at Salisbury a kindly refreshment trolley attendant used a single cup to give several of us a mouthful of water!

---

2   This route is now part of a light-rail system called 'Tramlink.'

The lady supervising our part of the train told us that no, we were not going to another country but to a place 'far far away from any war.' Perhaps she also had not been told where the train was heading. Even at that age I knew enough of geography to realise that unless a sea voyage was involved, we would still be on the same island that Hitler was threatening to take over! Towards the afternoon, Mr Maynard, the teacher whom I had failed to address as 'sir', came down the train revealing that we would arrive at Ilfracombe at a certain time. That was the first time I had ever heard the name 'Ilfracombe' – our 'secret' destination – and I had no idea where it was. The train slowed down and as we pulled into a station I heard some the children call out '*Barn ... Staple*', the principal town of North Devon, but our group stayed on board. I was bemused to read at rural passing-points *Stop, Look and Listen Before Crossing the Line*. Until then I had experienced only busy lines where *Passengers Must **Not** Cross The Line* was the rule.

It was late afternoon before our 'evacuee express' drew into Ilfracombe station and we were bussed to a large concert theatre, given a cup of tea and a slab of fruit cake, then volunteer ladies took us literally one by one from the seating rows to the families who were to foster us. We were assigned to billets rather than having prospective foster-parents looking us over to make *their* choice! Other stories from the earlier evacuation seem to have depicted total chaos in which the children were the main sufferers.

Not all families welcomed the children, but most made an initial effort. They couldn't really refuse those in need, but there were some strains over the interference in family life, and also cultural differences between city and small-town ways. The elderly lady who conducted me to my billet was a Miss Evelyn Griffiths, and the first thing she pointed out to me was the seaside and promenade close to the theatre. I was delighted that I had been brought to a seaside town!

After the busy streets in Croydon I was taken aback when she crossed Ilfracombe's main shopping street with hardly a glance to see that it was clear of traffic! In fact there was almost no traffic at all at *any* time of day. Miss Griffiths took a kindly interest in me for the whole of my stay in Ilfracombe and often invited me together with my friend Ronnie to her home. It turned out much later that she was a friend of a friend of my maternal grandfather.

I was billeted with a milkman and his wife, Mr and Mrs Tom Filer and their two children, at 10 Balmoral Terrace in St Brannock's Park Road. The family ran a one-man business; he delivered the milk in billy cans, and if it needed pasteurising, he warmed it in a large pan on the kitchen stove. Mr Filer ran a small van which, since a little petrol was still available for personal use, took us all to the beach at week-ends.

I spent my first day alone exploring Ilfracombe. Since Miss Griffiths had pointed out to me where the beach was on our initial walk, I knew which way to head in order to start exploring the harbour and many coves.

By the next day, school for Croydon children had been organised at the Wesleyan Methodist Church[3], adjacent to the theatre where we had been fed on arrival. Bearing in mind the shortages, we continued to learn passably well and I found lots to read. Outside school hours I enjoyed the freedom of roaming round the countryside and exploring the many little beaches tucked between headlands and mini-mountains. None of my five successive foster-parents seemed to think this was dangerous for a lone eight-year-old! Indeed it was quite liberating and it reinforced a life-skill – how to find my own bearings quickly around a strange place.

In fact this freedom of movement during wartime was remarkable considering the rigorous and suspicious security which overshadowed the enemy territories. Everyone in the UK was issued with identity cards, but only adults were supposed to be able to produce them at all times. The card numbers were quite easy to remember, and my number (which is still my National Health Service number) was CLKD/251/3. 'C' was for Croydon, LKD was for our area and street, and 251 was the number of the family, of which I was the third – hence '3'.

In 1941 all petrol rations for non-essential use were suspended, and most car owners who did not qualify for a petrol ration sold their vehicles at a heavy loss, or jacked them up till near the war's end.

Although posters at railway stations demanded of passengers *Is Your Journey Really Necessary?* there was nothing stopping anyone from buying a ticket to anywhere in the UK and travelling there without giving reasons. Only the areas along the eastern and southern coasts were restricted.

---

3   Now Emmanuel United Reformed Church.

The Filer household's weekend routine for children was Children's Matinee on Saturday mornings at the Scala Cinema, locally pronounced *Scayler*, and Sunday School on Sundays at the Parish Church, and occasionally we had a more church-like meeting. One I can recall was presented by the vicar about the conversion of St Paul. I thought he was giving his *own* testimony!

Two more evacuee children arrived in the Filer home, Ian Wheeler and his sister, and Mrs Filer soon made it clear we were all there on sufferance: "The London mothers they'm quite capable of looking after their own children!" My eighth birthday arrived, and my maternal grandfather in Wales arranged for me to receive a birthday cake from Ilfracombe's premier bakery, Southcombe's. I think I must have shared some of it with the family, but the rest sat in my bedroom. Sometimes I slipped up to taste a slice or just to read my few books. Mrs Filer felt strongly that bedrooms were for night-time, and were not to be visited during the day!

Naturally I did not understand her problems in overcrowding her home. But news came later in the summer that my parents would make their first visit, and that I was to meet them at Ilfracombe station off the night train from Waterloo. This was no luxury train, just ordinary seats where passengers could hire a clean pillow for one shilling. It was during my parents' first visit that they sensed the Filer household was understandably less than welcoming and somewhat overcrowded.

My maternal grandfather, Arthur Williams later visited me in Ilfracombe. Long retired, he had been Senior Goods Agent of the Taff Vale Railway (from an oil painting by one of his friends).

Shortly before the end of their visit, my parents spent a long morning at the Evacuation Office and a couple of weeks later I was moved to the hospitality of two older ladies, the Misses Hussell at No. 4 Cross Park. They took me on with two other Croydon boys, Michael and John – John was the first Roman Catholic that I was to meet. They were interesting ladies and kindly, and appeared to know everyone in Ilfracombe and their exact address! It was a very self-contained town, being at the extreme end of both the railway and the roads, and not en route to anywhere else. But soon the Hussell ladies decided they couldn't cope with my recurring asthma. (Others seemed to notice my asthma more than I did.) One day I was sent to a clinic near school. The clinic people suggested I should go to a 'home' at Torrington, also in North Devon, where evidently they specialised in medicating asthmatic kids. With memories of the Alfred Yarrow home at Broadstairs I wrote to my parents saying I did not want to go. Couldn't I stay here in Ilfracombe, or failing that come home? They managed to dissuade the clinic people from the Torrington idea. But to relieve the Misses Hussell, the billeting officer found me yet another place – which was to be my home for most of my stay.

Some friends of the Misses Hussell escorted me uphill from Cross Park to my new billet. On Montpelier Terrace stretched a Victorian row of spacious five-storey townhouses enjoying a view to the Bristol Channel. On the iron balcony of No. 18 were the words *Full Gospel Assembly*. No one seemed to know what that meant, except that 'Gospel' sounded like something from church.

My new foster-parents were Pastor Eddie Wright, an American, and his English wife – together with about a dozen other evacuee children around my own age. We called the Wrights 'Uncle' and 'Nanny'; and Mrs Wright welcomed me warmly and took me up to a small bedroom on the top floor. I was quite tearful because she was dressed in a blue and white 'deaconess' uniform somewhat like a nurse, and I was afraid that I would be back again in the restricted regime of the Alfred Yarrow home. 'Uncle' wore a clerical collar on Sundays and formal occasions.

Since I already knew my way around Ilfracombe, the Wrights had no objection to my continuing to explore the place alone. Until the Autumn 1940 term proper was due to start, the Wrights organised daily picnics to explore some of the hills and beaches. (They did not want us to play on the town's main bathing beach by the crowded Promenade as they suspected that scarlet fever could be contracted there.) The Wrights were childless but had the vision to rent this large airy terrace house with four floors and a spacious basement. One objective was to receive evacuee children and the other was to start a Full Gospel Assembly church.

Our large 'day room', which doubled as the Gospel Assembly room, was lined with large Bible texts painted onto white bed sheets. From there it was fascinating to watch the ships pass by, and it could not have been a better place for an enemy spy to sit and assess naval movements!

Down on the promenade, notwithstanding the war, the holiday season had continued. But as the autumn set in, there was the usual closing-down of an English seaside resort, plus the additional austerities of rationing and blackout. Ice cream and Devonshire cream were rated 'luxury foods' and banned from sale 'for the duration of hostilities.' Few homes had a refrigerator, but those that had them could home-make ice-cream — if they could get the ingredients.

The Wrights fitted out the vast house with camp beds, plus bedside cabinets made from curtained orange crates. The first German bombs fell over southeast England in July as summer faded into autumn; and as the winter drew nigh the German blitz started to shatter eastern London. More waves of children arrived at the Wrights, some quite well dressed, but a few wore just the louse-ridden clothes in which they stood; slums and abject poverty were very much an East London reality in those days. London's densely peopled and industrialised East End was heavily bombed while gentlemen remained comfortably dining in their clubs in the West End! The evacuation officers asked the Wrights to cram more children into the house short term — some were sleeping on the floor, and at one point some 35 children shared a single bathroom-toilet! Gradually a few were moved to other homes, and others were taken back to London by their parents until numbers stabilised at around 20.

The Wrights occupied a bedroom two floors above their downstairs sitting room, and decided to link the two with a battery-operated toy telephone. An older boy, John Warren, and I helped Mr Wright to drill holes in the floor and ceiling to link the two by wire — passing neatly behind one of the huge painted Bible texts! Few homes boasted a proper telephone, nor did I know anyone in Ilfracombe who had one. Indeed some politicians felt that it was not in the national interest for so many people to be able to talk to each other! No doubt Mr Wright, as an American sensed the lack of telephony and to him it came more naturally to make use of it.

As the household grew the Wrights took on a lady helper who arrived with her baby; her husband was serving in the forces. She needed a very early wake-up call to get breakfast ready for the children and one night

Mr Wright drafted me to help wire-up a further piece of communication – a bell in her room with the bell-push in the Wrights' room. The Wrights had the sole alarm clock in the house.

Fleas started to become a problem. The boys' hair was simply attacked with a toothcomb, but Mrs Wright doused the girls' head with kerosene and wrapped their hair in strips of torn-up sheets for the night. The next day many of them exhibited yellow blisters from the oil. Impetigo and foot-rot attacked many of the boys, no doubt as a result of overcrowding and limited bathing.

We children knew little about the war but as autumn turned into winter, we gathered from grown-ups that news was generally grim. Air raid sirens sounded frequently in Ilfracombe, but no bombs fell there. German bombers did roar overhead en route to attack industrialised areas across the Bristol Channel in Wales, just visible in clear weather. One day German raiders bombed Swansea, and from a prominent rock on the beach we could see smoke from the bombs mushrooming above the town.

Rationing kept catering frugal, though quite adequate. Lunches were padded out with turnips and swedes, the evening meal consisted largely of bread and butter, plus one half-slice per child with jam, and breakfast was almost always porridge. I could just about manage porridge as a little tightly-rationed sugar was sprinkled over it, but to many children it was unknown and unwelcome. I remember one young lad, Jimmy; as someone tried to help him by spooning porridge into his mouth, it just poured out again onto the plate! I received an occasional three-penny piece (three old pence = just over one current penny) from my parents which I could spread over six days. The Wrights did not approve of cinema entertainment even at one's own expense, so there were no more children's matinees.

Usually catering in large numbers enables a hostess to cook *more* interesting meals than would be the case with a small family. However, the Wrights did not seem to manage this, even though the government paid them a weekly allowance for each child in their care.[4] Undoubtedly rationing was part of the story, and possibly their own sense of frugality had something to do with it. I do not believe they could have been personally making a profit.

There was also the enormous physical task of feeding a couple of dozen mouths three times a day. Furthermore, being wartime, some items

---

4   Each child received the equivalent of 43 pence today, which should have been adequate.

like cheese, meat, fats and eggs were rationed even more rigorously in the winter. I do not recall the Wrights ever serving cheese, ham or cake.

One welcome attraction as winter drew in, was the visit to Ilfracombe of the self-styled Koko, The World Famous Clown. We watched breathlessly as he balanced a bottle on his upturned face, top downwards just below the nose. Reaching behind him to an assistant he lifted a sheet of glass onto the bottle, then two egg-cups at opposite corners, then two more, then another sheet of glass − more egg-cups and more glass then a vase of flowers! I cannot remember the conjuring tricks, but it filled an afternoon much more pleasantly than school's usual routines.

I was in the junior class under Miss Wilson, who was quite a good imparter of knowledge. She taught us all the usual subjects, in a school largely devoid of unruliness, and there was a daily 'assembly' when we sang a hymn or seasonal song, and a wide selection of English traditional folk songs. We sang *A-Rovin'*, *This Old Man*, *Strawberry Hill*, *B-i-n-g-o* etc, as well as the more martial *British Grenadiers*. As Christmas neared we learnt most of the usual carols. We also made slow progress with English and arithmetic and surprisingly, wartime frugality had yet to limit our supply of textbooks. There was a school library, and I received several books as gifts from my parents and relations. Since I was already quite an able reader I enjoyed these and picked up a lot of 'general knowledge' − not a subject widely taught in those days.

We observed that Miss Wilson and the Head, Mr Willoughby, were very friendly out of school; one could meet them wandering around the beaches in the evenings! Whether or not they eventually got married I have no idea.

From the other children I picked up some of the wartime songs − Miss Griffiths said that they were actually World War I pops. Some can still be heard today, usually to a light dance rhythm, on radio stations that play golden oldies. Among them were *Roll Out the Barrel* and *Rolling Home* with its opening line 'I've got sixpence, a jolly jolly sixpence...' Many more came across from America, especially in films.

Like many local people, Pastor Wright used to invite locally billeted soldiers to join them for a meal, and sometimes to help in his Sunday School. Miss Griffiths told me that those invited by the Wrights were all *conshies* (conscientious objectors). These men had to serve in the military's Non-Combatant Corps, mostly doing dirty jobs such as digging or peeling potatoes, and they were often openly despised or treated in a demeaning manner. On the way home I often passed an empty shop-front which had been chicken-wired over, and inside sat a couple of non-combatant soldiers disconsolately peeling potatoes by hand. Miss Griffiths volunteered to help in a forces canteen and commented that though the volunteers served the conshies the same food as other soldiers, they avoided pleasantries and minimised conversation with them.

I shall always be grateful to the Wrights; 'Uncle' taught me a lot of general knowledge and he was an interesting person for a growing boy to interact with, also a lot younger than my father. I found his vivid descriptions of leprosy (an incurable disease then) a bit frightening but otherwise I was very comfortable there. Above all the Wrights explained to me the simple Gospel of Jesus Christ for the first time in my young life. I understood some, but probably not all that they told me.

The Wrights ran a Sunday morning Sunday School for the children, where we learnt hymns from *Alexander's Hymnal* – costing only three (old) pence. We were encouraged to buy a copy. Both Alexander and Moody, visiting American evangelists, made good use of traditional hymns, but added many more with rollicking tunes. These hymnals gained great popularity in Britain's free churches, though many of the Anglican clergy looked down their noses at them!

Back at our temporary school, Miss Wilson decided that we should have a class newspaper – or rather a wall-sheet consisting of each child's item. (Copying machines were at least three decades in the future.) Anyone could write on any subject they liked. Fresh from the introduction to Christ that the Wrights had given me, I decided to write out some of the Bible texts that the Wrights had emblazoned around their home. My efforts were passed by Miss Wilson at first, but my second attempt was crossed right through, and I was firmly told to think of something else! (She did not think texts were news material, though at that time many newspapers *did* print a 'Daily Text' from the Bible.)

My sole evacuated Christmas (still in 1940) fell during my time at the Wrights, but I was confined to bed with measles – isolated in a single room, and largely unaware of the terrible bombing in major cities. Time passed slowly in the sick room, especially as we had no black-out on the windows, so my room became dark around 5.30 pm[5]. My presents from home included lots of reading material, a small electric motor and a battery, plus a perpetual calendar that looked like a radio set. I was indeed fortunate to have enjoyed the early years in the private primary school with its stress on reading. My books – plus some from the evacuees' school library – kept me from the worst of boredom.

Most of my time at the Wrights, I shared an attic bedroom room with my friend Ronnie Firmin, his younger brother Albie, and John Pitts who was two years our senior. The Firmin family had been bombed out of their Peckham, London home. John and his younger brother Frank were Londoners too and seemed to have a much broader background than others. They were well-dressed and had good vocabularies, plus a measure of social polish. As more recent arrivals, they attended another evacuee school in the Baptist Mission Hall[6] presided over by a Mr Price who John obviously admired for his sense of humour combined with strict discipline. One day it seems Mr Price called John forward and gave him 'six of the best' with his cane for 'playing up' – though that was untypical of John. Evidently the punishment was not too severe, and John's admiration for him remained undiminished. At times I wished I could have been in a class where the boys admired their male teachers – Croydonian junior school kids were taught entirely by ladies.

(One day strolling in South London, I remembered John's London address as I passed it. I rang the bell without response, and anyway it would be remarkable if the same family still occupied the house, after so many decades. In adult life I have never met anyone else whom I knew in Ilfracombe.)

In the early summer of 1941, the happy time at the Wrights drew to a close in a way I have never fathomed nor understood. One day the two of us from the Wrights who were schooling at the Wesleyan Hall were called singly out of class. The headmaster, a lady teacher and a policeman were standing in the entrance lobby and I was quizzed about life at the Wright's home. How many of us were there? Around 20 at that point. How many girls? About half. How many bathrooms? Only one. Who bathed us small

---

5   During World War II 'summer time' for clocks – GMT +1hour – continued through the winter, otherwise the room would have been dark before 4.30 pm. During the summer months our clocks were advanced *two* hours from Greenwich, giving us 'double summer time'.

6   Later Ilfracombe Evangelical Free Church.

kids? Uncle or Nanny? Did we ever see anything rude? No. It seemed that many of the other boys and girls living at the Wrights, but attending other schools, had a similar interview that day.

A day or so later all the children excepting the three who had been there longest – myself and two Croydon sisters named Budd – were re-billeted around town. Nevertheless for several Sundays afterwards many of them returned to the Wrights for Sunday School.

We three kids remained on with the Wrights for another couple of months, and the menu improved enormously! We even took a day's shopping excursion by train to Barnstaple, the market town a few miles away. But it seems the Wrights had decided that fostering evacuees was not to be their main occupation much longer. An evacuation official appeared one day to ask Pastor Wright if he could accommodate any more children, and he explained that he had found the task 'too much'. Nothing was said about my leaving.

Then one afternoon during the late spring of 1941, I arrived back at the Wrights after school only to learn from Mrs Wright that I had been re-billeted to a house at 9 Brookfield Terrace, a lane off the main shopping street which I had already 'discovered' in my explorations; and that I should move that evening. Possibly the billeting officer had acted too precipitately to a hint from the Wrights that they were no longer able to accommodate evacuees.

What exactly had happened at the Wrights to cause us to be moved out in two stages? I have never found out. If the policeman had come across something serious, surely we would *all* have been moved as quickly as possible? But three of us who had been there the longest remained. Anything with the least smell of impropriety in those days would have brought the wrath of the law on the Wrights without delay, and that plainly didn't happen. Moreover in a small place like Ilfracombe where everyone knows everyone, had there been a whiff of scandal, no one would have let their foster-kids come back to Montpelier Terrace for Sunday activities, yet they did. My mother later told me that she thought some of the older girls – say aged 14 – felt that Pastor Wright had been improper with them, and that after they returned home their parents had complained. But if any such complaint had been found to have substance, then surely action would have been drastic and immediate! My guess is that the 14-year-old girls had imagined problems – as girls of that age often do when away from their mothers.

On the other hand it may have been that the billeting officer decided that 18 Montpelier Terrace had been overcrowded and in need of relief, but nothing worse. Moreover by that time, quite a few families had taken their children home – they were always free to do this if they paid their own fares, so the overcrowding problem was reduced but not eliminated. The last three of us remained until, evidently, the authorities decided they could free the Wrights from evacuee responsibility entirely.

As with my previous moves I packed all my personal effects into my backpack plus my school satchel on one shoulder and my gas mask on the other. This was the way these eight-year-olds were moved between billets. A taxi was too expensive and few people had working cars during the war.

For a couple of nights I shared a bed with Mr Isaacs, a local bricklayer and stonemason, and then was moved into a room with four girls! The lady of the house, Mrs Hortop, seemed unable to get breakfast in time for school, and I recall running lest I get some minor punishment for lateness. I always managed to get in just before the register was called. On the plus side, Mrs Hortop served us well-cooked, tasty food.

After some five days the billeting officer found yet another family to take me on. As London evacuees themselves, this family was more understanding of the situation. Mrs Towers at 9 Greenclose Road, had a son away in the army, and her three daughters lived with her, all of them working in a 'scheduled occupation' as required during the war. They chose to be bus conductresses as Ilfracombe had a large bus depot. One daughter was married with a husband away in the army. Their son Freddy was about my age and we got on well together.

Each afternoon the three daughters would come home exhausted and had to complete long forms to prove that the ticket numbers tallied with the cash they had taken. Each value of ticket was a different colour, and the tiny discs punched out of the tickets were retained in the machine. If reconciliation failed, they could be counted colour by colour. At the end of their paperwork, if everything balanced, they would sigh thankfully, unlock the punch and pour the discs into the cooking range fire! Meanwhile I continued to return to the Wrights for their weekly Sunday School and always felt welcome there, but the other ex-resident kids dropped off until I was the only one left. Indeed, my parents decided on a different direction for my future.

At first Mrs Towers seemed a cheerful and motherly type, and welcomed me to their home. Air raid sirens sounded frequently but Hitler did not waste his failing supply of bombs on rural market towns. The Towers soon started to ignore the warnings; enemy aircraft only overflew Ilfracombe en route to industrialised targets.

Yet at other times Mrs Towers seemed moody and much less motherly. As a young boy, I did not know how to cope with this situation. Probably the strain of the war which was not going well combined with the stress of her son away; at one point I overheard that he had infringed some regulation and been given a minor punishment. Mrs Towers then took on a job ironing clothes at a laundry, and this no-doubt added to the overall stress. The house belonged to a Miss Goss, who scolded me for using the upstairs toilet by day; she felt children should use the outside toilet off the garden.

For me, my parents took their 1941 summer holiday in Ilfracombe, and decided that after my having had five different billets, and the London blitz being over, they would bring me back to Croydon. Ronnie's school let him take time out to see us off at the station, and Miss Griffiths was there to say goodbye too. I never saw either of them again.

It seemed a very long journey – even in peacetime it was a six-hour trip. Having realised the modest size of England from my many maps, I could not grasp why range after range of hills passed our train without, it seemed, our getting much nearer to London Waterloo! Restaurant cars were still running so we enjoyed a salad lunch. And as the train got nearer and nearer to London it became more and more crowded, especially with soldiers.

I corresponded a few times with Miss Griffiths. Regarding the Wrights, my parents were not churchgoers, and I sensed that when they had arrived in Ilfracombe they did not want me to join the Wrights' Sunday School during their final visit. Nor, I felt, would they have warmed to any corresponding with them afterwards on my part. I suppose the Wrights must have prayed for me – and for the three dozen or so other youngsters who had passed under their roof. Mrs Wright had read us the story of Mary Slessor, the pioneering Scottish missionary to Nigeria, and I think the Wrights would have been pleased that I found my vocation in a related, yet different calling.

Later my parents seemed to think that some kind of enquiry about the Wrights' household was due to start the very day that they took me back from Ilfracombe to Croydon. Certainly it was never in the news; I have checked the North Devon local newspapers in the British Library over the entire period.

Ilfracombe had felt far away from London, but occasionally evacuees would attempt to walk home, or maybe hitch lifts, but after a day's walking and no food most would give up and the police returned them to their foster-homes.

As a gift from our growing-up children, Ruth and I revisited Ilfracombe in 1992. We stayed in a guest house near the Wrights' former home, which had since been converted into flats. I wandered round a few old haunts: the Scala Cinema was empty and derelict, and Southcombe's, the former prestigious bakery and restaurant, where I had bought my daily ½d scone, was now a down-market snack-bar and bingo hall. The church hall where our school met was open for an art exhibition so I wandered in and around the former classrooms – almost nothing there had changed! The railway had long gone but the town itself was much as I had wandered around it 50 years before.

I could not find anyone who knew what had happened to the Wrights, nor what they did afterwards. One or two people could recall the *Full Gospel Assembly* sign in Montpelier Terrace, but it is not known whether the Assembly was ever affiliated to the mainstream Pentecostal church of that name. Since Ilfracombe was and is well supplied with good thriving churches, the Assembly probably just died a natural death.

Perhaps I shall find out when I get to Heaven!

School

When my parents got me back from Ilfracombe to Croydon, they decided I should still be evacuated, though much nearer. The Croydon Town Hall found a home for me just 30 miles away at Guildford in a small modern suburb known as Bannister's Estate, near to the half-built Guildford Cathedral. Mr and Mrs Cook took me into their home, and each day I walked about a mile to Westborough Junior School. No one thought there would any risk to a nine-year-old boy walking alone.

Most of my route to school was along the still-countrified Guildford By-Pass, and most of the very few vehicles which did pass by were rumbling tank-tracked gun carriers under test by the nearby Dennis Motor factory. One of my odd jobs was to walk the Cooks' dog up to the Cathedral Hill each evening. But I often wandered across the fields beyond Bannister's Estate to pick wild flowers or to gather blackberries. On a pedestrian railway-crossing I was well aware of the danger of the live rail from which the electric trains drew power. One day I saw smaller boys crouching over the rail as they had heard that they could 'stroke it gently' without serious shock. As a potential witness to a fatality, I did not want to stay around!

At Westborough the Croydon cohort of kids were a minority, grouped together within a class of nine-year-old evacuees mainly from Fulham, and under the eye of the dreaded Miss Chanell. In one way she was feared by her class, but also not taken too seriously. She demanded unconditional attention. Anyone who took his or her eyes off her momentarily was called forward and caned. She had quite an assortment of canes on her desk; most of them were fraying at the ends. When not beating the kids she used them to beat time on the blackboard while we recited our multiplication tables. Apart from those tables I learnt almost nothing. In fact, I was one of the very few in her class who could read. During my brief sojourn Miss Channel caned me on some eight occasions: just a single stroke on the hand. It taught us to laugh it off!

One day Miss Chanell's chosen subject was 'Singapore'. She told us it was a very hot place, and one needed only very light clothing. But although it was hot, the people were anomalously called 'coolies'. The land area was covered with rubber trees, and the inhabitants tapped them even though the countryside abounded with fierce tigers. Now, she continued, because it was well-known that tigers never attack anyone facing them, everyone in Singapore wore face-masks on the back of their heads. A decade later, landing in Singapore, I discovered otherwise.

The class above us was for boys only, under the rotund and cheerful Mr Pickbourne. He had a sense of humour and the boys said that he could 'take a joke.' However while quite a strict disciplinarian he always displayed a relaxed manner, and was not as arbitrary with his cane as Miss Channell. Our class spent one or two periods a day in with Mr Pickbourne's class, jammed three in a two-child desk. This was either in lieu of a proper School Assembly, or else to hear a BBC Schools Radio programme. The shortage of space and constantly changing logistics took their toll on the whole evacuee education system, and our schooling inevitably suffered somewhat.

By the late autumn of 1941 there were no signs of another German blitz, so my parents decided that perhaps evacuation was no longer necessary for my safety. The thing that finally decided them was when a few sores broke out on my chest. Mrs Cook just thought that she had caught her fingernails on me when giving me the weekly (summer), or fortnightly (winter) bath. (Such infrequent bathing was common among middle class families, especially with the wartime fuel shortage).

By chance one of the very rare medical checks intervened; the entire class was marched to a clinic where the eyes of a loud-voiced, ever-chiding sister alighted on the red spots on my chest. She addressed me in the hearing of the assembled company at the top of her voice. "Don't touch *anything*, get your clothes back on." Then to the rest of her staff, "He's *covered* with scabies!" A volunteer lady escorted me back to the Cooks' home and I learnt that I would have to 'go away' for a while because of the sores. Mrs Cook read me the passage on scabies in her copy of *The Home Doctor* and it proved to be a fairly accurate forecast of treatment during the next few weeks.

The evacuation department sent a taxi to take me to Durcot, a children's treatment centre which appeared to have been a sizeable, quite modern residence. Twice daily we were bathed and scrubbed all-over, then dusted with some cocoa-like substance. The sores very soon disappeared, and it seemed doubtful if they were scabies at all. (Scabies flourishes in dirty, unhygienic environments, which was not true of either the Cook residence or the school).

Just prior to Christmas, few children showed much in the way of remaining spots, and evidently Durcot was to be closed down. Good news indeed! Meanwhile my parents decided that with minimal enemy air activity, evacuation was *definitely* no longer essential, so my father brought me back to Croydon.

With so many evacuees returning, I was to experience Croydon's hastily reinstated schooling in temporary accommodation, because the Howard School had been requisitioned as an emergency fire station.

Shortly after that the Japanese armies brutally occupied Malaya and Singapore, so our teacher advised us to buy a pencil eraser before rubber – mostly sourced from Malaya – disappeared from the shops. But rubber erasers remained on sale, further mystifying us kids about the progress or otherwise of the war. Only later did we learn what Japan's conquest of Singapore cost in lives and suffering.

Howard School was fraught with endless changes of teachers, but finally we moved back to the refurbished Howard building with a Mr Williams as a long-term class-master. Mr Williams was quite an able imparter of the Three R's, and moreover we learnt a lot through almost daily general knowledge quizzes. But often he spent hours of class time talking about his stamp collection and tutoring us in the art of philately! As preparation for the highly competitive scholarship exams at age 11, it was a disaster. These exams were an opportunity to gain a free place at a selective-entry 'grammar' school or even at a prestigious 'public' (American 'private') school – this was my parents' fond hope.

Reading and writing were no problem, but maths seemed to elude me and I did not chase after them! I sailed through most of the 11+ exams but my poor mathematical performance meant I failed everything. Only a couple out of the class of 42 obtained scholarships. Much the same result came when I sat the entrance exam at an independent public school called Whitgift Middle.

Schooling in Britain in the 40s and 50s

After six years free and compulsory primary schooling, there was a three-way split in secondary education.

One might pass the highly selective 11+ exam and have a free place in a good school, your parents might be able to afford to enter you in a fee-paying school, or otherwise you would be consigned to a 'Council School' till your 14th birthday, from which the job prospects were very limited indeed.

Those who by brains or money arrived at the desirable public schools were the fortunate ones. These are in fact private foundations, usually with an Anglican outlook. A distinctive feature of public schools was the 'house system.' Boys lived in various 'houses' around the school campus. Each house included those from the oldest down to the newest arrivals and was presided over by a Housemaster. Some 'houses' became almost schools in themselves, apart from classroom, and fielded their respective sports teams. The youngest boarders had to 'fag' for the most senior ones (usually prefects) acting as a kind of personal servant or valet, and were always at their elders' beck and call while in the house.

The public school boys (usually called 'men') had a great advantage. They learnt first to obey their leaders and later to lead their juniors; they acquired immense loyalty to, and prestige from their school – their *alma mater*. They got to know people who would be important contacts for them in the future: the *old school tie* network. Nowadays, only a small minority of the state-sector institutions approach anywhere near the private sector's performance.

As I drew near to the end of primary schooling in wartime Croydon, my parents were at their wits' end. Then my parents remembered St Joseph's College, a 25 minute bus ride away. This time I succeeded in passing the entrance exam. A few weeks later I became a Josephian in my navy blazer, badged cap, grey flannel shirt, and school tie.

St Joseph's College was run by the La Salle teaching order of Roman Catholic monks[1], and totally independent of any state support. Thus my parents had to scrape and economise to pay £8 school fees per term –

---

1   The La Salle order was founded in France by Jean-Baptiste de la Salle. At first we new boys thought that our founder was John the Baptist!

expensive in those days – as well as extra money for unsubsidised lunches and travel. Academically St Joseph's performed well and enjoyed a large campus for sporting activities. It rarely related to other schools except those run by the same Order, They would bus a soccer team to Bournemouth (120 miles) or to Ipswich (about the same distance) rather than play local school teams.

Their financial strength lay in the fact that the brothers were all vowed not only to celibacy but to poverty as well, so their board and basic live-in lodging were the order's only cost. Since the teachers were all monks we had to address them as *Brother* rather than the customary *Sir*. The Headmaster was known as the Brother Director.

The Brothers were good with people, but poor administrators and the condition of the buildings showed it, though some of that could be attributed to war conditions. There was no orientation for new boys, and we 'discovered' the timetable by noting down the various teachers' appearances over the course of the first week.

On my first morning I found myself in a class with nearly 40 other boys. The class master, Brother Cuthman, after calling the register wrote the Latin verb 'carry' on the board: *porto, portas, portat* . . . . without explanation. The boy sitting next to me told me it was Latin. Later in the day the French master, Brother Dominic, appeared and expressively pointed out objects to be identified in French – a penknife, a book, a window and a door, plus the phrases 'I open', 'I close' and 'what is it that…?' He had flair and was probably the best imparter of knowledge that St Joseph's had on its staff. Alas, the syllabus was badly planned; many boys in my class had done much of the material before, and we repeated more of it a year later!

It was with Brother Dominic that I had my first brush with the rather relaxed and easy going disciplinary system; I failed to stop talking in the 'lines' in which we assembled to process into our classrooms, so I received a single stroke on the backside from Brother Dominic's sawn-off billiard cue! Despite the incident, I enjoyed his class because French was the one subject in which I was near the top of the class, and Brother Dominic was pleased with my good grades – I even won the French Prize one year. But with Hitler's armies in control across the Channel, visibly so from Dover, French had little apparent use. My parents wished that I were as interested in maths as I had been in French!

In my St Joseph's uniform – age 14, school blazer and grey slacks, at home in Croydon.

However by 1946, travel to Europe had normalised and the possibility of a summer 'practicum' in France was offered. My parents felt that French was quite peripheral to 'real' study and were probably put off by the (quite modest) cost. As for me I have always enjoyed languages, and unbeknown to me then, I was later to become familiar with a number of foreign tongues in far-away East Asia.

St Joseph's College was endowed with two playing pitches and a running track, so it was surprising that only a small proportion of the boys were involved in sport. But I preferred cycling and swimming with my friends. The annual athletic tournaments usually eliminated me early in the process, though in my final year I got as far as the high jump and came in third for my 'house'. Even the annual Cross Country Run was only nominally compulsory and I managed to escape it in four out of my five years there.

Sports Day at St Joseph's was one of the few interfaces with outsiders because parents and relations were encouraged to attend. In my final year, I took part in a 'pyramid' display. We marched onto the field double-decked – that is half the boys carried another boy on their shoulders – the upper boy swinging his arms as if the feet were his. I was a thin and weedy youth and rode on the shoulders of a heavier-built boy, Nichini. Like many children in Roman Catholic schools, Nichini was of Italian extraction – probably after several generations in the UK.

One morning as I entered the side drive-way, the soft drinks delivery lorry caught me between itself and some railings. I was spun round and round and found myself dizzy and then lying down. Someone took me to the Sick Bay, normally used only by boarders. I was laid on a camp bed, given an aspirin and a drink of water, and seemed to be none the worse. I was more frightened by the appearance of the unsmiling Brother Richard, the 'Brother Prefect', who was responsible for handling breaches of discipline – usually with a cane. I assumed the Brother would feel that it was my fault that I had got between a lorry and the railings and so

I'd be in deep trouble – it did not occur to me that the driver would be to blame. However, he seemed satisfied with my explanation and I returned to class. Brother Richard had impressed us all early in our first year after a complaint about high-spirited behaviour on a bus; a named boy was probably unfortunate in 'just being there' or in being the one to have his name taken. Brother Richard came into our classroom, with a stout cane under his arm, called the boy out, pushed him over the front desk and gave him the mother-of-all-thrashings, warning the rest of us to behave or else…! We boys knew nothing of sex and sadism then, but it did seem as if Brother Richard was never unhappy to have an occasion to wield his cane.

My only other brush with Brother Richard was for some minor misdemeanour in our class, when he was filling-in for another teacher. He told me to see him 'after school' when I expected one or two strokes of his cane. However he was not at his appointed place – it was a Thursday, when school ended 15 minutes early. We Protestant boys could go home but the Roman Catholic boys would attend a service called *Benediction*. Brother Richard was busy marshalling the boys in and out of Chapel.

I went home but realised that I could be in for deep trouble if I didn't take immediate action, so the next morning, I decided that a couple of strokes of the cane was a good deal better than a much more serious punishment for missing. I went up to Brother Richard and explained that last night I had gone to his office 'after school' and could not find him. He ignored me and I went away! A year or two later Brother Richard was replaced by a new Brother Prefect – Brother Elwyn Gerard – who discontinued corporal punishment for older boys but seemed to us to be both more approachable and also to be a more effective disciplinarian.

Another memorable event that got me into mild trouble was in my final year. As seniors the class-master, the cheerful, breezy Brother Rogatian, who was also Brother Sub-Director[2], entrusted small tasks to the boys. One job I was given was on the half-hours to call out, interrupting the teacher if necessary, *Let us remember that we are in the holy presence of God* – and invoke the name of the 'Saint for the Day' from a Calendar provided. The class would respond, *Pray for us,* and the teacher would carry on.

Not all the brothers appreciated these supererogatory intercessions so I had to learn who did and who did not. Brother Celsus (*Celsus* means

---

2   Or Vice Principal.

tall) taught geography – one of my better subjects – and I rather liked him. Once I had contrived to get a photo of him in class and made it into a calendar to send him at Christmas. I refrained from adding the current political slogan as a caption, as another boy had suggested: 'You've had one crisis, do you want another?'

One afternoon, in Brother Celsus's class, I called out the prayer as usual and saw a tall figure bearing down on me – evidently he thought I was 'taking the mickey' out of him. He clouted me across my ear and face and felt warm blood running down my nose. "Now get out!" he shouted. So I did – and standing dazed in the corridor dripping blood on the floor I was vaguely conscious of Mr Patten, the layman music master, close by. He sent me to the sick bay. No boy likes to 'report' on others – even on a teacher so I was glad to be sent by someone in authority. I was sat down, and given a glass of water and another aspirin. The bleeding stopped and I went back to class. Much later I learnt that the College had taken the matter of my bloody nose very seriously indeed, and it seems various other things led Brother Celsus to leave St Joseph's and to resign from the La Salle Order.

In the pre-Health and Safety days lunch 'hours' were typically 90 minutes long. One day some of us had brought packed lunches so that we could have extra free time. As we wandered round Woolworths[3] I thought it might be fun to burst the brown paper lunch bag. This was during the time when Hitler's occasional daytime raids occurred. My bag burst with a most satisfying, almost deafening bang. But it instantly became clear that the sooner I made myself scarce the better. Fortunately for me, no one reported the matter to the school. 'Six of the Best' from Brother Richard would have been a certainty.

By the spring of 1944 the Allies had shot down or grounded most of the Luftwaffe and their supplies, so the danger of even occasional bomber raids virtually ceased. But Hitler had a couple of extra cards to play. Quite suddenly in the summer of 1944, almost as the D-Day liberation troops landed in Normandy, air raid sirens started to become frequent – often several times in one day. German-designed pilotless planes (or flying bombs) were being launched from ramps in German-occupied France. They were known by various names: the P-Plane, the V-1 or the Doodlebug. Steered by a gyroscopic compass along a course for London,

---

3   A now defunct low-cost general store selling most things.

the fuel was cut off at a given point and the missile plunged to earth and exploded. They did not go deep but created an enormous and damaging blast. Where they fell was not allowed to be publicised as that would have given the launchers valuable gunnery feedback. Since no pilots were involved, doodlebugs could come at any time of the day and were a noisy nuisance as well as a serious danger.

Various British anti-aircraft gunnery was hastily readied again; more balloon-wires were interposed along the doodlebugs' main paths, and some intrepid RAF fighter pilots cruised alongside them and wing-tipped them upward so that they plunged into the sea. My parents and I hastily refurbished the air-raid shelter in which they had passed much of the 1940-41 winter blitz, and we slept down there most nights. Our borough, Croydon, suffered the most V-1 hits of any UK town. After a week or more of missing school, my mother accepted an invitation from Aunt Doily to be evacuated to her family living in Wales, outside of the V-1's range. So I spent the rest of the Doodlebug period, plus the long summer vacation, in Penarth, South Wales.

During the war, I inherited a very basic one-valve radio, originally constructed by my father for my grandparents. It was a great introduction for electronics and broadcasting later on! Listening on headphones in my bedroom.

I was quite used to rail travel locally, but this was to be a three-hour journey from London to Cardiff for a lone 11-year-old. A telegram from Aunt Doily told us to go to a Mr Hamblin. So my mother and I made our way into the office block of the lordly Great Western Railway's London Terminal. Mr Hamblin was very friendly; he escorted us down to the South Wales train and found me a seat in the Guard's Van, instructing the Guard to see that I got down at Cardiff station. There Aunt Doily and cousin Mary were on the platform to welcome me to their home in Penarth.

While I was in Penarth, back at Croydon my parents continued to sleep in the air raid shelter. One Doodlebug falling nearby demolished a large house and the blast removed much of the glazing in our home. A government agency made temporary repairs by tacking waterproofed cloth over the gaps.

My Penarth relatives taught me to swim in the sea and to explore by bicycle, and I enjoyed my 12th birthday next door with the Page family – their son Michael was exactly one year older than me. Meanwhile Paris was liberated, but the Germans were still holding out in Belgium and Holland and also in the small part of France opposite Southeast England. But as soon as the Doodlebug launch-sites were occupied by the Allies, victory seemed just around the corner. In fact Hitler still held out, even speeding up the deportation of Jews to death camps. However for me in Wales, summer was ending so I came home to Croydon and back to St Joseph's. Not much had changed but I was moved up one class. The new class master was Brother Adolphe, an elderly Frenchman who spoke good English, and was quite an exacting taskmaster on homework and class behaviour. However he was also an encourager, and a better teacher of maths – fortunately for me!

Nevertheless, although we heard no more doodlebugs, mysterious explosions were occurring, usually with no warning at all. Hitler's last, and in some ways most successful effort was to launch V-2 rockets from his still-occupied territory. Their trajectory was far higher than planes could go, and far faster and further. When the missile turned downwards to hit the earth and explode, the speed was so high that few were ever observed by plain eyesight. There was no defence against V-2s, and they caused civilian deaths much more seriously than the V-1s. If such a rocket were to be launched with a nuclear warhead, there could be untold damage, death and destruction.

One unique feature at St Joseph's was 30 minutes per day of religious instruction in which the roughly 50 percent Roman Catholic boys gathered separately from the others to work through the Catechism. The regime was that the Protestant boys (they called us *non-Catholics*) should study non-controversial issues such as the Bible and common areas of the Christian faith and ethics. The Brothers were quite conscientious in this but of course their own Roman faith shone through to us all the same. I recall the Brothers as men who walked closely with God, who prayed and encouraged us to do the same. They had no doubts about the authenticity of the Biblical narratives, nor were they in the least bashful in expatiating about Heaven and Hell – as well as Purgatory and Limbo! On one occasion I had a streaming cold and constantly blew my nose in this class. The teacher thought I was fooling around and I had to write out 50 times *It's about time I learnt to blow my nose in a civilised fashion!*

Though I've held onto my biblical and Protestant faith, I have never regretted what I learnt at St Joseph's. Years later during my Ordination in Singapore's Anglican Cathedral, two of the Brothers wrote me a warm letter of greeting, and it remains framed by my desk today.

For the last two years we had to choose between science and Latin. My father felt Latin would be more useful for writing and understanding English. With much hesitation I plumped for it – Latin was good preparation for later study in New Testament Greek. The science that I missed came up again later when I became involved with technicalities in Asia. In maths we had to struggle with simultaneous quadratic equations; we were not told what they were for, only how to solve them. About three decades later I had to re-learn them for studies in electronics – where I realised they actually had a purpose!

My 14th birthday present was a Kodak Hawkeye box camera, one of the simplest money could buy, but quite a thrill for me. Moreover the parcel included a film which was virtually unobtainable to the public at that time.

I decided I could afford the basic materials to make contact prints for myself. I still recall the thrill of seeing my first picture emerge under the surface of the developing solution. Later on I adapted our air raid shelter into a full-blown dark room. I often wondered if I could graduate to own a real camera – one with a larger, sharper lens.

However, affordable cameras in Britain were limited to cheap ones little

Early attempts at photography – my parents, Horace (Miles) Huntley and Phyllis née Williams with Tigger the cat, in the garden of our spacious home at 7 Barham Road, South Croydon, 1946.

better than my 'Hawkeye'. A neighbour lent me his press camera once or twice, but it was very bulky and the glass plates or film-packs were too expensive to sustain on my minimal pocket money.

One day at school, classmates returned after lunch with the news that there had been a major train crash at South Croydon Station (which I used daily). My mother had also heard and unbeknown to me, rang the school to confirm that I was indeed there. The crash had occurred in thick fog shortly after my usual train had left; a packed commuter train of older, wooden carriages had run at about 30 mph into the rear of a more modern train, killing nearly 40 people. Apparently a young, inexperienced signalman who had never worked in fog had over-ridden a safety device. A small error causing many deaths and injuries!

That evening I went to see the scene. Railway coaches were piled up and overhanging a suburban street, and I was able to shoot a rudimentary picture on my box camera. Steam cranes were working hard to remove the wreckage, and by next morning all signs of the crash had disappeared and the track had been relayed. Nowadays, many days would pass while the police and lawyers did their stuff.

One of my involvements at St Joseph's was with a project for a simple journal for our House – the Dunn House Magazine. Brother Cuthman, the Housemaster, pointed out that the school was poorly equipped for producing even a basic publication. I worked on a lino cut for the masthead, but there was no way to print it. Finally Brother Cuthman persuaded the school to allow us to use an ancient device based on jelly and hectographic ink, and the first edition of *The Dunlin*, printed in fuzzy purple-ish type was distributed to house members.

During my years at St Josephs I joined *Crusaders*[4] – a Bible Class movement aimed at middle class boys, and highly successful in nurturing future Christian leaders in the professions and into the ordained ministry. The Crusader Group grew appreciably and there was some suggestion that we should produce a Group Magazine. A former member owned a very basic roller-stencil machine requiring the user to manually brush sticky black ink onto the inside of the stencil drum, and to hand feed

---

4   Most Crusader groups are now co-ed and the movement has now been renamed *Urban Saints*. I remained in Crusaders after National Service till my early 20s when a Young Adults' Fellowship started at Emmanuel.

each sheet of paper! The Crusader leader in charge left it to me to edit and print, which stopped only when I was called up for military service.

One Sunday, one of the younger Crusader leaders suggested I sign up for an Easter Houseparty in Shropshire. I did not think my parents could afford it; however, my mother used some of her savings from the housekeeping for the fee. So I joined the group of houseparty-bound boys at Paddington Station. As the train puffed through the Midlands we experienced our first sight of old-style industrial Britain. I was shocked; there was almost no greenery or colour to relieve the slag heaps, the smoke and the blackened buildings.

The houseparty was organised by the energetic David Tryon and his team. It was partly to bring the Christian Gospel to the boys, and partly to provide an enjoyable break in the beautiful surroundings for games, hikes, and trips to the nearby aqueduct. I even tried horse-riding. David's *Pioneer Camps and Houseparties* were an offshoot of the former *South Africa General Mission*, now part of *Serving In Mission International (SIM)*. The camps also generated interest in the Mission's work in Southern Africa. On a subsequent camp, a small group of us had an unforgettable experience – a trip down a nearby coal mine. We donned helmets and miners' lamps and were escorted down the lifts for the underground tour. At the coal face a mechanised cutter filled the air with fine dust, but no one wore mouth masks.

Once the war was behind us, Crusader Camps under canvas recommenced, and I joined one on a cliff-top in the Isle of Wight. Some of us boys could earn a little pocket money with daily jobs and mine was to brush out the tent of the Chaplain, Norman Pateman, a veteran missionary to China.

It was the custom of each senior camp leader, to come to one of the tents to chat – usually something autobiographical – as we settled down to sleep. Norman told us of Hudson Taylor and the founding of the China Inland Mission 80 years earlier, and showed us a Chinese letter, explaining some of the hand-written characters. Most of us dozed off after that but I wrote to him after the camp to enclose a snapshot, and was surprised and pleased to receive a full and interesting reply. Norman, who held a first class honours degree in Chinese, had a photographic memory and welcomed me by name 10 years later to a CIM meeting in London.

Little did I know that my links with Norman and the CIM would be yet stronger as God led step by step!

Soon after that, my Crusader Leader suggested I come along with him to a *Youth Squash*, a gathering after the Sunday evening service, with refreshment and a talk. The venue was the Church Hall of Emmanuel Church, South Croydon where I had briefly attended Sunday school.

A friend from primary school days was helping with the refreshments and as we chatted he invited me to join the Youth Club – I had just attained the necessary age of 14 years to do so. Being in an all-boys' school and not knowing much about the opposite sex, I agreed to give it a try. At Club, we were encouraged to attend the Sunday Evening church services. Thus I joined Emmanuel Church, being confirmed into the Church of England a year or two after joining the Youth Club.

At the end of five years in high school came the School Certificate (the equivalent of an American high school graduation) which required a minimum number of passes in English, mathematics and a language. Subject-retakes were not allowed; one had to sit the entire half dozen or so subjects again! So passing the *School Cert* overshadowed my final school year.

When registration for the exam drew near, the Brother Director (Headmaster) came into our classroom and read out a list of names – fortunately mine was among them. Only these boys would be allowed to sit the forthcoming School Certificate examination *as pupils of St Joseph's*. Any others would have to register as private students. Here was a subterfuge employed by almost all non-government schools. When the results came out, the percentage of passes *from that school* would appear artificially high. Those not allowed to *register* under the school's name were those who the schools considered might not pass! This practice – with variations – still lives on in the private sector institutions.

I finished schooling at age 15 and was sitting the final Oxford School Certificate examinations over the time of my 16th birthday. Now, in 1948 with the war (but not rationing) some three years behind us, peacetime conditions were gradually reappearing, and there was the long vacation ahead before I started my first job.

Several weeks passed before the results from the School Certificate were posted; but while at a camp in North Wales, a telegram from my mother announced the good news of my pass. The favourable results said much for St Joseph's College and for the Brothers – after my scoring 3 percent for Algebra some years previously, I had passed the Oxford School Certificate with a credit in maths and several other subjects.

Now I became a school-leaver.

To Work

Along with my parents I considered an insurance company, promising security and a good salary, but I was dubious about confinement to paperwork and an office for life. I liked mapping so I wrote to the Ordnance Survey, but their salary would barely have paid my fares. But it was the railways that had always fascinated me.

Railways in Britain were then private companies. They manufactured their own equipment and rolling stock, and operated a chain of hotels as well as steamship links to Europe and Ireland. This was very different from the USA, or even Australasia, where many younger people today have never boarded a train, except perhaps on city lines or subways.

So I sat the Southern Railway's very basic entrance exam and was accepted as a junior clerk to start almost immediately. However, I was booked for the summer Pioneer Camps run by the South Africa General Mission at Benllech Bay in North Wales, so my father helped me to negotiate a later start-date. Benllech was a great place for energetic boys – there were various games, cliff hikes, lots of open country and beach to explore, boating in the sea and swimming in heavy surf, or in a large rock-hewn tidal 'swimming pool'.

A job at the camp was to organise the boys' luggage for their return home. I collected the forms and fees from the boys and took them to the tiny station. I suppose this was good orientation for my first job. A few days after the Pioneer Camp ended, I started with the railway.

The railway system was the 'signature' product of the Victorian age. Before this, all land transport was on or behind a horse which would also haul a canal barge. The Victorians' ruthless free and pure capitalism gave Britain a dense network of railways; poor tenants were tipped out of their homes without compensation as landowners sold the land to railway builders. Thousands of labourers used hand and horse to build cuttings and embankments as well as the tens of miles of brick-arch viaducts which still carry the tracks into Britain's major cities today. (I still ride these often myself, sometimes wondering if I share the guilt of the ruthless Victorian builders!)

Since sitting the exam, the system had just been nationalised by the Labour government, but my job offer was still open. After brief training I found myself inside our local station – South Croydon – selling tickets to early morning commuters, many of them my acquaintances. Though the trains on the Southern were mostly electric, we laboured under hissing gas lights because a former constituent company had signed a 50-year contract with a gas producer!

One chore was to answer the four phones. Our station was assigned the code '1-3' on all four phones: one ring, a pause and three more rings. After a while I remained oblivious to the almost constant ringing of various codes, but would immediately recognise '1-3' and answer it.

Our Station Master also had charge of three other stations, and one morning I was sent to one of these to cover for a sick staff member. I found myself in sole charge of a four-platform station served by very few trains – hence the day's takings for passengers and freight amounted to less than £1. I walked back to South Croydon proudly carrying the cash in the lockable leather bag.

Then out of the blue I was offered a junior position in the former Southern's Head Office at Waterloo, where working conditions were better and hours shorter. I was briefly interviewed in the department of a gentleman named Oliver Cromwell who enjoyed the resounding title of Chief Officer for Labour and Establishment. His department negotiated directly with the railway's trade unions – a task involving considerable legal cut-and-thrust.

Of course I only met the chief's number three – former company Chief Officers on the railway by now had become managerial eunuchs. 'Real' power lay with the three levels of bureaucracy imposed above them by the Labour government, mostly stuffed with former Trade Unionists. After nationalisation, the railways' own Chief Officers' functions seemed to be to await comfortable retirement, enjoying lunch and cigars with each other while their subordinates wrote and signed almost all the letters on their behalf.

My new job was in the file registry – typing up index cards so that files and letters could easily be recalled. Cross-referencing was the essence of this job as the registry could be asked to produce an old file from the vaguest of recollections by a senior officer. I was often sent down to the gloomy archives under the station to search for ancient letters which had established a precedent one way or the other decades ago, and the Trade Unions did the same thing with their files. It was good preparation for office work as I learnt to build a system where papers didn't get lost! In later years, including retirement, I realised what a useful skill I had gained in those early years. In other ways it was a rather tedious job and with no pecuniary advantage – railway staff at the lower levels were paid strictly by age, with no adjustment whatever for merit.

One of the few positive results of nationalisation was an enlightened Staff Suggestions Scheme with quite attractive awards for any suggestion recommended by a Suggestions Committee, whether it was actually implemented or not. The minimum award was about the same as a junior employee's weekly take-home pay. In addition to the cheque, the employee's staff record card was duly noted – to his credit should he apply for a higher job. The scheme was a breath of fresh air in an ossifying industry, whose ageing seniors increasingly felt threatened by innovation!

I submitted several suggestions, and as one or two gained awards I began to realise what areas were likely to get recommended and what would not. My immediate boss was worldly-wise in one sense so he sent the notes regarding my suggestion awards directly to the the filing cabinets; they were not passed up the hierarchy as they should have been, with the morning's more important mail.

One Saturday morning my boss was away and two letters came in – one advising a suggestion award I had received, and the other concerning a course I had completed. In my boss's place the Head Messenger sorted the morning's mail and included my two 'credits' in the paperwork to be passed up the hierarchy. So it went right up to Number Two who, obviously pleased, scrawled across the note *Who is Huntley?* (I had worked there for two years!) When he grasped that I had received several earlier awards, he demanded that he must see all such notes in future. This could have been embarrassing for me the next week when my boss returned but nothing was said. (During military service as I travelled round I submitted more suggestions and a few awards helped pad out the minimal army pay.)

In those early years, it did not occur to me that I would ever leave the railway. One of the positives of railway service was free travel. During our initial training I had met John Ede and together we planned a vacation in Jersey, one of the British Channel Islands but located deep into a bay on the French coast. We duly picked up our free tickets and took the night boat from Southampton. As the ship drew close to Guernsey, and then Jersey, the smell of decaying tomatoes enveloped us. The early autumn tomato harvest had just passed, and heaps of rejected fruit rotted and evaporated in the corner of every field. Interestingly after a day or so, our noses 'tuned out' the odour! Cycling, swimming and duty-free buying occupied our time.

Knowing that we were near to France, we had taken the precaution of getting passports for a possible day trip to the continent. For a 17-year-old, paternal permission was needed. I approached my father whom I knew would be very suspicious of small-plane travel, so I mentioned that there were sea crossings. We duly booked – a return air fare of only £2.75 – and made our way to Jersey Airport. Then our names were called for boarding the small eight-seat biplane. Window views were excellent, but conversation above the engine noise was almost impossible.

Twenty-five minutes later we landed at Dinard. It was a lovely sunny day for wandering round this old-fashioned, dignified town with its cream-coloured stone buildings and steep-sided sandy bay. Across the Rance estuary lay industrial St Malo, the future site of the world's first electric generator to be powered by a tidal barrage. Our few French francs sufficed for a simple lunch and a souvenir or two before we had to return to the airport. With this experience safely behind I was able to tell my parents about it. Air travel in those days did not have an image of safety!

My main free-time relaxation included 'Crusaders' on Sunday afternoons, and even more with friends at Emmanuel Church Youth Club. I loved to join the Club's hikes and cycle rides into the nearby countryside. These open-air excursions opened up a feel for Southern England and for exploring . In September, along with many suburbanites, we would cycle out to pick wild blackberries which we bottled for use in the winter, when fresh fruit would become scarce[1].

At this point I started to attend the monthly evening 'youth service' where the liturgy was a little shorter, young people read the Scripture lessons and the preacher was usually a young Curate. There was also an

---

1   Even now, each autumn I take our grandchildren 'blackberrying' in the countryside
     hedgerows.

informal youth programme after the service. I soon began to take in more of the Christian faith. I would have known most of the Bible Stories, but not where they fitted together. I had no other particular hobby, except for planning ahead for the next vacation trip and occasional photography.

The next summer John Ede and I decided on something more adventurous – to take a week in the Mediterranean sunshine and 'do' Paris on the way back. Our free travel extended to much of Europe, so this time we decided to spend the night on a French train. We were advised to book the lower bunks – some seats were convertible to bunks for the night (known in France as *couchettes*). Though basic, they are probably more spacious than present day business-class 'stretch out' seats in aircraft.

The sea crossing was just 21 miles from Dover to Calais Maritime, the ship-side station where trains departed for every point in Europe. The prestigious *Blue Train* was standing by to carry those who had paid for a supplement amounting to the cost of a first class hotel.

Ours was the next rung down – the *Azur Express* – with simple bunks, but nevertheless quite a comfortable way to reach France's sunny south. Towards the evening our train circled Paris, stopped briefly at Gare de Lyon and headed south. We drew into Cannes 17 hours after leaving Calais and negotiated our way to our youth-oriented camp, *Camps Volants*[2], which occupied a bombed site next to the beach. Accommodation included canvas beds in ex-US Army tents which were pitched double to cover up the rips and tears in the fabric. But in spite of its simplicity and basic facilities, it was a great base to explore Cannes and the off-shore islands, plus to take trips into the foothills of the Maritime Alps.

On one swimming trip, unaware of the force of Mediterranean sun, we got badly sunburnt. So on our sortie across the Italian border to San Remo we were somewhat more circumspect about beach time and bathing. The Italians were friendly and seemed anxious to forget their Axis orientation under Mussolini. This was the furthest point from London on our itineration: over 1000 miles by rail.

A hot, all-day train ride brought us back to Paris, and to another basic but adequate bomb-site camp in the Invalides area. Naturally our first trips were to the Eiffel Tower, Notre Dame Cathedral of *Hunchback* fame, and the Sacré Coeur hill. We survived on the simplest of menus, also on bars of Swiss chocolate and drinks of Vichy water mixed with a sugary lemon

---

2   *Camps Volants* roughly 'camps for travelling youth'

syrup, the Vichy *à syrop de citron*. We had been recommended a small restaurant in the student quarter that served a modestly priced omelette and chips[3]. The waiter seemed rather taken aback that we expected both items together; omelette and chips was evidently a two-course meal in France! The crossing to Dover this time was rough. John sat below and was badly seasick. On the open deck I only just managed not to be sick – and for the train ride from Dover to London we both felt decidedly queasy!

I went back to work on the railways, even though the war-exhausted system had started to run up huge losses. Politicians had taken it as axiomatic that improved transport would gain few votes. Bureaucracy now reigned supreme, but I saw no obvious job-wise alternative at that time. (It is worth noting that in the early 21st century the remaining railways were re-privatised and have regained popularity.)

However in the nationalised 'British Railways' of 1951, the weekly pay was better than a junior outdoor worker or an office boy earned, but still in the £3-£6 range per week (illustrating the enormous change in value of currency over my lifetime). Prices of most items had changed little between the Victorian era and the outbreak of World War II. But from the end of the war till now, prices started to rise. Today politicians seem to accept that inflation must continue, and cannot be minimised nor halted.

I was able to save up for a new camera. After examining many models, it seemed I'd need at least £20 to get a good camera, something with a multi-speed shutter, a quality lens, and sufficient aperture for the emerging processes of colour photography. Then new models arrived from Germany. I saw the Zeiss Nettar, a 'bellows' camera, taking the common size 120 film. It had all I desired plus a flash contact and cost a 'mere' £20.64. The shopkeeper found me a second-hand case for an extra £1.50. I used this treasure on holidays, Youth Club outings and activities and it was to travel with me round the world! Later I gave it to our son Andrew who still keeps it as a curiosity.

The Nettar was a versatile little camera, and I read in a magazine how I could adapt the picture-size slightly to get pictures of a size compatible with standard 2" x 2" slide projectors. It was to be nearly two decades before colour prints displaced colour slides and black and white photos.

---

3   *French fries* in North America

I still have most of the colour slides I have taken, and in spite of serious fading, some remain suitable for illustrations in this book.

However, after more than two years with the railway I was approaching the age of 18 and the prospect of conscription to military service. Most young men decided to make the best of it and there were few evaders. During their National Service, railway staff were allowed to retain their quite valuable travel privileges, so though in the uniform of the Royal Engineers, I would still be still a railwayman.

But for how long?

OHMS
On His (now Her) Majesty's Service

In 1950 I attained the 'ripe old age' of 18 and like all young men, had to register for National Service – two years in the armed forces.

I was just realising that the School Certificate which I had earned after finishing at St Joseph's fell just short of Matriculation – then the minimum entry level for university. Although the School Certificate allowed no re-sits of individual subjects, it did allow re-sits for upgrading to Matric. So I was granted a few months' deferment of military service to take one extra subject – Geography. Should I Matriculate, I would be able to study at tertiary level. I had no idea this possibility could ever open up, but in fact this brief step was to be a decisive factor in the future. I did obtain the desired Matric.

During my vacation with John Ede to southern France we had met a fellow young traveller, probably from a distinguished family. He was studying at Kings College, London; this brought me to the realisation that all these confident young people of my own age with their college blazers and longitudinally striped college scarves[1], had much better prospects than I had. This started my thinking again in the direction of studying for a degree. None of my family had ever been to university nor even considered it, so for the time being I had to put thought of further study behind me. Furthermore, the army's call was imminent.

A few weeks later I was summoned for form-filling and written test; not everyone could write! At the medical examination we were told to strip off all our clothes and fill a bottle with a urine sample. Some of us were a bit tardy with that and the doctor called out. "Come on! Hurry up, I only need a *mouthful!*" Then followed a very chatty interview with a relaxed and friendly officer, and the test was over. A few days later a postcard

---

1   High school scarves were usually knitted in school colours striped *across* the scarf, tertiary level scarves were made of flannel stripes longitudinally *along* the scarf.

assured me that medically I had passed grade '1'. Much later, when I was helping out in our squadron office, I saw that the doctor had written *Poor physique – underweight* in large letters across my medical record.

My call-up papers arrived – a form letter enclosing a postal order for four shillings (20 pence) and a railway warrant to Farnborough station in Hampshire. My mother took me to lunch at Simpsons, a famous restaurant in the Strand; then I found that the train from London Waterloo was filled with young men en route to their Selection and Basic Training Unit. An older man in the same compartment told us that we would receive our regimental number later that day; he could recall his numbers from both World War I and World War II.

Lorries trucked us from Farnborough station to Guillemont Barracks of the Royal Engineers, where we entered by a back gate. Just inside, in a high-barbed-wire enclosure some dejected looking denim-clad individuals were digging in the mud, belt-less and with unlaced boots. The corporal in our truck brusquely drew our attention to them and said we would join them should we not obey him. We were dumped from the truck at a long hutted office block and shunted past various registration desks with a soldier-clerk seated at each. What was my name? What sports did I play? Had I been in a school Cadet Force? Had I ever performed in a drama? What hobbies did I have? etc. It was assumed that all were Christians; it remained to say which denomination and anyone a bit unsure was marked down as 'Church of England'. I cannot recall anyone registering a non-Christian faith, nor did anyone claim 'no religion'. In the Quartermaster's stores we were issued with denim overalls, battledress uniforms (a smart belted-jacket suit) as well as webbing packs and belts and boots; mine were size '13 medium', which our sergeant commented looked like the crates that they came in!

Our billet corporal who was almost due for demob[2] gathered us round him and with somewhat vulgar parlance made us understand who was boss. The training ahead of us would be tough, and he would see to it that it was so. There remained little time before the evening meal, which was unexpectedly good.

Though the war was more than five years behind us, rationing and austerity were still part of the British scene, yet we were agreeably surprised that the food was excellent. The first few days were more like

---

2   Or 'demobilisation.'

lectures. The Commanding Officer 'welcomed' us and reminded us that we had to live and work together, to learn discipline, to rebuke anti-social room-mates if they needed it, but to be ready to do anything we really think to be right – for example to say our prayers at night even if the other men laughed. In fact I did this; no one laughed, but I now feel that one's overall demeanour probably reflects one's faith better than outward show. I had faith at that time, though uncertainly. Various other military brass lectured us, and the NCOs[3] soon had us blanco-ing webbing packs and polishing brass – with cleaning materials at our own expense!

Since every reasonably fit 18-year-old had to join one of the forces unless deferred for tertiary study, there were far more men than the forces could use – especially the conscripts like me, who could only spend a mere two years in the ranks. By this time the Korean War was almost over, and although the British military were active in the Mediterranean, the Middle East, Far East and Germany, and had even a few men in the African continent, many conscripts passed their whole service doing odd labouring jobs in the UK or simply killing time.

I soon discovered a typical example of the way the army used up surplus labour: in our case it was the floor-cleaning system, supposedly done weekly, if not daily, in every barrack room of the British armed services. The floor was to be dry-scrubbed and then polished to a short-lived shine. 'The short-lived shine' was the essence of military discipline. All of the Army's cleaning processes required frequent renewal be it polishing brass, whitewashing kerbs or cutting grass. The army was not interested in modern permanent-shine metal, nor any finish to webbing except the 24-hour-life, grey-green Blanco. (It was said that Blanco was manufactured by a company belonging to a senior general.) In many respects, daily chores differed little from those during the First World War.

If an NCO felt the men were hesitant in responding to an order they would yell, "Move! You're not paid to think!" Our problem was not whether we were paid to think, but that we were hardly paid at all. As a soldier, my remuneration (based on the rule that a soldier is on duty 24/7) was about two old pence per hour, or less than one penny today.

There followed occasional weekends when we were free to make our way home. My father was quite surprised that I 'enjoyed' i.e. 'cheerfully

---

3   Non-commissioned officers, e.g. corporals, sergeants etc.

tolerated' service life, but after all there was no choice. Moreover there was also something liberating about the new experiences, the broader circle of people and wider open-air life, which few civilians would experience at all.

The selection method for officership looked remarkably simple but was deceptively difficult to jump through. Traditionally the services recruited their officer material exclusively from the public schools – often directly from school-leavers. But with a Labour government in power, and the experience of much wider officer-recruitment during the war, something less exclusive had to be *seen* by the public to be in operation.

Thus all the men who held at least a School Certificate were assessed as *possible* officer material, and we were dubbed *OR-1s*[4]! Surprisingly the OR-1s were all placed in the same billet, Room 1, making it a kind of middle-class ghetto. We were not treated any differently from those in the other five rooms, although when out on mapping projects, one of us was usually allotted to lead a handful of the others.

In due course we OR-1s were sent in small groups to the War Office Selection Board, or WOSB (*woz-bee*). For three rather gentlemanly days we were asked in turn to lead small teams on open-air projects, to join in discussions or work out written puzzles and then sit through several longish interviews. Of the 80 or so in our intake-group only three made it as far as a commission. Two were from public schools and the third was older and had already qualified as an engineer.

Those in society's higher social echelons, such as officers, were then much more distinct than today, and accepted *noblesse oblige*[5]. For example, when on actual operations, officers were not supposed to eat until they had ensured that all the ranks had been fed properly – and this still applies. Nowadays *noblesse oblige* would be considered insufferably patronising, but then it was considered a cardinal quality for army officering – most of those who reached commissioned ranks displayed at least some trace of it.

The very few that did 'pass' WOSB – even those from public schools mostly failed – soon moved on to enjoy a comfortable billet in an Officers' Mess. Perks included a *batman*, like their 'fag' at school, a sort of mini-

---

4   OR: 'other rank (ie not officer) class 1'.

5   or the obligation to accept responsibility for the needs and wellbeing of their subordinates.

'Jeeves', who would be their valet to iron their uniforms and polish their leather and brasses – all at public expense! Not for them the petty repetitive chores which were the lot of ordinary soldiers. But there was something incongruous about NCO's with medals and many years of war experience standing stiffly to attention to salute these 19-year-old budding 'Bertie Woosters'[6]!

During our basic training, our platoon officer, a young Second Lieutenant, discovered that one of our batch of recruits, Arthur, lived near him and had attended a related public school to his own. When our group had the first prospect of a weekend's leave, he offered Arthur a ride home in his car. Alas, the Major came to hear of this and severely reprimanded the young officer for fraternising with 'the ranks' and had him moved to another part of the camp. Apart from not fraternising, an officer had to remain decorous at all times. He should not normally run; he should not 'do' a job but should order a soldier to do it, preferably via an NCO. He should not drive a truck; there were plenty of soldiers licensed to do that. Only in sporting events should an officer be seen to run, but he could rough up or be roughed up by a soldier on the rugby field or in the boxing ring!

From day one, soldiers learnt that officers and men were like different species. They sat separately in church and in-camp entertainments and belonged to separate Christian Fellowship organizations. In the mid-20th century English social ethos, this demonstrates how the small public school-educated stream still dominated the country's life. EJH Nash[7] noted that in the first half of the 1900s, the top 30 public schools (all boarding) produced virtually all of the country's senior professionals, industrialists, parliamentarians and business tycoons as well as most of the top brass of the military and church. Many also joined missionary societies including the CIM and OMF.

---

6   Bertie Wooster, an upper-crust young man, and his pompous valet Jeeves were the subject of many humorous novels by P.G.Wodehouse

7   Revd EJH Nash ('Bash') concentrated on spiritual ministries among the top 30 schools; his Anglican ordination gave him acceptance by the school chaplains and he was highly successful among the boys, especially on a person-to-person basis. For the summer he organised camps in Dorset to which he invited boys exclusively from 'the 30' and was assisted by Oxbridge student volunteers who had been schooled in the same stream. Many Christian leaders, even today are former 'Bash Campers.' The camps still continue.

The public school men had been *trained to lead*, which helped them feel at ease in any situation, in command or not. They were etiquette-wise, thus at a formal dinner they knew which wine and condiments matched which food, and easily navigated the ranged condiments and cutlery.

We had scheduled periods of running or sessions in the gymnasium, and one day the officer in overall charge of physical training dropped by and told our instructor that he wanted to see the men box. The instructor was supposed to have given us plenty of practice but in fact had done little more than pair us off one sunny day to box each other's shadows! We were hastily paired off by height. I was the tallest and the second tallest was a delightful guy named Scott, who happened to be the local boxing champion from a Welsh mining village. I had never boxed before, so the single one-minute round did not run its 60 seconds. Of course I got thrashed but managed to get a few blows in as well. Scott must have realised I was far, far below his opponents in Wales. I have never been in the ring since.

Rather different was the occasional brief visit to the barrack by an Army Scripture Reader (ASR). These men wear a military-style uniform but live more among the ordinary soldiers, and stress personal Bible study and Christian witness. They did an excellent evangelistic job; yet they had to be ready to go to the front line in active service. The Chaplains on the other hand are ordained ministers, and being officers, must observe a certain distance from 'the ranks' whereas the ASRs all work at the barrack-room level. There was never an ASR in the camps where I was stationed, but I got to know them better, years later on in Singapore.

After all this training we started to feel part of the Royal Engineers, and the sergeants made it clear they were justly proud of the fact and encouraged us to be the same. As the warm weather began we advanced into two months of field engineering – basic construction, blowing things up and rowing on the lake, which was far more interesting. I have never needed to use much of the knowledge gained, but it gave me a feel for things structural or mechanical. The 17 weeks were not unpleasant, but they represented a large chunk out of the 100 or so weeks' service required by law!

An instructional film usually preceded open-air work. With 80 men squeezed into the Training Cinema Hut it could became rather warm in summer, and the temptation to doze off was almost overwhelming.

On parade with rifles at the slope. As a tall guy I was often placed at one end of the column. Here I am immediately behind the sergeant, nearest row to the camera.

Occasionally the sergeant would stop the projector, put on the lights and ask someone to recapitulate the last point in the film. My turn came when I had to explain the basic principle of driving piles. Fortunately I had not snoozed that time. On the positive side with so much open air life and good food we became very fit – I put on 17 pounds (about eight kilos) in 17 weeks!

My introduction to explosives was 'learn by doing'. I was given a piece of Cordtex – a kind of explosive rope, to insert into a detonator, but I caused alarm when I withdrew it quickly to hand it back – apparently that just *might* have caused a detonation!

Next the instructor unwound about 50 yards of Cordtex in a large circle. We soldiers stood few yards back in an even larger circle to observe. Neither we nor the instructors wore any special protection, no hard hats, goggles or visibility-waistcoats. The instructor attached a detonator and a few inches of fuse to the Cordtex loop, lit the fuse and walked away. After a few seconds the rope exploded, making a bang and an instantaneous wall of flame about three feet high around the loop leaving a slight singe on the grass. Next he added real explosives to the ring and this time we stood much further back. When the fuse was lit, most of us blocked our ears and the loop plus all the explosives made a really big bang!

This field engineering was often hard physical work, but more pleasant than purely drill and rifle-cleaning. On one occasion while pushing a

Bailey Bridge[8] across an imaginary 'river', the sergeant bellowed at me for standing in the imaginary 'shallows'!

In basic training, our intake-group took its turn at what the army called *admin*, which was three weeks of full-time labour outside the strictly military sphere. Most of us were allotted to tasks in the vast cookhouse to relieve the qualified soldier-cooks of menial work, and a few of us were allotted to other jobs that needed unskilled labour. There were two shifts per day for all these jobs except for mine. I was the 'swill-man' whose job was to spend the normal working day tidying up the swill-bins, cleaning the toilets and washbasins, and hosing-down the swill area. Paddy (an Irish cook), my supervisor, dropped by occasionally to see if I was slacking. Daily the Swill Contractor came to empty the bins, and presumably paid the army for this non-stop supply of his raw material.

To clean the toilets I had been supplied with an old broom-handle-like rod, easily identified by a nut-and-bolt through one end of it. One day I couldn't find the rod, so I wandered into the cook house to see if was lying around. It was. Paddy was using it to stir the huge vats of soup.

Eric, a fellow recruit soldier, and I had become buddies and one Saturday we thought it would be fine to go out of camp when his early shift ended. I realised I would virtually have no afternoon duties anyway. The NCO nodded assent to my implied request for time off, but was careful enough, army-style, not to actually agree verbally! Thus one glorious summer afternoon Eric and I hiked across the woodland and heath surrounding the camp, past the lakes which had once formed part of the garden of a stately home, and on to the next town. We took a bus ride along a high ridge in Surrey, and then hiked back to camp. Experiences such as this were like a breath of fresh air in the army's stuffiness – an open window out of the confined camp life.

Another recruit-friend was Dick, who came straight from Fettes School[9] and from a leading family in Angus Shire. In spite of his distinguished background and privileged schooling, he, like most of

---

8   Bailey Bridge. A bridge made up of easy-to-assemble standard components, none of which require more than two men to carry. Many could carry roads or railways if assembled in such a way as to be strong enough. A simpler assembly could carry marching troops. Many still exist.

9   Fettes is 'Scotland's Eton' – its most prestigious school. Former Prime Minister Tony Blair schooled there.

us, failed to impress the selectors at WOSB and remained in the ranks for his two years. One weekend when we had leave, he came home with me for the night to visit the 1951 *Festival of Britain*, a kind of national 'we've recovered from war' exhibition and celebration. A rather run-down site on London's south bank had been cleared, but signs of war and austerity were still everywhere. Rationing had well over another year to run.

One of the leading recruits decided to organise a pre-departure party at the end of our basic training. Buses would be hired to take us to the *Ace of Spades*, a well-known 'road house', or main-road pub. It was to be a stag party, no girlfriends, but with alcohol as each could afford it. The majority signed up, either to be matey or because they could afford plenty of drink. This type of excursion did not appeal to the OR-1s and we opted out, preferring to make our way to Guildford by train, and enjoy a leisurely meal with a glass of wine.

When the 17 weeks of training came to an end, I was detailed with two others to take the train to Longmoor. Three of us were assigned to 'Movement Control' – the logistics arm of the British forces' then worldwide disposition. Here I learnt how poverty still reigned over parts of the UK. Jim came from a poor background and shared a jacket with his brother, while the only toilet in his home was shared with the neighbours. Also having had a very limited education, he was apprehensive about the course at Longmoor. We were able to reassure him that he would not find it a problem, and in fact he fitted in very well. For me it was a lesson in encouraging others.

It was decided that I should become what the army called a Traffic Clerk – someone who had basic literacy and could work on the army's logistics[10]. However, the next course for Traffic Clerks was over eight weeks ahead. As no one could think of anything for us to do, we were sent on two weeks' leave; and, as I could type, I then slipped easily into a job in the Squadron Office. It was an indoor job and considered to be one of the more desirable of the Army's time-fillers.

One of my first jobs was to interview those regulars (those who were not conscripts but had signed-on to the army) who were approaching

---

10   In those days military transport and logistics were part of the Royal Engineers. Nowadays there is a separate Corps.

demobilisation, with a view to the Army preparing them for a civilian occupation. Some were called to the office and others I visited at their place of work. As just an ordinary young soldier, I was interviewing men much older, and more senior to me. One of them was the warrant officer in charge of Physical Training. Even after the army's basic training, I remained a rather thin and weedy sort of guy, and during a chat he suggested I come and do some weight training in the evenings. This was a new activity to me and I found it became a life skill in later years and in warmer climes.

The six weeks flew by and then the 10-week Traffic Clerk's Course approached… and concluded as winter drew nigh. It seemed that I would be invited to stay on to lecture future traffic clerk trainees, and probably be promoted to the rank of corporal. It was a comfortable prospect not too far from home.

But this never came to pass.

To the 'Mysterious East'

*"Those whose names I have just read out," said the sergeant, "are drafted to the Middle East." That was one of the British army's most dangerous trouble spots, and I was relieved that my name was **not** listed, I had no desire to stop a bullet in Suez!*

I breathed a sigh of relief. "And the rest of you," he continued, "are going to the Far East!"

When I learnt I was to be drafted to a distant land. I was both fearful and excited. My parents were shocked, for the Korean War with its heavy casualty toll still overshadowed any thinking to do with the Far East. But to the Army the *Far East* was quite separate from *Korea*.

The British services of those days moved slowly, first shifting us to a remote and bleak transit camp at Barton Stacey in Hampshire. We killed time as we were allotted to 'General Duties' (GDs) – odd jobs ranging from peeling potatoes to digging holes then filling them in again, while repeated delays occurred to our departure. (A decade later, the Conservative government abolished National Service. This was largely because so many young men, voters by then, recalled endless time spent doing nothing military at all; in many cases tiresome jobs were created just to make the men look busy.)

Our intended troopship, the *Empire Orwell*, had suffered repeated mechanical problems, so four of us learnt we were to be among the tiny number selected to fly. This was marvellous news indeed, for flying, even in a military aircraft, was sheer luxury compared to a month of drill and washing-down decks on a packed, sweltering troopship.

I was offered a 36-hour leave pass to see my parents and I slipped out onto the main road passing Barton Stacey camp. Young soldiers enjoyed considerable sympathy then, and their uniform guaranteed them against any suspicion of bad behaviour. So a truck driver took pity on me and loaded me on top of his china-clay cargo. He dropped me off at Westminster just as Big Ben chimed midnight. Again I looked hopefully at passing traffic. A man with a rather unsteady walk stopped and with a slurred voice invited me to share his bed with him. I thanked him and declined. A rather opulent car stopped and the bowler-hatted driver offered me a lift. He was obviously a well-to-do professional returning to his Surrey house, and he dropped me off close to my home. I have often mused whether he was a stockbroker, a judge or even a Member of Parliament!

Back at camp a Warrant Officer told us to get our kit together and report to the Goodge Street Deep Shelter in London[1]. He had made the journey before and told us what the coming week would bring. Alas, when our inoculation cards were checked his was found deficient and he was held back. We wondered how many other hurdles we might need to overcome before we actually flew. Would some other hitch return us to Barton Stacey... and more *General Duties*?

From the Deep Shelter we were trucked to Paddington station for the hour's journey to Swindon; only when we assembled on the platform with our kit did we realise that most of our fellow passengers were senior officers, or *brass hats*. They dumped their expensive holdalls onto a large luggage cart and many of the pieces rolled off. This was embarrassing for them and also for us soldiers as we endeavoured to re-stow the items more securely. Our overnight transit accommodation was by military standards truly luxurious. With no chores or GDs required, we watched an old American film about one Willy Stark who had, apparently, contrived to buy up everything in town that mattered. He even ran the police force. From a British standpoint this seemed a bit far-fetched – we had never heard of anyone buying a police force, nor were any for sale!

Our converted Hastings bomber carried a couple of dozen passengers on fixed, rear-facing seats, and it lumbered noisily into the sky. Little was visible in the darkness and we dozed till the sun rose over central France; then we gasped at the spectacle ranging from the glistening Alps to the sunlit Pyrenees. The 'Air Quartermaster' brought us packed lunches and refreshments. We stayed the night in the RAF's 'Transit Hotel' at Castel

---

1   Such shelters were constructed at the outbreak of war as an ultra-safe retreat from bombs, with the possibility of its many tunnels being linked up post-war as an express tube railway line. The Deep Shelters with their distinctive fortified entrances are still clearly visible today.

Benito in Tripoli, the former High Command Base of Benito Mussolini's air armada. The camp was set out in a landscaped garden. Imagine the RAF having a base in Libya today!

The next day we re-fuelled briefly at El Adem, near Tobruk – an unlikely desert runway with barbed wire enclosing the terminal. Taking off from the desert, I was transfixed by such panoramas as the war-wrecked railways and vehicles left over from General Bernard Montgomery's North African campaigns. Then the Suez Canal passed slowly under us with the dredged approaches from the Great lakes clearly visible.

Our next night stop was even more remarkable: at the huge landscaped base of RAF Habbaniya, later the principal air base of Saddam Hussein's Iraqi Air Force. We were told that outside, many people's lives had hardly changed since biblical times.

Ascending out of Habbaniyah, we lumbered on past the oil rigs of Iran – then in world news headlines – and down to Mauripur, the Royal[2] Pakistan Air Force base outside Karachi. Sand and dust were everywhere; we took a trip into town and experienced wall-to-wall crowds in every street. Men spat betel nut – we thought it was blood. Petrol-driven trams were the main street transport. A boy cleaned my heavy army boots, rubbing the blacking on with his hands. He asked about half a penny – later I was told I had been overcharged!

The next stop was RAF Negombo in Sri Lanka (then Ceylon). Still wearing our heavy British battledress, we tasted the steaming equatorial heat for the first time. In the hutted terminal, the Ceylon Tea Board welcomed us with a cup of strong, hot sweet tea. There was little to do for the rest of the day but attend a film show in a hangar – torrential rain on the tin roof made it difficult to follow the sound. Finally we crossed the Indian Ocean, and circled over Changi, with its notorious gaol being the main landmark. We landed in Singapore, then one of Britain's largest-ever air and naval bases and then still a Crown Colony. Our journey had lasted a week!

This had been a special experience indeed. As young conscript soldiers, we had been privileged to travel a third of the way round the world, in a small group of mainly officers, with comfortable night stops and courier guides.

---

2   Pakistan was then a Dominion.

A logistics officer, Captain Thorpe, met us and we were loaded into the back of a jeep-type truck. It was late afternoon so the heat was moderated.

We were soon installed in Tanglin Barracks, which were converted from former cavalry stables. The accommodation seemed spacious by British military standards, and the hilltop location meant it caught every cooling breeze. My parents imagined me fighting in the snowy wastes of Korea, or locked in deadly jungle conflict with murderous Malayan communists. I wrote to reassure my parents that I was doing neither. I did see a few rubber plantations, but no tigers, nor coolies with masks behind their heads!

The next morning the Sergeant gave us remarkably wise insights on living in Singapore. He extolled celibacy for young men, and made it clear what he thought of those who ventured into the few out-of-bounds parts of town. Finally he cautioned us about leaving valuables unguarded at night, concluding in a hushed tone with "remember, *this*... is the... mysterious... East!"

Since Communist terrorists were still operating in Malaya – of which Singapore was a kind of self-contained part – we were considered to be on Active Service and it was compulsory to wear our Campaign Medal on our jackets. (Not the actual medal, but a small slice of the medal ribbon: purple, green and purple). This was a multi-purpose medal for campaigns that were less than a full-scale war. When worn formally, complete with the solid silver medal itself, a bar for 'Malaya' was added.

The Malayan campaign was a jungle-based insurgency to take over Malaya for Communist rule. However this 'war', unlike those in Russia, China, Indo-China and elsewhere, ended with the Communists' defeat. There were several reasons for this:

1) Only a few of the population were motivated to take part in guerrilla warfare[3].

2) General Gerald Templer was given command of both military and civilian affairs, and he formed a clean government, neutral towards all ethnic communities.

3) Templer also won the hearts and minds of the civilian population with

---

3   At that time the population of Malaya-Singapore was approximately: Chinese 35 percent, Malays 45 percent, Indians and others 10 percent. However, the Chinese were thick on the ground in towns and cities, and also in market gardens; the Malays were concentrated in the rural areas though they dominated political life.

lots of schools and medical services, combined with good conditions for businesses. These things mattered far more to the ordinary people than politics[4].

4) The scattered rural Chinese population of Malaya, on which the Communists preyed for supplies and personnel, were resettled into some scores of fortified 'New Villages.' They were allowed out during daylight, mostly to tend their market gardens, but forbidden to take any food or supplies outside the villages lest they be of use to terrorists.

5) Independence for Malaya was in the pipeline, with future local leaders already receiving training.

Thus the Communists had little to offer to the people at large, and tensions between races could not be exacerbated by the terrorists. The victory over terrorism and Communism was largely completed before independence from Britain and is the sole example of a major communist insurrection that completely failed. Alas, not all the lessons learnt there were noted in, say, Indo-China!

I was to spend my remaining working year at Embarkation Headquarters in an ancient, but refurbished dockside office in the Singapore Harbour grounds. Here the army's logistics and drafts of personnel were handled. The first thing that struck the visitor on entry were three signs above the main gangway between the desks:

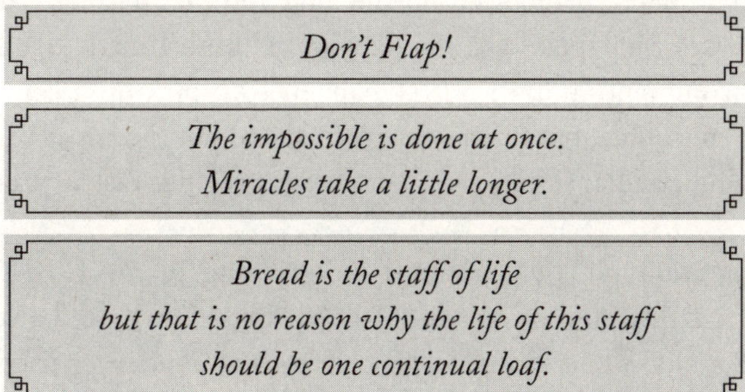

My first task was in the file registry, something I had become familiar with in my work with the railways. To introduce some kind

---

4   By contrast, in Vietnam the Americans were on foreign soil and dependent upon a corrupt and self-serving government who cared little for mere villagers; moreover, the Vietnamese military proved to be riddled with political fence-sitters and collaborators with the Communists.

of system, I started by making up an index-book with a 'laddered' right hand edge, and had a few copies run-off on the stencil machine. The cover paper included the badges of the Royal Engineers and the RAF. The Office Manager seemed quite taken aback. "But Sapper Huntley," he exclaimed, "I'm not saying that this isn't very well done, but you were not *told* to do this!" The *you're not paid to think* syndrome had reared its head again! I learnt that he had taken the index to the Colonel. But the Colonel was known to favour the young, often enterprising National Servicemen and at any rate shortly after that I was promoted one rank to lance corporal.

In those days no one had heard of recycling, but each day the civilian messenger-boy emptied all the unit's waste paper into a drainage ditch just outside. My old files went the same way, but I had not chosen tides well, for they remained clogging a grating across the ditch for some days. There could have been serious trouble, because all military files were deemed to contain operational secrets which could be the object of espionage. This was rather like the position of Civil Servants in the UK who can, for example, be prosecuted under the Official Secrets Act for revealing how many cups of tea are served in their office.

One early incident stands out in my mind. While working on a late evening duty, I typed a wax stencil and ran off copies of a circular letter to send home. I reported on the long and exciting flight out, some impressions of Singapore and my new job. I think I made one less-than flattering comment, and an officer happened to pick up a copy. I could have been in trouble, but he merely grinned and put the paper back on my desk! Typing circular letters was to become a regular task at a later stage in life.

Embarkation HQ was a small unit lacking in much of the usual military formality, and on Wednesday evenings they hosted a social and bar for all ranks. The officers' wives taught us to dance – or tried to, it's a skill I have never mastered! To make a dance surface, the concrete floor of the NAAFI[5] canteen was sprinkled with the army's medicated talcum powder!

---

5   NAAFI stands for *Navy, Army and Air Force Institutes*, the army's canteen and recreational facilities organisation, somewhat parallel to the American *PX*.

One day when a few us were passing the Capitol Theatre – then one of Singapore's best known cinemas – we noticed an advertisement for a film about the French Foreign Legion: *Ten Tall Men*. Tall passers-by were invited to be measured in a height contest. I duly submitted and the newspaper announced I was a prize-winner with two free tickets on the opening night. The next day a group photo of us 10 lanky young men appeared in *The Straits Times*.

Since we were part of the Royal Engineers, we were moved to a vacant barrack room at Gillman Barracks, the base of the Singapore Engineer Regiment RE. We were assured of breezy upstairs barrack rooms, a swimming pool and breathtaking views of the distant mountains of Sumatra.

The former Gillman Barracks looking from the hilltop towards Labrador Beach. The chimney of Pasir Panjang Power Station (then under construction and now in reserve) is visible – upper centre. The entire Barracks area is now swallowed up in a jungle nature reserve to provide a 'green area' in a built-up city.

There was less insistence on regimentation at Gillman Barracks than at Tanglin; moreover, Gillman was within walking distance to Sandes Soldiers' Home, a Christian club with a canteen, swimming pool, comfortable lounges, a library and if desired, overnight accommodation. (This building is now the Temasek Club for Singaporean officers.)

An interesting reflection was that Gillman, like Tanglin, and indeed most of the UK forces' camps in Singapore and many in Britain, had no border security at all. There was really nothing to stop anyone from walking through the camps. Yet theft or vandalism were almost unknown. Nor was it considered that such openness would be a breach of military security.

A minor problem was that once we were billeted at Gillman, we were expected to undergo a 'physical efficiency' test annually including series of runs, jumps and swimming – none of which were any problem to me. But when it came to rope climbing, the sergeant had to give me a good shove from below ("come on, lofty!") and I reached the top. His encouragement was verbal, vertical and physical!

My next job in Embarkation HQ was to track His, and then Her[6], Majesty's military hardware being unshipped from commercial freighters, trucked off to the military depots, and occasionally pilfered. Letters were written in the pedantic army style and long lists of cargo were typed and re-typed and circulated to all parties concerned. I suggested to my superior officer that we no longer laboriously hand-copy and then type them a second or third time, but refer to them in subsequent letters by date. He agreed (i.e. he didn't refuse) and this cut down my work considerably. Initially, I had to work late to clear-up the arrears, but even this had its compensations – we usually got a bigger plateful when we booked a 'late duty' evening meal.

I occasionally went to the office of our haulage contractor over a problem. I would be referred to the owner's son, who usually managed to say nothing at all! He was more or less a place-holder for his father. The Contractor found a loophole in customary procedures, which exonerated him from compensating us for several weeks of losses in transit. My boss, Captain Jervis did not seem to know what to do; many military men find civilian situations baffling! One day Captain Jervis suggested that we visit the contractor together over several outstanding issues. A truck was duly called; Captain Jervis sat in the front while I squatted in the back carrying the relevant files. The office manager welcomed us with coffee as usual before we got down to business. 'Coffee' (today's *Kopi-C*) was a thick, black tar-like liquid, or *sock coffee* brewed in a long sock-like tube that

---

6   The death of King George VI came to us on an evening news broadcast relayed in the Barracks, we could hardly believe our ears. He was not an old man but his serious cancer had been kept very quiet – he was a heavy smoker. In a day or two a message from Queen Elizabeth II appeared on poster sites throughout Malaya including Singapore. Obviously those in authority had some premonition of the impending change in the Monarchy and had planned accordingly!

holds the coffee grounds in the urn – with a spoonful or two of sweetened condensed milk added. We drank this coffee from a thick china mug. "Huntley, isn't this coffee ghastly?" asked the Captain. Actually I quite liked it and still do!

(Interestingly, it was through the transport company that I experienced my first Chinese wedding feast – of the contractor's son, and also my first taste of spirits which I was unaccustomed to. Guided back by my fellow soldiers, I have ever since avoided this kind of refreshment. About half a century later, while researching in Singapore I opened the newspaper and there was the former bridegroom's photo and obituary!)

At the Embarkation Headquarters, a diversion within the desk-based freight-discrepancies job was to visit one of the many military depots scattered around Singapore Island. Usually this was necessary when it became clear that depot papers showed unsolved discrepancies, or that we were possibly being bamboozled by the contractor. I enjoyed getting out onto the then cross-country roads among the green rural scenery which still carpeted much of the island.

I usually tackled the problem with one of the respective depot's Asian civilian personnel. But one day I was ushered into the office of the depot's boss, a senior officer. After my usual formal standing stiffly to attention and saluting, he told me that he, too was mystified why 'that rascally haulage contractor' was able to get away with so much quite patently abstracted army stuff that he was missing. This was a difficult situation, for lance-corporals should not normally instruct officers, but I answered his questions, and explained what legal problems we were having with our claims. He was quite warm and chatty and seemed appreciative of a mini-lesson in local law. We returned to our correct formal positions with salutes before we parted.

I finally got to a point where I was sure I had incontrovertible evidence of a clear, though small loss in the contractor's hands – a consignment of 11 buckets. Surely action would be taken? I was looking forward to 'finalising' this shipment with the usual pedantic form-letter to the War Office in London. But no. I was shifted to another section!

I served briefly in the Personnel Movements Division; at that time Britain chartered some 16 elderly ocean liners as troopships. Sometimes the British civilian ships' crews, wanting the company of fellow-countrymen, would slip us into the saloon for a full ship's evening meal. We learnt to avoid being plied with liquor later, or joining the crew in their quarters!

It was very pleasant riding on a launch in Singapore Harbour – and still is. One duty was to disembark an officer arriving from Australia before the ship actually docked. A second military man wanted to come ashore on the launch too. *Should we let him? Won't that generate headaches?*

"Well," came the reply, "if we get headaches we can always take aspirins!" And so came my first introduction to the easy-going Australian indifference to bureaucracy. Little did I know that 15 years later in Singapore, I would meet and marry an Australian... and later become one!

Then I heard that missionaries were beginning to arrive in Singapore from newly closed China. This was to be far more meaningful to me later than I realised, when I was assigned a duty on the Queens Birthday holiday 1952. Two of us soldiers were detailed to disembark a British intelligence officer from a small coastal steamer, the *Szechuan*. What I did not know till years later was that the *Szechuan* was also the steamer bringing the advance party of the China Inland Mission, or CIM. Their leaders had come to Singapore to prospect for their new international base. They are still there!

Back in Croydon, my home church was keen on supporting missionaries and supported about a dozen of them. Some 10 speakers per year representing various societies came and challenged us. Many had us sitting on the edge of our seats, and a continuing stream of younger people responded to the call to serve overseas. In those days places like Singapore seemed very remote from England.

I held the missionaries in high regard, but unfortunately in the UK, many societies exemplified their schools and hospitals as the *principal* opportunities for service. Thus the straight planting of the Gospel among the *totally* unevangelised did not always come to the forefront. By contrast the China Inland Mission, having been forced out of China and starting work in East Asia, would continue their China policies: they would seek out some location where there were few or no Christians, and work by invitation with any who were there. They would aim to move on when a viable congregation was planted among the people locally. They still do this. I saw all this 'through a glass darkly' during my army service in the Far East.

One of the perks of army life in Singapore was the occasional free ride 'up country' into Malaya, notably to a military vacation centre in Penang, or to explore the much more 'oriental' city of Kuala Lumpur (KL). A long train ride was usually involved – over 30 hours' journey to Penang. Even the leisurely steam-hauled 'Day Mail' took all day over its 248 mile journey to KL. Our office corporal, Dave Ward, was approaching demobilisation and suggested a visit to the KL railway works before his departure for the UK. He was a steam-train aficionado (and still is) and made arrangements to get us free travel.

Malaya, consisting of about a dozen States was then a British Protectorate. However, Britain was not sovereign over every internal matter. For example, Malay religion and customs remained the prerogatives of the Malay Sultans and were unaffected by the British presence, so through the decades an absolute ban on any evangelisation of the Malays has been strictly reinforced. Singapore was considered part of Malaya for some purposes, but quite separate for others and its colonial status made it a bastion of religious freedom – which as an independent republic it still is. Travelling between the two then required no documentation, and only a perfunctory one-way check by Malayan customs officers.

Britain then kept about 100,000 security forces in Singapore and Malaya, including a number of local personnel. By 1952 the period of rural terrorism

David Ward and I travelled to Kuala Lumpur by train. We had to carry an (unloaded) gun but with five rounds of ammunition.

was ending, although we were each required to carry a rifle and a few rounds of ammunition on rail journeys in case there were attacks from Communist bandits.

In KL our economical night-stop was in a shophouse hotel, the *De Luxe*. Shophouse hotel rooms usually had walls stopping a couple of feet from the high ceiling – making for both economy and coolness, so snores and conversation were common background noises We were fortunate in having no all-night gamblers as fellow-patrons.

Our guide, a Malayan-Indian railway officer, explained that the KL railway works was very well equipped with the most advanced technology east of Suez; they built almost all of their rolling stock there except for the imported steam engines. One fruit of those expeditions was to learn something of the country and people, most of whom seemed to be friendly, charming and welcoming.

The curious 'steam carriage' between Kuala Lumpur and suburban Ampang in 1952.

There was one railway curiosity in KL on the branch to suburban Ampang: the steam railcars (a kind of one-coach train with a built-in steam locomotive). The ride was only a short one, notable for the amount of coal dust in the passenger cabin. The ticket collector was friendly enough but warned Dave and me that there might be terrorists in Ampang, so we returned on the same antique specimen of locomotion.

On our return from KL to Singapore, the train started to lose time, and night was falling. Because of the occasional Communist guerrilla attacks on night trains, we were parked in a rural station until the 'night pilot' could be brought along. This was an armoured gun turret coupled to a flat wagon full of heavy ballast in front of it, and with a locomotive propelling both from behind. The ballast wagon was intended to explode any mines placed on the track. Authority to depart was given and we continued with the 'night pilot' just in view ahead.

The camp chapel at Tanglin was closed, and non-existent at Gillman. There appeared to be no Chaplain, and we were left to find spiritual activities on our own. Occasionally on Sundays a few of us would find our way down to St Andrew's Cathedral or the much nearer Sandes Soldiers' Home. However, the same four of us who had arrived from England by air together decided to take our leave due at Sandycroft[7], the forces' seaside

---

7   At the time of writing Sandycroft is now Dalat School, started for children of the Christian and Missionary Alliance, a sizeable American denomination.

leave centre in Penang, nearly 500 miles north. At Sandycroft on the northern coast of Penang, we could borrow bikes to cycle round the island – a hilly but spectacular ride. There was a bathing beach and various attractions in town, plus the funicular railway to the top of Penang Hill. Just outside town lay the Snake Temple where live, though not poisonous snakes lay around, and tourists were encouraged to hold them.

Four national service soldiers enjoying leave on top of Penang Hill. 'Bud' Abbott, Frank James, David, George Hedworth. The shorts were typical off-duty garb.

My snake turned inquisitively towards me and I'm afraid I dropped him on the floor, but he seemed none the worse. One of my friends recorded the incident on my hand-turned 9.5mm movie camera.

A diversion for me in Singapore was to be ordered to undertake some errand for our superiors. Our small unit of about 20 army and air force men, plus about the same number of civilians, was commanded by one Lieutenant Colonel Saunders. He and his wife enjoyed a spacious bungalow along the shore near Changi; he decided that the flower beds needed enhancing and the gardener had prescribed horse manure. Thus I was despatched with a small truck and Malay driver, plus a 'coolie'. There was a standard joke that the army would use four men to do the job of one: a soldier to do the job, someone to supervise him, a truck driver to get them to the location, and of course an officer-in-charge. We managed this assignment with an economical three.

We drove to the Singapore Turf Club, a gentleman's club which owned and operated the race track and horse racing monopoly. No one seemed to expect me, but I was ushered into the manager's office – he seemed perplexed and suggested I phone my unit for he was not in the horse dung business. Unusually, the Colonel himself picked up the phone. He was unimpressed: "No, NO!" he shouted. "You should have gone to the Singapore **Saddle** Club." I discovered this rather downmarket facility just a few minutes' drive away and the coolie started shovelling manure into sacks. Suddenly, and again atypically, I had a severe bilious attack and was sick into a small stream – the driver and coolie thought this most entertaining, and they stopped work to observe my discomfort more closely!

Colonel Saunders was, again, typical of the life-long military man – excellent at military procedures but rather out-of-depth in purely civilian activities. One evening I was on the occasional task of Duty Clerk and so had to sleep the night in the office. For some reason I was checking the Colonel's desk trays and noticed an unusual letter – he had been consulting an astrologer in India about his small child's future!

Another diversionary time-killer occurred when I was Night Duty Clerk at the docks and the doorway framed the dreaded Brigadier Montgomery. Whether he was related to the D-Day and North African 'Monty' of fame I did not know, but he was noted for impatience with any soldier who omitted the correct formalities. With him was a Captain Gould as his 'staff officer'. It seems that the brigadier wanted to send a 'signal' – the army's equivalent of a telegram. In fact it transpired that the two men had just seen off a friend so I wrote as he dictated. 'Best wishes, Bon Voyage, Montgomery Gould'. I phoned this 'vital' military communication through to Royal Signals, and lest they query the social nature of the text I was able to quote Brigadier Montgomery as the authorisation.

Many servicemen took advantage of the excellent local tailoring and I had a formal suit made.

While National Service in Singapore was by and large pleasant and much better paid than army life at home, incidents such as this explain how much labour and time was spent on simple, even peripheral jobs ostensibly to defend the Queen and Commonwealth from her enemies! The warm climate was attractive, not to mention the floodlit swimming pool at Gillman. Moreover, Singapore was a free port with minimal currency control. Watches, fountain pens, cameras and other luxury goods sold at about half the heavily taxed UK prices, and beautifully tailored clothing cost much less. And nothing was rationed. Many demobbed National Servicemen subsequently returned to East Asia, and I wondered if I might do the same. But whether on the railway or through some other channel, I could only ponder.

Independence for Malaya was then on the distant horizon, but many local people seemed ambivalent about it. They went along with the idea that should it come about, it *might* be good, but also that it might not! Others felt that some kind of local independence could be better. Meanwhile most were pleased that everything was in much better shape than in any neighbouring nation. Very few people sympathised with Communism or with the terrorists in Malaya, whose insurrection was pro-China oriented. The local Chinese were understandably loyal to their great nation's culture, but in general feared the as-yet little-understood Communist rule of Mao Zedong. On the whole the jungle terrorists were considered to be holding up and delaying progress towards independence.

There was free fraternisation across races and cultures though the major ethnic groups tended to each have their own social clubs and business associations. We young men from the UK enjoyed swimming in a local Chinese swimming club. There was none of the ethnic separation found in for example, parts of Africa. A few British soldiers even brought Singaporean brides home with them. Now in the 21st century where Singapore is a glittering and successful metropolis, and a rightly proud independent Republic, older folk who can remember the colonial time kindly comment that it was a favourable launch-pad for their present prosperity.

Before leaving my Army job, I was told to train local civilians to take over my tasks. I left the freight claims worries with a Chinese bachelor and an Indian Christian, a family man. Both of them farewelled me sumptuously according to their traditional cuisine, and they corresponded with me a few times after my return.

The *Empire Trooper*, an old German vessel, originally named *Cap Norte*, had been torpedoed, sunk, salvaged and refitted as a troopship by the British. Now she was standing-by in Singapore harbour for her 28-day voyage back to Southampton. My job aboard was in the ship's orderly room. It was far from arduous since it was not felt necessary to 'keep the men fully occupied' as it had been on outward trips. It was warm enough to sleep on the open deck most nights until Suez, rather than on the triple-decker bunks in the bowels of the ship, and by day the sea breezes moderated the tropical heat. The sun became less fierce after Aden, and by Suez the night air had turned too chilly for deck-sleeping. On a grey and dismal day late in the afternoon, we berthed at Southampton in a grey and dismal dock. I was assigned to Tannoy[8] duty and spent the evening in front of a microphone calling up various functionaries, clearing areas of troops, warning that import of any kind of firearm into the UK was prohibited and so on.

A leisurely but well-filled steam train trundled along lines now long closed, taking us back to Andover and the bleakness of Barton Stacey. I found a seat and a woman next to me in the compartment grumbled that troops were causing overcrowding. I commented that she should remember that some of them had seen active fighting on behalf of their country, and the rest of the occupants warmly concurred – unusually conversational for Britain!

We were matured, sun-tanned and demob-happy, and after a couple of days were given a week's home leave. Ration Cards were issued and we were back in the land of austerity. Bleak, cloudy, chilly weather emphasised the contrast with far-away warm and sunny Singapore. Then it was back to Barton Stacey while slowly and step by step we were prepared for return to civilian life. 'Prepared for' simply meant we spent days doing almost nothing while the army's bureaucracy completed paperwork.

At last we were free – and on a fast train back to Waterloo I enjoyed a hot meal in the restaurant car, a service that has long disappeared.

It was notable that out of the two years of conscription, I was actually doing a job for the army for only about 10 months. The rest was spent on various kinds of unrelated training, on waiting around and on travel. In due course I received my Campaign Medal – silver, engraved with my number and name, complete with its ribbon and the 'Malaya' bar.

Few, if any, young men would have entered the Armed Services had there been no compulsory National Service. Once the Korean War was over there was very little fighting, so casualties were minimal. For some it seemed a waste of time. Nonetheless, the military taught young men

---

8   *Tannoy* is a brand of amplifier, which had become the eponymous name of public address systems used by the forces and others.

self-respect, team-spirit, fitness, discipline, loyalty, dress-sense and a new kind of confidence. For many, service in Europe, the Middle East and Far East – and even further – were a form of education for world citizenship too. Even today, I find that men with some military experience are the easiest to work alongside.

My next steps were unclear but proved to be completely unforeseen.

Back to the Railway

It was early 1953; out of army uniform and back into my office suit. I returned to Emmanuel Church and to old and new friends in the senior Youth Club – and back to British Railways. I was well received, having won several prizes under their Staff Suggestion Scheme, and an illustrated article of mine entitled *Railways in Malaya* was published in the staff magazine while I was on military service.

A fast-track cadetship programme was in the offing, and my boss suggested that I spend the first few weeks looking round various aspects of the railway system to be ready for the scheme's entrance tests. Twice I passed the scheme's preliminary exam and initial interviews, yet twice failed the final selection.

At this juncture I joined the Railway Service Christian Union (RSCU) which fitted its short lunch hour meeting into a spare basement space below Waterloo station. Members or visiting speakers brought us a spiritual challenge or encouragement week by week. Complementing this was the weekly lunch time 'service' with excellent speakers at St Mary Woolnoth Church in the centre of the financial district. I learnt a lot from both.

My boss then suggested that I move to the Continental Department, and I was allocated to a small sub-department which booked cars onto railway-run ferries to France and Belgium. It also dealt with 'real business' companies such as travel agents who brought a breath of fresh air and challenge into the office. But I was disgusted to discover that in summer when most of the ships were fully booked, many of the staff did very well out of 'advance thank-you's'. On one wintry occasion when the boats were far from full, I was completing a booking for a would-be passenger who slipped me a 10 shilling[1] note in his final handshake. I shared this

---

1   Ten shillings would have bought about six canteen two-course lunches at that time.

instance with our Curate, who as a student had worked in this same office. He warned me that this man would come back in the peak season. (He did!) So I wrote him a letter returning the 10 shillings, and explained that while I could not accept it, I valued his kindness and would be pleased to be of service on his further trips.

For relaxation my church friend, Dennis Norris and I would mount his motor bike and go camping in some open country or woodland. It was pleasant leisurely Christian fellowship; we were united in learning more about overseas missions. Several of us in the Youth Club had become increasingly interested in these ministries. In fact, in Emmanuel in those days one could never be ignorant of 'the mission field' as it was then called, because of the frequent and riveting missionary sermons we heard – about 10 times a year! Later Dennis and his wife Daphne spent most of their working years as missionaries in Pakistan.

My main social outlet was still the Emmanuel Church Youth Club (14 to 26-year-olds) where I helped to organise relaxing activities or visits of interest – one was to the printing works and export centre of the British and Foreign Bible Society. On another occasion, after a London tour we planned to hold our concluding 'epilogue' in St Mary Woolnoth Church adjacent to the Bank of England, where I had been attending lunchtime services. As I made my request, the Vicar was leaning over a table looking some paperwork. Without looking up he cut in, 'yes, that's fine, tell him to collect the key at lunch time. They can let themselves in when they arrive in the evening and then lock themselves out and drop the key in the letter box'. I had a similar experience when we were welcomed to use the private chapel of Queen Elizabeth the Queen Mother for our 'epilogue.' One wonders what insurers and Health and Safety bureaucrats would make of that today! Other opportunities for spiritual refreshment came with hikes and an annual houseparty. Here too, we were challenged to consider working overseas by speakers who had given lifetime service as church-planters or overseas mission trainers.

At that point car ownership was increasing exponentially, so it was taken for granted that rail travel must continue to decrease[2]. During the 1980s, Prime Minister Margaret Thatcher opined that any young person who had not become a car-owner by age 25 must be utterly devoid of ambition indeed!

---

2   As I write in 2012, several routes abandoned for decades have been reinstituted.

Youth Houseparty at Wiston Hall, a former 'Stately Home'.
Breakfast in the Great Hall as seen from the Minstrels' Gallery.

I could not afford a motorbike, let alone a car. However, with my
21st birthday money I bought a Trojan Minimotor for £16. This was a
small two-stroke engine which fitted behind the saddle of a bicycle and
was equivalent to a low-powered motor bike. It had just three moving
parts and a small drive-wheel pressed on the top of the rear tyre. It
occasionally needed pedal-help on steep hills, nevertheless for four years
I Minimotored around southern England until the machine was near-
worn out.

In 1954, my friend John Ede and I decided to go to Italy. This
time we booked places on the prestigious Golden Arrow to Dover: 'the
train of the diplomat and the financier' – and Hercule Poirot! Crossing
Switzerland, we appreciated breath-taking views as the train climbed
magnificent bridges, tunnels and a circular viaduct towards snow-
capped mountains, then down to Italy.

In Venice, we were delighted to find that our guest house was right
on St Mark's Square, overlooking the famous bell-Tower and the Grand
Canal. We walked or rode the ferries to explore the maze of canals and
managed one short gondola ride. From Venice to Rome we sampled the
high speed of Italian railways; even the second class compartments were
quite luxurious. On Sunday, we located a tiny English chapel run by
Scottish Presbyterians!

The final leg of our journey was on the remarkable Night Ferry,
whose specially built Anglo-French sleeping cars were shipped across

the English Channel complete with somnolent passengers; it was hauled off the other side for the last couple of hours to London, with breakfast en route. The Night Ferry was popular with businessmen since they could travel outside of the working day.

Even though I enjoyed vacations on the Continent, I had often wondered whether it might be possible to revisit distant Singapore. But the cheapest sea passage would have been far beyond my means, and the air fare was about triple that! Moreover the sea voyage took three to four weeks in each direction, and my annual vacation was only 12 working days.

In my job with British Railways, I was promoted to a section at Waterloo concerned with ever-ongoing branch-line closures. The 'close it if at all' possible philosophy was being implemented, 'the smaller the system, the less the loss' despite some sectors of the industry being quite profitable.

Should I consider going back to the Far East? Perhaps with the railway? At that time Malayan Railway still recruited in Britain for their more senior posts, and I had had a brief chat with a senior manager before leaving Singapore. Though I had often considered this possibility, I found no confirmation either way.

No immediate alternative to a future with the railways had presented itself, although one older man suggested that I pray and read the Bible and see if a passage might 'hit' me with a message about leaving the railways or otherwise.

'You might for example,' he continued, 'read, *arise, take up your...*' and stopped himself abruptly, realising that was a passage taken out of context. It was from Jesus's words to the paralysed man whom he had cured: 'arise, take up your bed and walk.' (Mark 2:11 in the King James Version – the only version we used in those days).

That passage came in my daily Scripture Union reading a couple of hours later! Exegetically it was unrelated to a young man's calling to change his job. But the remarkable coincidence struck me! Other 'signposts' were to follow.

I related well to John Bickersteth, our Curate, and I often sought his advice and counsel on my future; we prayed together several times for clear guidance. With so much interest in overseas missions, he invited about a dozen of us teens and 20's to a country vicarage to meet Leslie

Lyall, the CIM's candidate co-ordinator, and he outlined to us some of the practicalities and difficulties of missionary work. Among those he instanced was an ex-China couple who were now on loan to the Far East Broadcasting radio station in Manila – broadcasting locally and to China. This was my first intimation that missionary radio stations existed at all. At that time independent broadcasting was unheard of in the UK.

At work, office politics took me from the moderately interesting branch-lines job to the drudge of handling public complaints. My new boss handed me a thick, yellowing pad of ageing carbon copies which were the standard replies with which to respond to any complaint. 'David', he said, 'take this as your bible!' From a Christian standpoint I felt most of the complaints were justified; but very little could be done to remedy the problems complained of since most railway investment was barred by the government. So I could merely trot out the standard anodyne replies. It was becoming clear that, though they would have vigorously denied it, senior railway officers were increasingly in the task of 'managed decline.'

At Emmanuel Church, the first Emmanuel Missionary Committee was formed under the chairmanship of a retired lady missionary, Elsie Webster MBE ('Auntie Webster'). To us younger folk she seemed like the ideal aunt. As a senior youth member and one who had been to a 'missionary country', I was invited to join this Committee, and also to encourage the youth club to foster prayer for missions. Each year, at the annual Missions Weekend, the young people prepared a striking exhibit about missions, and this became part of the parish's teaching on service overseas. It was excellent training and brought many of us into contact with mission societies.

One year we built a model New Village, as in Malaya – fortified against Communist guerrillas and yet wide open to churchplanting, especially by the CIM. Another year we researched and featured missionary broadcasting with a tall balsa-wood 'radio-mast' displayed in the Church Hall.

Obviously money for living and fees in any missions college course would amount to a considerable sum and my family did not have that. But again, God knew the future! I decided that a first-hand visit to some missions would help me, so I used my rail travel concessions to go down through France, Spain and Gibraltar, then across the Straits to Tangier, just then being merged with the Islamic Kingdom of Morocco. I enjoyed visits to the two 'mission' radio transmitting stations then operating there, Radio Ibra and Voice of Tangier[3] – quite an eye-opener to one accustomed to a strict BBC monopoly! The possibility of mission radio seemed to open up all sorts of potentialities.

While a guest in the Tangier Mission Guest House I received warm invitations to visit some missionaries where they served. This was to be my first experience of the Arab World and its overwhelmingly Islamic ethos. Several other guests were about to make their various journeys and I felt quite confident about mine as an elderly man prayed for 'travelling mercies' for each of us.

But the journey proved to be anything but uneventful! I was ejected from the train because apparently my passport lacked a stamp, but a friendly French official sorted that out by phone and asked a passing motorist to take me on to Port Lyautey[4] where I could re-join the railway. My car-host had warned me to be cautious for my safety as it was already dark, and to avoid crowded places. So I was relieved when a friendly station-master at Port Lyautey invited me into his office. He made some unflattering but possibly true remarks about safety – or the lack of it – under the new government. The train deposited me in Fez late at night and there was only one small taxi waiting. Already, two hooded ladies were sitting in the back and I had been warned that it was inappropriate to sit close to them.

However, the driver beckoned me into the front seat and seemed to understand the instructions which the missionaries had given me. We were stopped by an armed guard at a Moorish gate in the wall, but he simply waved us on, and indeed the driver easily located the missionaries' building and was quite happy with the fare that I had been told would be reasonable. I was starting to get a good impression of Morocco. The missionaries were quite used to people getting delayed, and weren't fazed by my unearthly hour of arrival. They commented that such experiences were GMT or 'good missionary training!' In retrospect I thanked God for

---

3   Soon after Moroccan independence, these stations were asked to move away. The
     Sultan said, "There is only one 'Voice of Tangier' and that's me!" The organisation is
     now Transworld Radio.

4   The town was named after Lyautey, a Frenchman. It is now called Kenitra.

the three helpers who had solved problems during the journey: the French official, the motorist and the station master! The old man's prayers for 'travelling mercies' had been answered.

The Fez Mission house enjoyed a magnificent view across the old city towards the Kairouine University and the major mosque. However, the Fez Christian Church was tiny – about eight people met in the mission building. The two lady missionaries, Lily and Grace, spoke good Arabic and took me sightseeing around the old city with its craftsmen, butcheries and donkeys. I bought a soft leather cover for my Bible. Next I boarded a bus for Rabat, the capital of Morocco. It filled up with soldiers and a young man in uniform sat next to me; he offered me a cigarette which I did not take, and then a glass of mint tea which I did! Moroccans seemed to be delightful people.

In Rabat I met my next hosts – two more lady missionaries, Dora and Winifred, serving with Crosslinks[5] who invited me to their mission centre at Sidi Bettache, an hour or so's drive away. A former missionary had built an impressive old-style mission station, transgressing all the missiological wisdom of earlier decades that missionaries should live as simply as practicable, preferably in properties similar to those of local people. There were three courtyards: one for the missionaries' private domain; next, the clinic, and the third received casual local callers including tradesmen. There was no electricity but we enjoyed hot baths by virtue of solar heating. Here I gained some insight into rural Moroccan life. To chat with real missionaries in a 'missionary' land was both an education and an encouragement to me.

On the homeward route I made a diversion to Lourdes, which I had learnt about at St Joseph's College. Many pilgrims visit this healing spring where St Bernadette is said to have seen the Virgin Mary appear. The nightly candle procession was about to start, with loudspeakers carrying the rosary prayer, but I had to catch my onward train to Paris and home.

A day or so later I met our Vicar, Revd Bertie Rainsbury. I did not think he would be interested in my Moroccan trip, and I suspected he would consider it a waste of money and time. But he was very much interested! As a speaker at the annual Keswick Convention, he had met Ralph Freed,

---

5   Then called BCMS – Bible Churchman's Missionary Society

the founding director of Radio Tangier, and Bertie encouraged me to think positively about overseas service.

My father retired and my parents decided to move north to the English Lake District. They found a small cottage plus a spacious garden with a magnificent view of some 27 mountain tops. They felt that at 24, I should be able to find my own accommodation, so I moved into 'digs' in a large house owned by an Emmanuel family. Nonetheless I did not feel that this lifestyle was to be long-term for me, even though my parents saw my position on the railway as an iron rice bowl[6]. Like many who had lived through the 1920s Great Depression, they felt that such a job should not be quitted lightly – if at all!

Then I went for an interview for a study trip to visit railways in North America, but the funding body decided not to make an award that year. If this had come to fruition, I would probably have been committed to the railways for some time. I continued to learn that God knew differently.

In fact, my remaining time at Waterloo was to be very short indeed.

---

6   Iron rice bowl – a Chinese expression for a secure job with a sure future.

The New World

"Mr Huntley, we'd like you to spend the summer in New York," announced the urbane executive interviewer at British Railways' lordly Marylebone HQ. There was a partnership with Irish State Railways to operate a network of sales agencies across North America: *British and Irish Railways Inc.* They brought single young men out for the busiest season.

I had to present myself at the American Consulate to apply for a visa. An official made me raise my right hand and repeat after him an oath that neither I nor any friend or relative had ever had anything to do with Communism. I was fingerprinted and then issued with the necessary passport stamp.

The Curate invited me to speak to the Emmanuel Youth Club to share my news and commented that just as my move to the USA was unexpected, so Christians should always be ready for the unexpected.

Apparently the Tourist Class cabins were all taken, so I found myself in a business class luxury cabin aboard the RMS *Queen Elizabeth* heading for the USA – a land which few Brits had ever seen apart from on the large screen. The voyage was a leisurely five-day interlude between the frenzied packing up and having to settle in to American life.

In those days dollar-shortage all but prohibited *any* funds for travelling across the Atlantic. So I left Britain without a cent of American currency in my pocket, and had to live on pay advances for the first couple of months. 'The East' may have been dubbed *mysterious* but to most Britons there was much more mystique about America!

My impressions of the USA had been by conflicting bits of hearsay, plus brief encounters with American visitors. I knew that the US was vast to cross – though my England to Singapore journey was even further. We knew that cars and household gadgetry and such luxuries as German cameras were widely affordable, and that large families

Gala night on RMS *Queen Elizabeth*. David (left back) with
fellow passengers.

were common. I gathered that church-going in the USA was a bigger
feature of life than in the UK, with whole families driving considerable
distances to worship.

On the fifth morning, the ship glided into Manhattan's West Side
alongside a shore-side expressway at its peak. I was amazed at so many
large cars, so fast and so brightly coloured! Not one mile of motorway
existed in the UK then, neither were there any major road-over-road
intersections, let alone spaghetti junctions.

The Englishman from British and Irish Railways Inc. who met us
off the boat warned us that in spite of the largely familiar language, we
would find New York 'much stranger' than any European city. Some new
thinking would be called for in this strange and exciting land.

The enjoyable and unfamiliar world of French fries, garden parkways,
turnpikes, fried-two-over-light, sunny side up, wheatcakes, elevators,
pumpernickel, redcaps, dimes, cheeseburgers and subway tokens lay ahead
for discovery. Till then 'coke' had been a dusty, black solid-fuel that was
tipped into the hot water boiler!

The most surprising thing of all that greeted my eyes in Manhattan
were the ubiquitous air raid shelter signs – a large white 'S' and legend
on a black background which appeared to be identical with the long-
disappeared ones in Britain during the war. But this was 1957 and the
American government was conscientising the public to the danger of
missile strikes from Russia. I needed to buy a radio and noticed that every
radio had two 'CD' markings on the tuning scale – frequencies to which

listeners should tune in the event of enemy attack, to hear Civil Defence announcements.

Everyone knows that Americans are friendly and helpful, but on about my second day I got a rude shock when a barber (financially speaking) scalped me. But that was my sole such experience among Americans then and after a lifetime of working with them and visiting their homeland.

The job was in a way the easiest part: I worked behind the counter of British and Irish Railways Inc, selling rail travel to Americans in our Rockefeller Centre ground floor (American 'first floor') shop in the Time and Life Building. My task was to make up itineraries for enquirors, and hopefully to sell them tickets, railway hotel reservations and through journeys to Europe.

For me this was no problem. I knew the UK rail system quite well, and enjoyed explaining the wrinkles of British travel to Americans; they often asked me for suggestions for sightseeing. A large proportion already had a shortish list of places they wanted to see; typically, an aspiring tourist would walk up to the counter with an engaging smile, stub his finger on the counter map, and ask 'how can I see Londonengland, Dublinireland, Glasgowscotland and Yorkminsterengland?' A less expected, but quite common addition to their wish list was Tunbridgewellsengland, not forgetting Cardiffwales!

I had imagined that American railways would be modern marvels far ahead of anything I had seen in Europe, and in a few respects they were. But even in 1957, America had already advanced in the 'managed decline' of their long distance railways. On a recent visit I discovered it is possible to drive over a hundred miles in any direction without entering a rail-served city!

With the very high American labour costs there was little room for bureaucracy. In British and Irish Railways we signed our own letters – and occasionally even typed them ourselves; there was no 'typing pool' as in Britain but 'secretaries' were hired by the hour to take our letters in shorthand as necessary. This was a breath of fresh air after Waterloo! However, enjoyable as I found it, the work-day regime was somewhat routine. My spare time activity and vacation travel was far more exciting.

Initially I was placed in a hotel but was asked to find somewhere cheaper, and settled into the Biblical Seminary in New York – a much more 'Christian' environment. Moreover, I had my own wash basin and a view across to the Empire State and Chrysler Buildings. Getting back late at night I would make my way to the 10th floor vending machine with a dime (10¢) to buy a cold Coke… I just felt I *had* to get that bottle into my hand. It did seem that Coke's accusers – claiming that the bottlers added an addictive ingredient – had a case! I'm no longer keen on Coke but the Americans did wean me from tea to coffee.

Since my arrival had been dollar-less, I soon discovered the Horn and Hardart Company's economical but excellent *Automat* restaurants. These displayed various fresh hot and cold dishes in glass-fronted cabinets with instructions such as *drop 3 nickels in slot* to release the catch and take out the dish. Hot breakfasts were served at any time from a cook-to-order cafeteria, and I still think back with pleasure of the mouth-watering wheat cakes with butter and syrup that formed my daily breakfast. Automats no longer exist, but their distinctive grey-tiled buildings can sometimes be spotted.

To Church on Sunday

On the eve of my departure from Britain I had attended a China Inland Mission (CIM) meeting for new missionaries from North America as they joined those from the UK for the voyage to Singapore. The Americans at the reception advised me to look out for Calvary Baptist Church in New York City. What was most memorable for me was Calvary Baptist's broadcast service. In England a broadcast church service would be a chance in a lifetime – and probably still is! But Calvary broadcast their services for a full hour morning and evening, *every week*. The congregation were used to the broadcast part, but on my first few attendances I watched open-mouthed as the immaculate maroon-robed choristers waited for the signal lights to change colour and the music to begin.

Soon after the opening exercises of the service, the 'on air' time drew close.

The ushers closed all doors. Dead silence reigned.
The choristers stood breath-held.
Brother Gbeka, the Choir Conductor, held his arms aloft.
The signal light changed. Green… Orange… Red.
And the ensemble struck up:

Years I spent in vanity and pride,
Caring not my Lord was crucified,
Knowing not it was for me He died,
At Cal…va…ry…!

As the organ softly cooed the chorus melody, the Assistant Pastor (a former commercial radio announcer) took the mike:

"Good Morning ladies and gentlemen, this is the Calvary Baptist Hour
Coming to you from New York City's evangelical cathedral
At 123 West Fifty-seventh Street,
between Seventh and Eighth Avenues
Conveniently located for all modes of transportation.
And in these warm days you'll be pleased to know that our auditorium
Has been comfortably… air-conditioned …
Yes… Calvary's air-conditioned comfort beckons YOU!…"

…At Cal…va…ry…" responded the choir.

I was gobsmacked yet awed and impressed at the harnessing of modern means in the church; the polish, sparkle and even a dash of opulence. All of Greater New York was within the station's hearing and the programme was evidently popular, generating phone calls and mail. But I did feel that the juxtaposition of the Crucifixion with 'Calvary's air-conditioned comfort' was in poor taste. Staid English Anglicans still emerging from wartime austerity with gloomily lit, draughty[1] and poorly maintained churches could never have conceived such an approach. I thought of my home parish, Emmanuel, in a moderately well-to-do London suburb, where the Treasurer's response to just about anything new was a morose and predictable "That's all very well Mr Chairman, but what are you going to use for money?"

That extroverted American vigour was exhilarating. I decided that I liked it all – or *almost* all.

---

1   Even today with a modernised boiler, our UK churches rarely pass this test: 'the building is warm when older ladies remove their top coats', and that's something we almost never see!

The members were welcoming, and a deacon invited me to stay for Communion despite being 'unbaptised' by Baptist tradition. He did seem a bit perplexed at first, asked a few more questions and finally came up with 'Are you saved?' On the affirmative answer his face lit up: 'Then you stay!' They explained about their all-age Sunday School (something unheard-of in Britain) and at age 24 I quickly fitted into Calvary's 20+ fellowship.

I had a lot to learn, and if English conservatism across the sea looked a bit claustrophobic, then Calvary's extrovert 'can-do' was thoroughly envisioning. The journey which brought me to New York would later lead far away. I started to wonder if this was another 'signpost' towards moving away from the railways.

But New York became claustrophobic in in the sense that I longed for open countryside or somewhere pleasant for a hike! One weekend a Calvary group member invited me to a Inter-Varsity Christian Fellowship[2] camp in New Jersey. I was to meet up with a carload starting at the George Washington Bridge.

To the Countryside

It was dark by the time we drove across the bridge to New Jersey and through what I was told by one of the girls was 'fairyland'. It proved to be a mile or so of brilliantly floodlit second-hand car lots, but it was indeed colourful and spectacular. This was my introduction to a superhighway with its neon direction signs and peremptory commands: *Stop – Get Ticket!* and *Unlawful to Deposit Trash on Parkway.*

An hour or so later we pulled into the YMCA's Camp WayWaYonder, a hutted campsite alongside a beautiful lake. The next day it was so refreshing to dive into the lake, and singing campfire songs around a barbecue was the sort of relaxation I had imagined would typify America. I enjoyed the fellow campers, relaxed and friendly American college students of roughly my own age who mystified me as they talked of being at (or returning to) *school* – meaning their tertiary-level studies.

---

2   IVCF – Inter-Varsity Christian Fellowship, now known in the UK as UCCF (Universities and Colleges Christian Fellowship).

Food was excellent – truly American-style – and we were all recruited into dishwashing teams. Our team's machine plainly was not up to the job and it became clear that manual washing would be far quicker. I set about this and with lashings of hot water (always available in America) it was easy to keep a couple of the dish-drying team busy. This seemed rather odd to my American friends, who had taken it for granted that un-automated dishwashing was old hat and inferior to that done by a machine!

We didn't sing the rollicking songs from the Billy Graham Crusades as I expected; Fred, our leader, though an American himself, took the view that they were not really "worthy" for worship. We sang more traditional hymns from Wesley, Watts, etc that were being rediscovered among young Americans.

While treading water and chatting in the middle of the lake, a fellow camper offered me a lift by car to Keswick, New Jersey, to the CIM weekend conference in two weeks' time; I accepted gratefully because no one seemed to know how to get there without a car. The USA's 'Keswick' is a Christian conference centre named after the annual convention in England's Lake District. It was a far more polished establishment than Camp WaywaYonder, and many of the participants were twice, even thrice my age. But several of the younger ones were new candidates for service with CIM. I shared a room with their lone bachelor who was soon to sail for Asia.

The CIM's Director for North America, China veteran Herbert Griffin, was presiding over the conference. It was here that I had my first serious conversation with the CIM Candidate Director, Elden Whipple, about possible service in Asia. I was to meet him, and the new missionary candidates many more times during my all-too-short stay in America.

I enjoyed many more excursions to New Jersey with IVCF – mostly Saturday trips culminating in a barbecue and a singsong. They remain among my most happy and vivid memories of American friendliness, and usually included a stop at a roadside diner along the way. Originally these were old railway restaurant cars moved to a roadside site; patrons sat along a counter on high revolving seats and waitresses served what we call 'fast food' today or else steaks plus American apple pie. There was always a wide choice of ice cream – one diner enterprise featured 28 flavours. Nowadays diners are few and far between and enthusiasts eagerly seek them out and 'spot' them – like old steam engines or cars!

The diner stops, however, were just another pleasant aspect of the Christian fellowship which I was enjoying. I met many young Americans who, like me, were seeking God's plan for their future.

Were Keswick and the many weekends with IVCF to be further divine signposts to the future? Well, that's jumping ahead with the story!

Billy Graham

Early in March 1957 in New York City, still wet, wintry and cold, I learnt that a Billy Graham Crusade was approaching. I was invited to join something unheard of then in the UK, a small gathering called the Christian Men's Breakfast. One of the Crusade staff spoke up, "Why don't you take the Crusade Counsellors' Course?"

At first I was hesitant to answer, because in my home church, we had been linked to a Billy Graham Crusade by an audio landline, and there the Crusade Counsellors, all more than 10 years my senior, had all been personally selected by the Vicar. My friend continued: "It's so hard to get enough committed Christians." This sounded to me like the 'acute need' which English Christians were drilled never to ignore – how could I 'pass by on the other side'? Later I wrote and told Bertie Rainsbury, my Vicar; I was relieved that he was more than pleased.

In spite of my late enrolment, I completed the course and filled in the final application form. "We Americans fill *out* forms, the British fill them *in*," chuckled Dan Piatt, the cheerful lecturer on the platform. The next week I joined the queue to be interviewed. Had I learnt my verse cards? Let's hear some! How many chapters are there in John's Gospel?... 22? Only 21? Well let's look and see; you do have your Bible with you, don't you? Well worked-out questions and perceptive interviewers were just a small part of the thorough filtering and advance-processing that was to impress me with the Billy Graham organisation. And despite hearing some of its detractors, I have never changed that opinion.

My job offered overtime at about five times the UK rate, so I grabbed every opportunity to work evenings at British and Irish Railways, and afterwards made my way to Madison Square Garden[1] – to help as a

---

1   The old 'Garden' at 49th St and 8th Ave; Madison Square Garden is now above Grand Central Station.

NEW YORK 1957
BILLY GRAHAM CRUSADE

DAVID A HUNTLEY

COUNSELLOR

My Badge as a Counsellor. I had a similar one as an Usher.

volunteer Counsellor and Usher. 'The Garden' as it was known was a girdered oval, seating about 11,000 people and claiming to be the world's largest air-conditioned building and have the organ with the world's most powerful amplifier. Friendly students from Fuller Seminary formed a warm-hearted team in the counselling office and especially Jim Ziervogel who invited me to help mark the simple Bible studies which new 'enquirers' were given. I had not been an assiduous marker of my Bible but I had made a start – in red ink. Jim commented on this and later invited me to his home in St Louis. (I'm still in touch with him, 40 years later.)

For nearly three months, packed Crusade meetings continued six nights a week, and it was my first experience of frontier evangelism. Though I had been selected as a Crusade *Counsellor* I had only my own routine church life plus the Crusade Counselling Course as background. After determining an enquirer's spiritual need, we were encouraged to introduce him or her to an *Advisor,* mostly ordained ministers, and a great strength in our relative weakness. For some years I kept the tear-off slips from the cards of the dozen or more people I had talked with, and prayed for them. One enquirer had been on active service in the Korean War, and was fretting over the fact that he had shot a Korean prisoner when he should have handed him over as a prisoner of war. Another was a Greek immigrant who seemed overjoyed at Billy Graham's message. A third was a boy aged about nine whose mother broke in at everything I said, so I handed him over to the Advisor who told her quite sternly to let the child answer questions for himself!

Time shot by, but I found time to accept Jim's invitation to visit his home in the Midwest – a 24-hour train ride to St Louis. The train was fairly old, but the overnight bunks were spacious and comfortable and the next morning passengers changed to American-style chair cars. My adjacent seat was occupied by a GI[2] who had recently joined the Baha'i

---

2   GI: a colloquial term used by foreign and Americans alike for American soldiers. I was told it could stand for *gentlemen inlisted* or possibly *government issue!*

faith, but he failed to convert me! So I was discovering the wider world of sects and cults.

Jim introduced me to the Midwest with its attractive spoken accent. Journeying out to the Missouri countryside, we joined a children's camp for a few days and helped with games and activities. On the final night our camp fire had a wooden bridge built over it; the lady camp-leader explained that Christians must 'burn their bridges' and not go back to life without Christ. We were invited to cross the bridge before the camp fire was stoked up to consume it. Here was another insight into American life. Back in St Louis Jim farewelled me onto the night train with, "Maybe we'll meet later in Asia." We did!

St Louis receded as I sat back in an ancient chair-car of the Wabash Railroad for the night's ride to Des Moines, Iowa, where I enjoyed small-town hospitality with a future CIM missionary, Darrell Eddy and his parents. They took me on a side-trip to Boone, where President (and former General of D-Day fame) Eisenhower's mother had been born. For some reason Darrell's hostess asked me to look at her faulty washing machine.

Jim Ziervogel and I by the School Bus taking us from St Louis to the children's camp.

This ancient device incorporated a powered mangle above the round tub. She was disappointed when I showed her that the gears driving it were completely worn away!

Most notable was Darrell's valedictory party in his church – with typical American entrepreneurship everything needed for his packing list had been provided, plus a share of his budget. Life in a relatively small American town was interesting and Darrell took me round in his spacious six-seater car. We were invited to a meal about 200 yards away from a friend's church. Then started a long discussion as to who would ride in whose car so that we would all be in the correct vehicle for the return trip. I suggested that it was so near, why didn't we just walk? We could sort ourselves into cars after

the service. My comment was greeted with blank incomprehension –
no one had ever *walked* to church from there!

My next train ride was in a sparkling new 'silver liner' i.e. a stainless
steel train with an all-glazed observation car at the tail end; one of the
Rock Island Rockets speeding me to Chicago. Gary Reid, whom I had
known in New York, met me and showed me around the famed Moody
Bible Institute. A few were training to be pastors of American churches,
but most ex-Moody students served across the world. All seemed to be
excellent advertisements for their college.

Gary had volunteered for a street corner evangelistic service that
evening. The law required the display of an American flag, and an
understanding that the sidewalk not be blocked, but there were no
other formalities. Gary brought a portable amplifier and the team
leader drove us to the appointed place, and led us all in prayer aloud
while driving. A few enquirers gathered around; American passers-by
were quite responsive, and were given booklets and tracts. One or two
who were the worse for drink were a little more difficult to handle. But
it was all more GMT (good missionary training)!

I spent the night in the pleasant, hotel-like Lawson YMCA, and my
room looked across to the floodlit Wrigley Building – of chewing-gum
fame.

Gary saw me off back to New York at LaSalle St Station, but there
was a problem: my free ticket proved not to be valid beyond Detroit
where I was told that they *might* allow me to continue. At the Detroit
office, hearing my tale of woe, the clerk just smiled; "you're a long way
from home, aren't you?" he quipped, and was already typing out a chit
for me to have a seat.

These two weeks' experience in the Midwest, especially in the
pre-Vietnam years, gave me further insights into the attractive 1950s
American 'can do' approach to Christian missions, evangelism, and
indeed just about everything. I decided I liked it all.

Back to Asia?

My visits to Philadelphia, the US Headquarters of the China Inland
Mission, excited me. I enjoyed relating to the candidate-missionaries

taking the orientation course there. Much later I was tickled to learn that the Candidate Secretary initially wondered if I was eyeing his lady candidates for a possible wife. With that misconception assuredly out of the way, he warmed up significantly!

In that ethos, seeking future guidance laid stress on viewing one's current circumstances as well as prayer, Bible study and the like. I had gathered that fasting and prayer might also be appropriate, so I decided to do without a day's solid food, and limit myself to coffee. And some helpful advice arrived unexpectedly – in a way I could never have foreseen!

It was Sunday breakfast in the Automat[3]. While I was manipulating the dime-operated coffee dispenser I felt a fatherly hand on my shoulder. It was Herbert Griffin, the China Inland Mission's US Director, up for the day from Philadelphia. In his humble and gracious way he asked, "Brother Huntley, won't you come and sit with us? I've got Sanders with me and we've come to hear Billy Graham preach at Calvary Baptist Church." Having trained as a lawyer in New Zealand, J. Oswald Sanders was the Singapore-based General Director of the 1000-strong China Inland Mission, by then fully redeployed in East Asia.

As the two men tucked in to a typical American breakfast, they noticed my apparent frugality which unintentionally put me on the spot! Fasting was to be done in secret and not boasted about, so I could not mention that. On the other hand, young Christians were warned against failing to eat properly – even to save money – as that could generate health problems and expense, as well as difficulties for others. Fortunately Mr Griffin moved on after chatting about the Crusade. Four years later in Singapore, Mr Sanders recalled this breakfast encounter.

In the church, well ahead of time, my two senior friends commented that with so many church officials running round and talking there were distractions from pre-service quiet. I had not noticed this in America but back in the UK 'pre-service quiet' was still the rule!

Before I could think any more about missionary service one thing became clear: I'd need to train in a Bible College or similar. Why not study in the USA? It was apparently quite easy for young Americans to take a job that would earn enough for general living expenses *and* pay for

---

3   On 49th Street diagonally opposite Calvary Baptist Church. The building is still there – it is now a fish restaurant.

full-time study, but enquiries revealed that as a foreigner, I would only be permitted to stay and work *on campus* – where the jobs would pay less than half of my current salary.

I made several applications. Fuller could only take graduates; Moody could not let non-citizens take the radio course I was interested in; Toronto Bible College did not seem to offer more; so the doors seemed to shut one by one. Interestingly enough, Elden Whipple didn't seem to think that going to an American college was the best way ahead for me anyway. He even opined that UK Bible Colleges were more 'serious'. However, a study possibility opened up back in the UK: London Bible College[4] assured me they had no money for bursaries, but they drew my attention to a grant that would probably be given by my own Town Hall.

So my stay in the USA was not to be long-term after all. The manager of British and Irish Railways Inc offered me an attractive package to stay on in America, but on the last day that I would have had to respond, a letter arrived from Croydon Town Hall informing me that a study grant for a degree at LBC had been approved. The Manager was kindly and understanding. This seemed to be my complete answer: (a) it would enable me to study for a degree; (b) it was a training course acceptable for missionary service; and (c) there would be enough of a grant to pay fees and (just about) live on!

In longer retrospect, Moody and Toronto would not have given me the qualifications I would later need, while opportunities at Fuller were to open up later. Step-by-step guidance again!

I found myself homebound on the RMS *Queen Mary,* and among my fellow passengers were the new CIM missionaries who had been candidates during my visits to Philadelphia! This time it was they who were on unfamiliar ground – struggling with the UK's pre-decimal currency, aerograms, early morning tea, syrup-less breakfasts, and other transatlantic eccentricities. Docking in the palatial Ocean Terminal at Southampton, they were surprised that the mere 78-mile journey to London was to be by rail and wondered if we didn't have roads! But they enjoyed the train's at-seat elevenses – in those days served on china plates and from silver coffee pots.

---

4   Now London School of Theology at Northwood, Middlesex, but at that time in
     Marylebone Road, London.

Thus the return from New York to England was much more congenial than my return from Singapore aboard a troopship, and my American brethren obviously decided that the British knew a lot more about comfortable travel (other than car travel, that is) than they did.

For me, that day of arrival back in London held a decisive step.

A Tertiary Student at Last!

On the day I returned from New York, I made my way to the China Inland Mission to talk with their Candidate Co-ordinator, Leslie Lyall. He extolled the virtues of the frugal, missionary-oriented 'traditional' colleges. I explained that a letter funding my prospective time at the younger, more academic and scholarly London Bible College had arrived just as I had to give my boss an answer about leaving New York. Then Leslie begrudgingly agreed that, yes... well... perhaps in my case I *should* go to LBC! So I made my way over to the College.

The Director of Studies assured me I could start a degree course if I had matriculated[1]. As mentioned previously, I had fortuitously delayed military service in order to secure it. Thus I found myself embarking on something I had longed for – and which I trusted would fit in with a growing sense of call to missionary service in the Far East. God confirmed that step early on; my first college room-mate was Alfred, a Singaporean, who was full of encouragement and still is. We were joined by Gérald, a Frenchman from Algeria. We have all remained in touch.

I had cashed-in my last American dollars and I proudly joined the students of the day, disporting the distinctive longitudinally-striped scarf in the College's colours. Jeans and T-shirts were definitely for well-away-from-college attire. It was an exhilarating experience just to walk down to Oxford Street wearing my scarf! No longer was I a prisoner of bureaucracy, but a liberated student!

There was little spare money in the bank, but back in New York I had laid this matter before God. He assured me I could trust Him for the funds and strength for the necessary study before heading for

---

1   *Matriculation* was a school-leaving certificate (now discontinued), and was the minimum entrance requirement for university.

With Gerald Sanchez (left) and Alfred Yeo in the entrance mural at London Bible College when it was at 19 Marylebone Road.

missionary service, so I felt a complete peace about financial provision. During my first year, my living allowance was only £160 plus tuition fees, but subsequently it was nearly doubled to a more comfortable £305 per year.

Then bang! A few weeks later the Director of Studies told me there was a mistake. I could *not* register for the degree! But the University ruled that I could make up the entrance requirement on top of the first year of my degree course. It was a slog, but did enable me to catch up with lots of things in the Bible that I probably should have already known. In the long term it proved to be a step forward rather than backwards!

The regime at LBC did not compare to the military life which most of the male students had experienced, nor to the monastic frugality of some other 'Bible Colleges'. But we certainly had to observe 6-9 pm for study, followed by Chapel and lights-out by 10 pm. Morning Chapel was at 9 am sharp. We were required to wear gowns to all lectures and in the dining hall, where we stood at our seats till the teaching faculty had processed to the Top Table and Grace had been said.

The Principal, Revd Ernest Kevan, combined formality and correctness with pastoral kindness and fine scholarship. He was a good organiser who had built up the college, from a handful of students meeting in a rented room to the force in theology that it is today.

Time at LBC passed quickly. Though I never mentioned my American experience to fellow students they seemed to spot it, and anyway the cross cultural exposure proved to be useful in such an international body.

I quickly discovered that I had joined a widely varied student body ranging from both Americas across to antipodean New Zealand. The young London Bible College (and later most of the other, older colleges) pioneered a path more akin to universities or the American 'seminary'. I never regretted LBC's rigorous theological workout, combined with complete loyalty to Scripture. It was to stand me in excellent stead for 37 years in Asia and beyond.

The College later moved from central London but the building at 19 Marylebone Rd remains, and also the foundation stone on the corner of Nottingham Place.

Though the College was young compared to most others I was glad to benefit from its mixture of mission vision and academic excellence coupled with free discussion of any and every controversy. Just a few years later it was gratifying to hear that LBC had mentored for his doctorate George Carey, soon to become Archbishop of Canterbury!

Study-wise I was on new ground and had to find my way around an unfamiliar syllabus. The timetable terminology mystified me; I had encountered *dogma* in my Roman Catholic schooling, but what were *dogmatics,* I wondered? Far more mystifying was *Theological Prolegomena* which proved to be an easy introduction to the syllabus for those who were newcomers to theology. In addition, French and English were required for the London University Degree, but there were twice as many more lectures again for the College's own diploma. Here I faced pastoralia, homiletics, Greek, and various set-books plus practical work assignments.

I was fortunate to be allotted residence in one of the adjacent college hostels. Perhaps as students we were quite naïve world-wise – one evening a well-spoken man dropped by our hostel and asked if anyone had an Apocrypha as he was reading the Lesson in his church the next day, and needed to review the passage. As potential pastors, we invited him in and chatted while someone found the reading he wanted. He took only the most cursory look at the Bible before thanking us and excusing himself. We thought no more about it, but a day or two later the hostel was burgled. Our guest had obviously 'cased the joint'. We had learnt something about pastoral security!

My first year's practical assignment was not a great success. Three of us were sent to the Paddington Wharves Mission, in a run-down and very poor area near the canal, presided over by an ageing widower. He was a kindly fellow, and glad to have us trying to keep a Sunday School running. Sadly he was quite beyond supporting us, and was only too aware of the forthcoming closure of the Mission. (One small boy, Peter, got into a photo that I took, and

Outside Paddington Wharves Mission; 'Peter' by lamp post (This canal-side area has long been demolished and replaced with high class flats).

some years later I woke at night feeling I should pray for him.) Now the area has been 'regenerated' with the poor families shifted away into low-cost flats, while the old houses were replaced with costly luxury apartments around a yachting marina.

Interestingly at LBC I found myself as one of the Anglican minority, and wondered how, among so many free-church members, I could gain a placement in a church during our middle year. Moreover the assignment should include some preaching. I visited my Bishop, the kindly John Hughes who prayed for us till the end of his life! He set me a couple of essays and then I was licenced to officiate and preach in an Anglican church in much the same way an ordinand could.

My placement was in St James Parish, Clerkenwell, then a down market residential area just outside London's financial district. The Vicar welcomed me warmly though he was not really a trainer! It was my first experience of door to door visiting in Victorian blocks of flats, many with common toilets – very discouraging. But the church itself was great experience, getting to know a congregation that reflected the area. Then with my home church, Emmanuel in South Croydon, taking much greater interest in their potential missionaries (myself included), I remained in membership with them, and am still a member as I write.

Unexpectedly my (maternal) Aunt Doily offered me either to be a beneficiary in her will or, she suggested, giving me £150 immediately to purchase a Italian Lambretta[2] Scooter. A relation of hers who was a Lambretta agent found me an ex-demonstration model with just 30 miles on the dial! The motorbike took me (and sometimes a pillion passenger) on trips to church, to Aunt Doily in Wales, as well as the long trips to visit my parents up in Cumberland. Had I taken her other option, when she finally passed away the sum would have bought only a fraction of such a vehicle! The trips to my parents in Penrith took eight to 10 hours, and on one of them I was caught in thick sulphurous fog outside Manchester. With wet black grime on my face I night-stopped in at a Bed and Breakfast place.

However Ted Malcolm, a fellow-student, lived near Leicester, where his father was Vicar, and the family occupied a large, old-style parsonage. On several further northward itinerations I stopped there, they were the epitome of kindness and hospitality and Mrs Malcolm was a good cook and a motherly soul. On one icy day I sat down to lunch with them – formal but ever friendly. Clergy were poorly paid in those days but the meals were always delicious. Some meat was brought in on a silver plate with a silver dish-cover bearing the family crest, and placed before Mr Malcolm. He lifted the cover off and carved us all a generous helping of corned beef. Never did such a simple meal taste so good! Many of the Malcolm family are still serving in ministry and overseas missions.

Students were expected to join in a church 'mission' or evangelistic event in a village, small town, estate or parish. During my first Christmas vacation I went to a rural Methodist chapel in Kent with Desmond Hales, a fellow student from Kenya. The church was far from flourishing yet it seemed to us quite an adventure when the villagers invited us to hold a 'mission' there and offered us board and hospitality, and even more so when Leslie Groves, the Minister of the main church in Gillingham encouraged us. Leslie suggested we invite Keith Ranger, a young Methodist preacher on his circuit. Both Keith and I were to serve in Asia later. Villagers offered us simple but comfortable hospitality, though the home in which I stayed had neither electricity

---

2   The then-popular *Lambretta* was similar to the still-current *Vespa* scooter. It was a 150cc two-stroke machine with a pillion seat. I added a rear luggage-carrier and two panniers. In 1958 a new machine cost £180 on the road!

nor modern sanitation. Perhaps another gentle preparation for simple living overseas?

It was January and the chapel heating had long ceased to work, so we borrowed an assortment of paraffin (kerosene) heaters to at least get the dank chill off. 'Making do' was considered part of the challenge of missionary preparation!

We successfully filled the chapel for several consecutive nights, partly in response to prayer and possibly by our unorthodox publicity – printed invitations as well as making announcements from a loudspeaker on Desmond's car! Messages were aimed at lapsed Christians, for although church attendance in the UK was falling, few people would have openly said that they weren't Christians at all.

As a result of this mission, our team was invited back later that year to the Methodist chapel at Twydall, a new Council Estate on the same Methodist circuit. This time we invited a Scottish evangelist, a former hardened criminal, who related very well indeed to the local people, especially to the children to whom he must have seemed like a kindly grandfather. His punch-line was 'From Crime to Christ!' In both Hartlip and Twydall we gathered quite a following for the meetings, but we were to discover later that one of the issues of visiting student-evangelists was that small churches often invited them, hoping for a kind of 'instant cure'. They lacked either the ability or the application to continue the spiritual momentum, prayer and biblical teaching.

One lovely summer evening, I was driving back to London with Desmond when we started to climb the steep face of the North Downs, softly illuminated by the low sun. The view was magnificent. Desmond verbalised both our thoughts: 'Wouldn't this be a lovely evening for courting?' In fact for both of us matrimony was a few years away in both time and distance, for we both married and started a family overseas – he in Kenya and I in Singapore. Keith did the same in East Asia too.

One more assignment came from the College. The Director of Evangelism asked me to lead a team of four on an Easter Mission in a rural chapel: Great Barton Free Church in Suffolk county. Unlike most village chapels – and indeed British churches – this was a modern building with proper heating. The congregation seemed starved of solid Christian teaching. Perhaps they thought that the right preaching – maybe tinged with the emerging charismatic doctrines of the day – would rebuild the congregation and fill the Sunday School. We tried tactfully to disabuse them of ideas about instant solutions; nowadays something like *Alpha* would probably have envisioned them on the right lines. We departed with a charge to recall Paul's reminder to Timothy to concentrate on true teaching of God's Word. But there *was* spiritual encouragement; during our mission there had been one or two clear-cut conversions, and Norah Lovelace, the organist, prayed for us till the day she died.

Though Britain faced financial strife and strained international relations during these years following the first Suez Crisis (1957), the Christian scene was quite optimistic. Newly established biblical colleges were gaining academic honours, and missionary societies were glad to take these graduates especially as scholarly levels overseas had also climbed. The Inter Varsity Fellowship[3] organised *Missionary Breakfasts* – a new American-flavoured venture and well attended by tertiary students – where returned mission leaders stirred the students to consider the claims of God's service abroad.

Around this time I knew that my father's health had been deteriorating. He smoked a pipe, then considered to be a 'relatively healthy' option; the health danger from smoking was little-known in those days, and definitive research was only just surfacing. Smoke filled most restaurants, theatres, pubs, offices and most of the space in public transport and public buildings.

Suspicion of a throat problem took my father to the local doctor, and it emerged that his condition would probably be terminal. As was the custom then, the specialist told my mother but no one told the patient himself. The carcinoma deteriorated to the point that my father lost weight and could only eat porridge-like meals. He passed away quietly at home after the local doctor had called to give him one of his occasional pain-killing injections. He had never held any Christian profession, and was in fact quite blunt to 'gospel messengers' who would call at the door from time to time. Only after he died did I learn that the Hospital Chaplain had struck up a friendly conversation with him, and that he had joined in the Chapel service and received Holy

---

3   Now *Universities and Colleges Christian Fellowship* – UCCF. There was also the Student Christian Movement – SCM, which was associated with a more theologically liberal, socially-oriented agenda. Though SCM was to go out of existence a decade or so later, it was re-started at the end of the 20th century.

Communion. I am certain that in spite of the conspiracy of silence, by that time he knew he was dying.

After three academic years came London University's final exams. Everything depended upon those nine days of written tests; coursework counted for nothing at all. I never felt sure of a pass, and so on the appointed day I rode my scooter with Ted Malcolm to Senate House. There was the notice board. Yes

Last Days at London Bible College. (L to R): Reg Piesse, Ted Malcolm, Peter Kingston, David (below). All passed the BA final exams.

my number was among the passes, though not with such an exalted grade as Ted's. But a pass was a pass, and I no longer had to think of possible re-sits or delays to service overseas.

Some 5000 graduands assembled for the formal graduation by London University at the Royal Albert Hall. Each was allowed two guests – in my case my mother and Aunt Doily from Wales. The bumper attendance was due to the presence of the Chancellor: Her Majesty Queen Elizabeth the Queen Mother, widow of King George VI. We each in turn bowed to her as our names were read out.

That night, a dozen or so of us candidates were formally received into the China Inland Mission.

East Asia suddenly seemed near!

France

Before leaving studies in London, I'd like to take you on a couple of my visits to France.

Since I had enjoyed French at school and on holidays, I decided to take this language as part of my London University degree. Again, in the Lord's kindness, the third occupant of our room (besides Alfred from Singapore) was Gérald, the Frenchman with whom I could polish my grammar. I was advised to spend some time in France itself to become immersed in French and become more 'at home' with the language.

My first trip was to take a short course at the Alliance Française in Paris, whose programme fitted LBC's Easter vacation well. I looked dubiously at the cost of the fare, but then an enterprising company offered the public an economical choice; they bussed us to Lydd in Kent, where an aged DC-3 Dakota plane lifted us across the sea to Beauvais with a final bus ride to Paris. Meanwhile I had prayed that God would help me to empathise with French ways and understand their distinctive culture – which after all is basically Christian.

Two of us visiting from London Bible College lived-in at the suburban Nogent Bible Institute, and we commuted into the city centre daily – I was relieved that the weekly cost of the ride was but a fraction of a similar 'commute' in London.

The Institute itself is contained in a fine, dignified French-traditional mansion; my room *John Calvin* was on the top floor and I shared it with Reg, a New Zealand postgraduate student.

Soon after we arrived it was obvious that there was a culture-wise hitch. We were a he and a she – though there was no relationship between us! In the Institute at that time men and women students did not mix, and for meals sat at separate huge tables, with the principal and his wife presiding over each. Moreover, the fact that we would normally commute daily to town together was obviously *non bon ton*[1]. Moreover the 'she' had arrived with cut hair and a less-than-ankle-length skirt. In those days uncut and bunned hair was expected of French Protestant ladies! But there seemed to be little that could be done about the situation, and the bosses at Nogent evidently concluded that since the English were all quite mad anyway, they would just let it pass. Indeed they were very kind, and as with the American experience, it was good orientation to the cultural gulfs that separate seemingly similar peoples. We did manage to rug up and stay warm, for the heating boiler was only fired up twice a week – once for the ladies' weekly bath and laundry, and the other for the men's! The two of us from London appreciated the kindness, and as we left we presented the elderly Lady Dean with some flowers.

(Fifty-one years later in 2009, the opportunity came to take my wife Ruth to see the institute. We were graciously given a guided tour. The stately old house retains its historic features and the Institute has acquired all the accoutrements of a modern tertiary institution. The students even wear casuals. Nevertheless, the spiritual tone and world mission vision are more than ever to the fore.)

Now back to London. A year later in the summer of 1959, a further French trip was prescribed by my tutor: this time to a Christian teaching and retreat centre. The *Foyer Missionaire*[2] overlooked La Bourboule, in the Auvergne Mountains of Central France. Travel would be no problem thanks to the scooter. So I watched nervously as my Lambretta was craned aboard the ferry to Le Havre, and rode across France all the next day – about 500 miles without eating. There was then no motorway so after tucking into the ship's (English) breakfast I passed right through the centre of famous cities such as Chartres. A point I noticed was that in spite of the reputed secularity of France, each town's church services were advertised at the main-road approaches. I woke up my prospective host around midnight!

The *Foyer's* Director was one Monsieur le Pasteur Franc Barral, the father of a fellow student at LBC, Jean Marc, and a minister of the French

---

1   *Non bon ton* literally 'not good tone' or in this case, inappropriate proximity between sexes.

2   Roughly translates as *Missionary Centre*.

The Barral Residence and *Foyer* above La Bourboule. The Renault van is in the carport – Franc's workshops were either side. My room was in the top right section. The ground floor below the balcony was the living space.

Reformed Church. Franc made his living by carving beautiful hardwood candlesticks and dishes, plus collecting modest fees from the retreatants and paying-guests such as myself. I had planned to stay there for about six weeks. But soon after arrival it was announced that we were all going on an evangelistic mission near Drôme, a day's journey away, so unexpectedly my itinerary was to be widened.

We loaded ourselves into a huge Renault van, and as the vast sun-drenched central valley unfolded, my host told me about the Christian scene in France – the story unrolled largely as a tale of secularism overtaking both Roman Catholic and Protestant Christianities. Franc explained how the paternalism of the Roman Catholics had combined with a militant labour movement to turn the populace against organised religion of *any* kind. Russian-style Communism was disconcertingly vibrant in a few parts of France.

By late afternoon we drew into Le Mazet St Voy, a bucolic village in one of the few Protestant enclaves of mainly Catholic France. A farmer agreed to our setting up camp in a field, but we men slept in the *grange*, the piled straw in a barn loft. We washed and shaved in the village horse-trough and dug an earth lavatory. The Swiss members of the team who joined us were appalled at the backwardness of things generally, but as one who had just read Hudson Taylor's life, I felt I should do my utmost to fit in without criticism, real or implied! I enjoyed it all even though I agreed with the Swiss!

The *Temple* or Protestant Church at Mazet was vast, and could have sat hundreds if, that is, the thick cobwebs had been dusted off more of the narrow benches. There were almost no hymn books – one was expected to have one's own. A dignified old gentleman with a long white beard duly gowned himself and appeared in the lofty pulpit; the charismatic movement was hardly born then, but he implored us to consider this theme with which many Christians of that time – us students included – were grappling. Surprisingly, most of the village turned up in honour of our visiting team.

Rehearsing for a meeting – David (right) with musical team members on the French Camp.

Afterwards our Director, Franc, rounded us up and drilled us on visitation. We were to knock at every door in Le Mazet, and ask the occupants if they had a Bible at home. If they had no Bible we were to offer to sell them a Gospel, and anyway to invite them to a Sunday afternoon programme to be held on top of a large rock.

They would know when to come as our van would tour the area with the Director's sons on the roof-rack, playing a guitar and banjo into loud hailers. The Barral brothers' rollicking musical treatment of *Stand up for Jesus* captivated people and they followed as if it were the Pied Piper. Indeed the whole neighbourhood came! We in the team were to wear blue jeans, white shirt, and the team's orange scarf; and Franc Barral spoke on the theme *Le Repos Qui Fait Boum! – The Rest Which Goes Bang*! He invited people to stay on and chat.

I found there was much to observe and learn from the French team. But the follow-up in France seemed to us students somewhat tame: enquirers were simply invited to subscribe to *Rainbow,* the Foyer's magazine. Though to be fair, those who wanted to talk at length found sympathetic and helpful pastoral ears. There was obviously a great loneliness in the lives of many middle-aged and older parishioners, and uncertainty among the younger folk. It was a mission field indeed and Franc seemed like a prophet sent from Heaven to these certainty-seeking people; we felt privileged to be part of his team.

Time to return to La Bourboule. One of the Barral boys started the van with the caravan still attached – so he thought – but only the copper brake-pipe had actually been connected. There was a rush of air, and a solder-joint lay limply protruding from each vehicle! I helped push the two pipes together and we patched up the joint with sticky tape and enjoyed a long, but evidently safe, ride back. Intending missionaries must indeed learn to 'make do!'

The Barral van was covered with warnings about alcoholism, so I was surprised when red wine was produced at Sunday lunch. Evidently in France, wine with a meal was not considered to be 'drinking'. Another cultural difference! Time in France proved to be yet one more orientation to comprehending the endless mountains, valleys and ravines of cultural differences, and was to stand me in good stead when out with young people in Asia.

A few days later I rode my scooter via a Paris night-stop to board a remarkable means of transport across the English Channel – a boxy wartime aircraft carrying three cars and a few motor cycles with their passengers.

I have never been able to revisit the Auvergne, and cannot find the *Foyer Missionaire* nor the Barral family in the online phone book. I wonder what my La Bourboule hosts are doing now?

Back to Asia

With the degree behind me, there was one further commitment to London Bible College. At the end of each summer season the Christian Holiday Crusade took over a Holiday Camp at Filey on the Yorkshire Coast.

I wondered what I would find – in some ways it was a bit like the military. All meals were provided on a mass feeding basis, waitresses served six plates on a wire rack to each table for six, the plates went and the sweet course arrived the same way. The recreational activities of this 'camp' included fairground type rides – all free, plus an indoor and an outdoor swimming pool, cinema shows, and light-hearted entertainment each evening.

Most of the camp's entertainment and recreational activities continued as per the normal programme. But the evenings of light-hearted entertainment closed with a talk on Christian living. Certain courses and seminars on subjects such as Sunday School teaching were also available. The serried ranks of cigarette vending machines did negligible – if any – business during that week!

On arrival I was allocated a 'chalet' boasting a camp bed, a wash basin and minimal lighting. My bed was within sound of 'Radio Butlin' – really just a huge loudspeaker system, but the idea caught my imagination as being something to bear in mind should I eventually serve in missionary radio.

Most Christian organisations in the UK were represented at Filey, and I had been invited to staff LBC's stand in the 'Colleges and Missions' exhibition. There was a gratifying number of people enquiring about training courses, as well as preparation for missionary service – plus one or two who had landed drudging jobs, and wondered to me whether missions would be more exciting!

On duty at the London Bible College exhibit in Filey Holiday Camp. Each mission or Christian organisation mounted a stand.

In September 1960, I rode my scooter across England to visit my mother, and then down to the China Inland Mission's centre, then in Newington Green, London. I had – wrongly as it turned out – anticipated a certain frugality about life at the CIM, and stopped at one of the new motorway service stations for a full plate!

For the next 10 weeks I was one of a dozen paying guests of Mr and Mrs Leslie Lyall; the Lyalls had served for many years in China. During this 'Candidate's Course' various lectures and visits enabled the CIM and us to understand each other and to assess our suitability for overseas service. Leslie Lyall was a warm, interesting person to interact with and was gifted with a commanding presence. Before the course, we had been pre-filtered by earlier encounters. A weekend stay with the Lyalls included Scrabble games, interviews and a medical check. Was the Scrabble just a social interlude, or a subtle part of the selection process? At any rate some of the candidates who seemed slow at Scrabble got accepted too!

Mrs Lyall was an excellent cook, and she decided that the young men would cook breakfasts and the girls would cook in the evenings. We were free to order any ingredients we liked and make up any recipe! We successfully made omelettes, and we were encouraged to try the newly-popular kippers which were sealed in a plastic sheath to be dipped in boiling water. We learnt how much cheaper Scottish porridge was compared to packet cereals; one or two other dishes were less successful!

Before the final interviews, each of us had had to spend a day with one of the CIM's Council Members. I was allotted to Mr and Mrs Paul Broomhall. (Paul, a successful businessman, was a descendent of the CIM's founder, Hudson Taylor.) During the delicious evening meal I had used my sweet fork in one of the earlier successive courses. "Would you like another fork, David – or can you manage?" asked my hostess. I thought quickly: should I be 'correct' and await the proper weapons, or manifest missionary initiative and make do with the spoon? I chanced on the latter, and I was accepted.

Although an affable man, Paul was a bit absent-minded. When we were chatting by the fire, he started to read aloud some of my referee's confidential comments! The next morning he drove me in his snazzy sports car back to London.

CIM candidates were then asked to attend the Wycliffe Language Camp. We needed to grasp the principles of phonetics so that we would be able to pronounce the sounds of *any* language correctly. We learnt that, for example, in some languages an (English) adjective could be a verb, and that there are many, many anatomically possible sounds not found in English. I was truly thankful for the linguistic tutors' teaching when I started to tackle Asian languages, and much later when I taught linguistics at Singapore Bible College.

After I finished College, with College tie and Crusader badge, I started at the CIM Candidates' Course in London.

The camp leadership took pains to emphasise that those who had only basic academic qualifications would not be at a disadvantage. One young man slept in the next camp-bed to a Cambridge graduate from a distinguished family, an ordained Anglican minister. He seemed to find he could rehearse linguistics best by interlocution with his new neighbour! The five weeks' camp shot by.

I considered getting some work before our scheduled sailing for Asia. So I offered for 'supply teaching' in a government school – teachers were then in desperately short supply. I was accepted on the basis of an arts degree plus Sunday School teaching experience.

My assignment to Finsbury Park Secondary Modern School proved to be an eye-opener. The school was a dumping ground for those who had failed to score well at the competitive 11+ exam, and students stayed there, some motivated and some not so, till their 14th birthday. What was I to teach the children? Miss Dumville, the headmistress's advice was a model abnegation of responsibility: "Teach them anything you like as long as you don't send them to me!"

The actual vacancy was one that I could hardly fit into exactly – the girls' physical education mistress! I began with some geography about the Far East, and soon discovered that Religious Studies (supposedly a compulsory subject) was conspicuous by its absence. So I took the opportunity to teach some of the main Bible stories, as well as some Three R's sufficient for a normal 40 minute lesson; the final written or drawn assignments were often surprisingly well done. Adding-in a few class games in the playground, I just about managed to fill the time for seven exhausting weeks.

It was a pleasure to find that in spite of generally low standards, the law on daily worship in schools was actually implemented. Fifteen minutes of daily worship started off the morning assembly with a hymn, a short Bible story and the Lord's Prayer.

It was fairly easy to keep order since most of the children were small, though those in the third (and a few fourth) years were a bit more difficult. I finally ventured to explain that I too had 'failed' the 11+ exam[1] but that they should not necessarily consider this as the sole lost opportunity which would restrict them for ever. This was received with remarkable sympathy.

The pay was fantastic; I received more than double the daily rate had it been worked out on a normal annual pay packet. This proved to be part-provision for some items on the CIM's packing list. In the few remaining days before sailing, I completed a car driving course and got my licence (in addition to the motor-bike one) which was valid almost anywhere for life.

Passages for four young men and eight lady missionaries had been booked. My dream of returning to Singapore after nine years was soon to be a reality. We presented our heavy luggage at Waterloo station for loading onto the *Ocean Liner Express* – a special train to take us to the P&O *Canton*. Late that afternoon, the *Canton* steamed down Southampton Water and out into the choppy water of the English Channel. Now we were *really* en route for Asia.

---

1   In 2011, at a local clergy gathering it came to light that at least three of us had failed the '11+', and so had the former Archbishop of Canterbury, George Carey!

Escorted by the kindly Revd and Mrs Max Orr, veteran missionaries from China, we met for prayer daily in one of the cabins; Max presided at the Ship's Sunday Communion service, and we all ran a shipboard Sunday School. The P&O Steamship Company were prepared for this and provided the song books and the children's attendance cards. One of my diversions was to set up a deck-chair in a corner of the deck and practice my Hohner harmonica. I had taken a few lessons at the London College of Accordionists, and I enjoyed trying but did not gain proficiency. The four men in the party, still bachelors, had all been to the Far East before, mostly as soldiers. The stops were not quite the culture shock that they were to the young ladies.

Then one morning we faced a dilemma. Our early morning tea trays bore invitations to take cocktails with the Captain that night. Should we accept? I knew there was no pressure at all to imbibe alcoholic refreshment; in those days most anglophone evangelicals were total abstainers. I knew moreover that the Captain's company would be polite and very 'correct'. We asked our seniors what they thought, and Max articulated his gut feelings in his soft Irish accent: "There will be alcohol; there may be lewdness – and liberties taken with the ladies." He added, "My wife and I will not be there." But to make it clear we were not under orders he continued, "But we shall be perfectly happy if any of you feel the Lord would have you go."

None went.

(But on subsequent voyages I have always accepted these invitations, and never found them anything but a pleasant few minutes of 'getting to know you' in the most 'proper' of atmospheres.)

One evening the crew organised a fancy dress party, and our group decided to dress-up to represent the nursery rhyme *The Old Woman Who Lived in a Shoe*. The Captain announced that we had been judged winners! The prize was a voucher for the bar; we bought cordial to moderate the foul-tasting drinking water taken on at Aden.

We passed the Bay of Biscay, the Straits of Gibraltar, Suez, Aden, Bombay, Colombo, down the Sumatra coast, and then on to our first taste of Malaya. Here in the island port of Penang there was time for a day ashore. Max suggested going up the Hill Railway to the fantastic view from the top. After lunch I proposed a visit to the Kek Lok Pagoda which I had recalled from my military days, and so conducted the group on a tour of that famous and mystifying piece of China-in-Malaya.

Singapore OMF Language School – David (sixth in back row), Ruth (third in front row), Frank and Irene Wuest (Superintendents) and family (second row, centre).

As we were watching the coast of Malaya passing by, some chatty university students quizzed us about our jobs. They were quite interested that we were missionaries, and one or two of them were Malays – therefore Muslims by law and, in Malaya, not to be 'proselytised' under pain of deportation. One Malay, however, seemed quite curious about Christianity and chatted freely.

Once the boat had docked in Singapore , we went up on deck before breakfast to meet Frank Wuest (pronounced *weest*), our new OMF host. He seemed to feel that we should forego the ship's breakfast so that we could attend the daily morning Prayer Meeting; many of the old CIMers felt this way about scheduled meetings. A phone call evidently persuaded him that we may just as well get our breakfast on the boat. In fact, most ex-China missionaries were relaxed and hospitable – especially when there was no scheduled meeting!

It was indeed like re-living the dream, for Singapore had not changed much in the nine years since I had been a soldier there; even Embarkation HQ, my former workplace, remained functioning. I recognised much that had faded from memory. From now on 'CIM' will rarely be mentioned. In Asia we were *Overseas Missionary Fellowship* or OMF, as we are known everywhere today.

Frank's minibus deposited us on the steps of the OMF's Language and Orientation Centre, a large compound along one of Singapore's many leafy lanes[2]. We were enjoying our first iced drinks as the door framed my college room-mate Alfred Yeo. Had I brought the souvenirs he had requested from the Suez Canal? Yes, I had. With him was his 12-year-old nephew Charles. As rain started to patter down he told Charles in Hokkien to go and close his car windows. I listened aghast… would I to have to learn and understand *that* kind of language? Yes, I would!

OMF's first task was to 'designate' each of us 35 new workers who hailed from the UK, USA, Canada, South Africa and Australia to a country of service in East Asia. With my strong interest in Christian broadcasting, I was tentatively earmarked for some kind of venture with the Far East Broadcasting Co.

But before any 'institutional' work could absorb our attention, we were expected to spend a year or two in a conventional missionary situation – that is, working in a small emerging church in a village or small town. Some language fluency was also required. So started another chapter in my missionary service.

But where?

---

2   This is now the home of the Discipleship Training Centre.

Malaya

My 'designation' with OMF was to *North Malaya*[1], mostly rural areas towards the north and also to the south of Ipoh the capital of Perak State. It was designated as the OMF missionary district within the Anglican Church, along the lines of the former CIM's Diocese based in Sichuan, West China. All of the 40 or so OMF missionaries in that area were Anglicans, or sympathetic to that tradition.

Two of us plus a senior missionary from Language School, Joan Wales, journeyed up from Singapore to Kuala Lumpur (KL) in bunks on the night train – quite a pleasant experience. Alfred Yeo came to see us off at Singapore rail station before we entered our bunks. At KL the local OMF Secretary picked us up and took us for breakfast before the onward journey to Perak, three more hours by day train. There were open windows but no air-conditioning, so we got thirsty quite quickly. I managed to order coffee for the three in our group using Hokkien Chinese – much to the pleasure of Joan who had been a kind of linguistic mentor to us.

After a hill break in the cool of Cameron Highlands, I made my own way downhill to St Luke's Church in Teluk Anson (now Teluk Intan), which was to be my home for a year. St Luke's was a well-established Parish under Bob and Amy Harper, who had served in China for 12 years and spoke fluent Mandarin – the standard language of China. My job was to help take services and get to know the younger folk. In China the CIM team had worked under their own CIM Bishop and his Chinese successor-Bishops, but in Malaya the team was much smaller. Moreover, the OMF were 'newcomers' among an established Diocesan structure.

---

1   The country was then known as *Malaya*, which for many purposes included Singapore. The area is now known as *Peninsular Malaysia*, part of the country of Malaysia but excluding Singapore.

The Bishop, Kenneth Sansbury, an expatriate, was kind and welcoming – and we soon got used to understanding each other!

The Anglican Church in Malaya had been planted in the various state capitals and major towns by the former Society for the Propagation of the Gospel in Foreign Parts, (SPG)[2] with a strong emphasis on ordained ministry, the structured Church and on the sacraments. The SPG men who had been there a long time included many spiritual giants who were able to bridge the gap between themselves and the 'newcomers' in OMF and other societies.

The SPG leadership were quick to realise that OMF could supply partners who understood Chinese language and culture, and who were willing to live in quite basic conditions. They felt OMF was a team who could continue spreading the Gospel far wider than they had done. There was a kind of warm regard between the two traditions, but each groped for understanding of the other, sometimes with mutual bafflement; however, the differences were more in emphasis rather than opposites!

Most mornings during my year in Teluk Anson I sat sweltering on the church veranda with Mr Mah, my Chinese teacher. I learnt that Singapore's (then, not now) main Chinese dialect, Hokkien was also known variously as Amoy, Minnan, Ban-lam, Xiamen and Fujianese. Now I was grateful for the tuition at Wycliffe Language Camp back in England.

Our textbook was DuPree's *Amoy Primer*, written in China in 1920. It rehearsed us in reciting such 'useful' sentences as: *This clergyman has 30 sheep*; and *These eggs which the cook bought are stale*; and longest of all: *How many coolies are needed to carry this mandarin's sedan chair?*

Bishop Kenneth granted me lay-reader status so I could officiate at some of the many services, mostly in English; but I preached once in Hokkien as part of the language course. It was a simple poster-illustrated sermon, well rehearsed with my teacher before presenting it to the congregation. I also enjoyed learning a little basic written Chinese.

In North Malaya, operating within the Anglican Diocese, a chain of preaching stations (or embryo churches) was developing across Perak State, with slowly growing congregations. Under God almost all of these

---

2   The Church Missionary Society also worked in the KL area – their outlook was similar to OMF's.

early outstations have now developed into a viable branch church or outreach centre run entirely by Malaysians.

I took many photos – then colour slides only. Most of my slides have now degraded, but many will produce a usable picture.

Soon after my arrival, I was invited to join a cycling evangelistic tour in the northern reaches of our missionary district, beyond Taiping and Ipoh. The tour was to be headed by Revd Ray Flatau, an Australian. The cycles and loudspeaker gear were loaded into a 'Willy', the Willys station wagon, for the first part of the journey to Taiping.

We slept our first night on school desks and then pressed on to Selama where a team of lady missionaries was planting a new congregation. At intermediate villages along the road we held open air meetings, distributed tracts, and then retired to a coffee shop for a meal. In Selama we had a rented room, no furniture but quite comfortable grass sleeping-mats. Our third and final night was as guests of a British estate-manager's family who were sympathetic to our mission. So we enjoyed soft beds that night – plus a swim in the family's private pool. Our Chinese team found they quite enjoyed corn flakes followed by an egg-and bacon breakfast!

From a very faded slide. Revd Ray Flatau (second right), Stephen Choo (later my Best Man, second left) and self at front, Ding Zer Tian (left) plus two other cyclists. The Willys station wagon has the cycles and PA system piled inside and on top!

As a single guy, it was no problem to make many friends among the local Chinese young men. Independence had come, and there seemed to be no anti-colonial sentiment. Schooling and public services were still not unlike those in Britain, and the country was prosperous. There were seeds of sensitivity on the part of the some communities, though they were all delightful people to get to know.

With Alfred Yeo's help I had bought a bicycle in Singapore; my machine was a China-made substantial steed, of the type mockingly known in Britain as a *bedstead*. But it was comfortable and could carry a little luggage. I armed it with a dynamo lighting system so I could go anywhere, anytime.

It was Easter 1962 and a youth fellowship member, Ding Zer Tian, suggested cycling from Teluk Anson to his home in Sitiawan in another part of Perak State. This sounded exciting and the Harpers felt it could be a useful experience. We set off early for Bagan Datok, cycling downstream to the mouth of the broad Perak River which was still without a bridge for many miles upstream.

We negotiated a fare for ourselves and our cycles on a *sampan* (small motorised boat) and were soon purring across the crocodile-infested estuary. Just beyond the far side was an oil-palm plantation whose manager was an outstation member of our Parish[3], so we enjoyed a chat and cup of coffee before setting off on the gravel roads. A brief but torrential storm utterly soaked us, but cycling in the ensuing sunshine we soon dried out. An hour or so later we rode into Sitiawan, Malaya's most-Christianised district.

Zer Tian discovered that a group of his former classmates were planning a cycle trip to Pangkor Island and would we like to join them? We enjoyed the days of fellowship, cycling over Dickson Pass, onto the ferries to Pangkor, across the island for lots of lobster and crab meals in a fisherman's hut. We swam and dived in the crystal clear sea. We slept on the thin grass mattresses again, and I have never found this a problem; they are adequate for a good sleep, and they afford well-ventilated coolness. Cycling back, a couple of the party decided to accompany me to the jetty to re-cross the Perak estuary. Sure enough there was a crocodile

---

3   The genesis of most English-speaking Anglican Churches in most former colonies was that they were first built by the British expatriates who would support Chaplains – some based in a town, but sometimes roving. Teluk Anson Parish still roved a bit around Christmas, but our visits to outlying estates were rare. Early ministry was also extended to Indian immigrants, many of whom were already Christians, and clergy from India were brought in to serve them. The immigrant Chinese Christians were usually numerous enough to build their own churches and support their own sinophone minister.

below the pier – the only one I had ever seen in the wild. I was relieved that I had arranged to cross on the much larger Estate ferry.

On several occasions we loaded up the Willys station wagon with equipment and literature for a village visit. Even arriving without any notice did not prevent a good audience. I recall how, as I drove into a village,

Another very old slide – Pangkor Beach – now all built up! Zer Tian (left) with friends from Sitiawan and David (second right).

the children would shout '*Bok-su lai liau!*' ('The pastors have come!') We set up a simple bamboo-framed screen plus a projector lit by a kerosene pressure lamp; someone proficient in Chinese commented as we showed a filmstrip of *The Prodigal Son,* acted as in a 'modern' (i.e. pre-Communist) situation in Shanghai. We handed out leaflets to bystanders and stocked a few Bibles for sale too. But without some kind of foresight, consecutive teaching at these outstations became difficult.

Meanwhile, our spiritually strong senior missionaries were starting to find Malaya more difficult. They had all learnt standard Mandarin Chinese and spoke it quite well, meaning their initial welcome by the Chinese in the New Villages was warm indeed. But the local Chinese spoke southern Chinese languages at home, and, increasingly, English, yet still displayed Chinese courtesies and friendliness.

Some of the senior ex-China CIMers found these Anglophone Chinese intimidating. Perhaps they felt out of their depth with the bright, precocious, questioning fifth- and sixth-formers[4] in the English-speaking schools. So these seniors tended to withdraw to the simple rural market-gardening communities, where easy-going schedules could be worked out on a day-to-day basis. I myself enjoyed both environments.

On the downside there was little advance planning for the Field as a whole; we younger ones had been taught to plan carefully and to look as far ahead as practicable. We felt, justifiably, that we needed to see some clear template for developing our outreach centres for national leadership and the future church.

---

4   Fifth and sixth forms were the two pre-university years in high school.

A particular problem for us all was that our well-organised and visionary leader of the 'North Malaya' field, George Williamson, had been invited to take on leadership-level work at OMF headquarters. Thus we lacked a clear aim for our congregations.

With no one to speak for the Anglican side of the OMF team, the Bishop and Diocese saw OMF as delightful people, and willing to live simply, but rather unresponsive in decision-making. The Diocese saw them as espousing a kind of twin loyalty, divided between the Church and the Mission. As I write, this 'two hats' misunderstanding is fortunately fading into history, and I personally have been made more than welcome by the Bishops and the Diocese, both while serving and much later on my many retirement visits back to Asia.

Some vindication was to come later when Bishop Chiu, himself a Malaysian, took the lead and commented that in villages where OMF had worked, the congregation may have been small and apparently weak – but it was well-trained, and would continue to function whether an ordained minister were available or not. Quite a tribute! The next Bishop, Moses Tay, became Chairman of OMF Singapore, which sends out high calibre Singaporean missionaries to work in church-planting teams.

Sadly by 1967, Malaysia's new visa rules were pushing *all* foreign missionaries out of the country altogether. The effect, however, was to force younger Malaysian Christians to take full responsibility, which they have done. With their vigorous church planting, membership is growing exponentially.

On my retirement visits back to Perak, I find that OMF's former missionaries are seen in a very favourable light today. In fact one Malaysian Anglican missionary society has been formed to complete the tasks of village evangelism. Many of the children and youth in our Sunday Schools and adult congregations are now church leaders.

Earlier on in my time at Teluk Anson, I was sent down to Singapore to meet John Wheatley of the Far East Broadcasting Co. (FEBC), an American-based missionary radio organisation[5]. A project for a programme recording studio in Singapore had been on the back burner for some years and John wanted to make firm plans, and to form a governing committee of local Christians. At this point OMF confirmed my designation to work

---

5   FEBA Radio in the UK was formed to support FEBC and later took on responsibility
     for several overseas centres in India and Africa.

along with FEBC, based in the proposed new Singapore studio. The rest of the year in Malaya passed quickly.

All too soon it was time to move on to my orientation period with FEBC in Manila, the Philippines. In early September 1962, I was booked on a near-new Dutch freighter to Manila. So I found myself with just seven other passengers in first class – the only class on this ship – all in spacious comfort and with the use of a small swimming pool. We ploughed through four days of choppy water under grey, leaden skies, docking in Manila in drizzling rain. Wrecked and rusting ships dotted the harbour, and everything else looked gloomy and run-down.

Could this really be the Pearl of the Orient Seas?

Manila
– Pearl of the Orient Sea

I disembarked from the *Schiekerk* in Manila. Clearing three pieces of luggage through customs took all day. Clearly, not everywhere in Asia shared Singaporean ideas on efficiency! FEBC's minibus crawled along pot-holed mud streets, sometimes axle-deep in water, passing some stately Spanish-era churches. But most of the scenery comprised dusty, unpainted wooden or breeze-block row-houses, shops and shacks. No wonder we had been warned on the ship to 'avoid flies and boil drinking water.'

Exhausted by tea time, we reached Christian Radio City Manila, which I had heard and read so much about. FEBC was known in Christian circles chiefly for its giant international missionary radio transmitters in Manila – 16 of them. It claimed to be the largest non-government radio system in the world. The much-photographed Eiffel Tower-like transmitting mast towered above the compound. This was indeed an exciting place to be: here was a completely non-government, all-Christian broadcasting station, covering all of Asia. Britons, brought up on the then-BBC monopoly, would have found it difficult to conceive a private radio station, let alone one operated by missionaries and audible across half the world. Yet that's what we had in Manila[1].

As I settled into my room above the studios the window framed the tower reaching 300 feet above us; its red navigation lights glowed as the sky darkened. A few years earlier the FEBC engineering team had priced such a tower, but there was none available in the Philippines, nor could one be affordably imported. There was much prayer and counting of funds. Apparently they even emptied the coins from the Coca-Cola machine! Then one day a shipping agent phoned. A steel tower had been shipped to Manila mistakenly. The local agent's instructions were to sell it for the

---

1   At that time FEBC also operated stations in Okinawa and San Francisco, and later in Korea.

Aerial view of Christian Radio City Manila (CRCM), dominated by the 300-foot transmitting mast. Also the Far East Bible Institute and Seminary (FEBIAS).

best price he could get – or scrap it, if need be. It became FEBC's for only $300, then just over £100 – about an eighty-fifth of its true factory-price in the USA. Was this a coincidence, or another missionary tale of God's provision?

I found my new working neighbours, mostly American warm, friendly and hospitable, very anxious to involve me in their work, and excellent teachers. It was almost like being back in the States. Although the Philippines had inherited an American system of government, the Filipinos did not always run it with the usual American élan. Apart from the 'jeepneys' that ploughed through the muddy downtown shopping area, there was almost no public transport. There was little or no street-lighting, and we were advised to have all our inoculations up to date. Government offices were very like my initial experience of the customs house, and the Post Office often ran out of stamps – sometimes for weeks. Once in a barber's chair I watched alarmed as in the mirror I saw one man pulling a knife on another!

Nevertheless in spite of pervasive appalling political and governmental corruption, things got done. Indeed, from the vast reservoir of American military surplus, we could buy almost everything needed for the station – often at a flat price of a dollar a ton.

I was quickly drawn into the routine of an international radio station: scriptwriting, recording continuity announcements for overseas English, gaining insights into the philosophy of constructing a programme schedule, and doing simple yet intricate electronic repair.

I particularly enjoyed reading the late night international news. An hour or more before the newscast, I would go into the teletype room, and pull off several yards of typed news. I tore off the individual items with a ruler, and then those to be used I put to one side and sorted into geographical order; the rest were used as economical toilet paper.

We usually started our newscast with the Philippines and worked westwards across Asia and Europe to the Americas. Most of the news stories needed drastic shortening. The preparation was complete when there were about 180 lines selected, just right to read in a 15 minute newscast. After typing up a few short headlines I was ready for the microphone.

Unlike the staid BBC's deadpan "Here is the News" of those days, we started off with a lively news theme – a band backed by the chatter of a teletypewriter, and as this faded down our standard recorded announcement played:

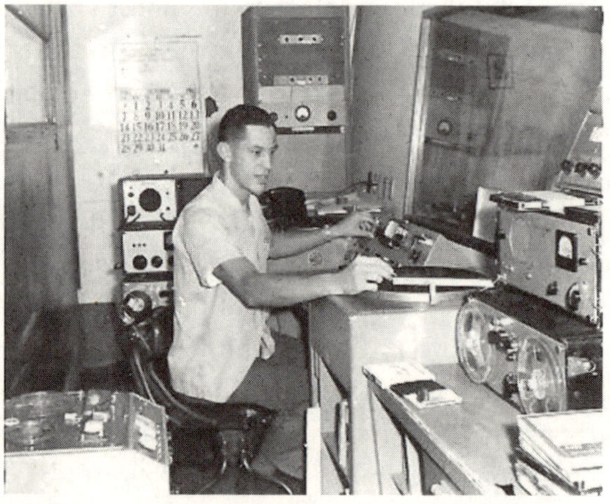

Leaning to use the equipment in the Control Room of FEBC-Manila's best drama studio. Note the sloping walls, ceiling and control-room window – to avoid opposite parallel sound-reflecting surfaces. The two reel tape recorders (behind me and right) are the early American 'Magnecorders' and (left front) the then more modern but obsolescent British 'Ferrograph'. The record turntable was capable of playing 16" discs, an earlier broadcast standard.

From the news-capitals of the world, here is the latest world… news… roundup…

and I would cut-in with: Good evening, here are the headlines.

After reading the 180 lines of teletype, I concluded with FEBC's formula:

and so goes the latest world news – the news that will make tomorrow's headlines as brought to you from the worldwide facilities of the Far East Broadcasting Company's news room… in… Manila… your newscaster David Huntley wishing you… 'good evening!'

The operator faded-up an instrumental, *Seventy-Six Trombones*, to conclude the newscast.

Our quite effective news-preparation technique became known disparagingly as *rip n' read*. But virtually all comments from our overseas listeners were, and remain, favourable. After all, FEBC offered the only international radio newscast in Asia not subject to control by a government agency. Some career news journalists were appalled at what they saw as such unprofessional presentation; but in retrospect I'm not so sure. *Rip n' read*-ers quickly gain an excellent grasp of world affairs, and the method gives a far wider, more detailed coverage of the whole world, albeit with shorter, less fully-expounded stories. And of course, all at a fraction of the cost.

Most mission-type radio stations in those days funded themselves by *time donation payments* – a polite form of selling airtime – just ambiguous enough for us not to be regarded for tax purposes as a for-profit business! I learnt that News was seen as 'dead' time as it produced no sponsors, though it certainly pulled in listeners.

On the production side I learnt there was about a score of well-known English-language Christian programme producers in the USA (as well as hundreds of lesser-known ones) plus a few more in the UK and Australasia, all producing similar 'Gospel' broadcasts. There was a musical opening – the theme or signature tune – followed usually by a mixture of short biblical expositions interspersed with more music, and perhaps a closing prayer and closing theme. Many would offer literature to any listener who wrote for it. Some programme producers strongly hinted that they would appreciate some money too, though we did not allow direct financial appeals. On a different plane we received high quality *Jungle Doctor* dramas from Australia – popular in their own right but the more so for being in a refreshingly different format.

This English-language scenario provided both broadcast content and money without too much effort, though a few scripts were superficial and unsubtle. However, one 'gospel' programme was very much like another, and a concatenation of these was hardly the way to draw totally unchurched people to our transmissions, nor to keep intelligent Christians tuned in. But there was a growing recognition that while we needed to maintain our distinctive Christian ethos, we also needed to cater to a much wider range of interests. On the vernacular side things were very much better; a network of FEBC recording studios across East Asia supplied us with tailor-made recorded programmes, all voiced by nationals and many of them producing some excellent regional music. Some Asian broadcasters came to help us on a live-in basis in Manila.

My practicum there was under John Wheatley's tuition. I scripted and produced a series of dramas from early Church history: *Echoes from Rome*. I also remember operating the control desk while John produced his daily live breakfast slot *Four Cups of Coffee*, a chat-and-news show incorporating occasional short taped interest items from our studios around East Asia. Two or three others joined him, literally with coffee and buns on the table.

John was later appointed to direct the construction of a huge new transmitter in the Indian Ocean island of Seychelles. But back in Manila it was hard to find any replacement who could match his breadth of vision for the Manila Overseas Service, his thoroughness with correspondence or his willingness to travel twice a year to our wide-ranging service areas.

We had an excellent team of Filipino staff; however, their interests were with our separate Philippines vernacular network of stations developing up and down the archipelago itself.

In Western countries most of the promotion of FEBC and its British sister organization FEBA majored not on general coverage of Asia but on broadcasting to China (then a tightly closed country) and to India – which then forbade all Christian use of broadcasting. Only in the last decade has there been some easing-up, but local radio and TV communications in Burma, Malaysia, China, Vietnam and Laos are still staunchly shut to Christian content.

An interesting task for me was to fill a need for economical recording equipment, and John Wheatley had the idea of converting a local hi-fi mixer for broadcast use. We worked on a prototype which we found gave broadcast-class quality, and many more were adapted. I had always enjoyed this kind of electronic work; perhaps it was fortuitous that it started when I inherited a couple of ancient radio receivers from my grandparents. But this Manila job seemed so much more satisfying – and indeed a privilege: it was for the end-purpose of spreading the Gospel, to God's glory.

He knew from the beginning!

Another interesting assignment was to accompany FEBC's elderly rattlesome 'Glory Truck' (*Ichabod, the glory has departed*[2]) to the airport for the state visit of the President of Mexico.

The Philippine President welcomed his Mexican counterpart in Spanish with great stress on the common Latin-American heritage of the two countries. Eric Parsons and I took it in turns to commentate, and evidently our efforts were well received. Again one wonders whether anywhere else, a private radio station would ever be allowed such close proximity to a visiting head of state!

On the church scene, I was attending an Amoy-speaking church in town and was invited to speak to the children at their related school further down in Luzon. We travelled there by the Philippine Railways in a surprisingly luxurious first class coach. In the east coast town of Siain, the Headmistress explained to the children that I had learnt their language because I loved Chinese people (true!).

Another outside trip was to be rowed up the Pagsanjan River in small wooden boats – a couple of local boatmen took the oars and lifted us and the boats over rocks along the gorge below the magnificent Pagsanjan Falls, a great place for a leisured swim!

I enjoyed one more trip, up to the mile-high resort of Baguio to the rice-terraced canyons at Banaue – said to be of prehistoric origin and claimed by Filipinos to be the eighth wonder of the world. Eric, the Canadian fellow programme worker and I travelled by bus: a truck chassis with a wooden box-like body. Passengers sat five abreast on transverse wooden benches, each seat having an un-doored exit to the right hand side. The bus crawled along a ledge just wide enough for itself with no room to pass anything. An un-walled 1000 feet drop was to our

---

2   From the biblical Book of Samuel, 1 Samuel 4:21.

right, and occasional fading wreaths bore witness to someone who had tumbled off the edge.

Our mountain hosts, who were studying tribal languages with a view to Bible translation, suggested a visit to the nearby cave system at Sagada, site of a mission endeavour by the Episcopal Church of the USA. We were hospitably received and a young student pumped up a kerosene lamp to give us a guided tour of those amazing lofty caverns.

The Philippines was an interesting place to be, and I learnt a great deal about broadcasting, but the time was drawing nigh for my return to Singapore. Orientation was over, and now I would be working. But in a sense learning has never stopped, nor will it till I see Heaven!

The Chinese have a proverb: '*Xue dao lao, xue bu liao*'.

Though you study till you grow old, you will never learn everything.

Singapore Studio

My Manila time was up. FEBC's American management decided to fly me to Singapore; this was my first air experience since the RAF had flown me to Singapore 10 years before.

Chris and Catherine Ellison, who had served 20 years with the CIM in China, welcomed me back in Singapore to the newish Church of the Good Shepherd. Under its Hokkien-speaking Vicar, Revd Lau Teik Oon, an English-language service was to start. Young Singaporeans were increasingly enrolling at English-language schools and using English as their first language.

Chris's age, humility and maturity attracted young Singaporeans, and an informal youth fellowship soon grew into a proper congregation. Several of the original members are still there today. I was again welcomed by Bishop Kenneth Sansbury, who licensed me so that I could preach and assist at any service, and that later led to ordination. I was invited to read one of the Scriptures at the Chinese service as well.

It was here that I became involved with Singaporean young people; I often took some of them with me as I travelled to speak about the Singapore Studio in Malayan churches. Some of the young men married within the congregation and several are currently leaders in Singapore's churches[1]. There were also spare time activities such as a cycle-riding across the Causeway to Johor Bahru; no documentation was then needed to cross into Malaya, though none of the youth had been there before.

My reason for being in Singapore was the radio recording studio, but Dale Golding, who had started the FEBC studio in Singapore had been hospitalised and reassigned to Manila. That left me alone to head

---

1   Derek Hong (and Su Lan) went on to pastor a large church, and Kuan Kim Seng (and Ai Mai) is Dean of the Cathedral and Diocesan Director of Missions. John and Alice Wong are active in missions. Allan (and Mae Chan) Wong is a lay leader in the church and in many other Singapore Christian activities.

up the Centre, with the title of FEBC Field Director for Singapore and Malaya. There were only three staff, but with a team of unpaid volunteer broadcasters we recorded a healthy tally of programmes, mostly in Chinese. These, on seven-inch tape reels, found their way by surface parcel post to the FEBC transmitters in Manila or in Okinawa; and each was aired at least once right across China.

The studio flat included the traditional servant's quarters at the back with its own shower-toilet and mini-kitchen – a comfortable 'bachelor's pad' for me. Apart from breakfast, I took my main meals at the OMF Guest House, just a couple of minutes away on my Honda Cub motor bike. Singapore was still a low-cost place to live; the local *Malayan Dollar* was fixed at $8.57 to £1.

After installing the recording equipment, one of our first jobs was to set up a shortwave receiver in order to monitor reception from our transmitters in Manila. For technical reasons, short wave stations have to 'hop around the dial' at least twice a year, and only in the reception area was it possible to ensure that we had clear reception. I recall one evening moving across the dial to see what other stations I could find. Many were jammers, usually based in countries behind the Iron Curtain. Government stations such as the BBC were often jammed, and one could hear behind the jamming 'noise' the faint Morse signals as they communicated with their master control – it seemed to me like the sound of evil itself! In fact, FEBC's transmissions were rarely jammed. Jamming is a costly and complex process, which was kept for use against government stations.

For the studio, money was always the big problem. From the outset the Singapore FEBC venture was told there was 'no' money at all: they must find it in Singapore itself. This was a radical idea. Singapore Christians and churches were used to the idea that missions or missionaries came with all the necessary funding for their projects. A local governing body had been appointed for the studio on a more or less ad-hoc basis, consisting mainly of members of the Plymouth Brethren, still a major Singapore denomination today. Happily in due course, churches of almost every denomination would support us in prayer and finance. That we successfully did so was due to a general informal opening-up of fellowship through planning for the various non-denominational gatherings across the island.

Early in my time in Singapore we were privileged to receive a visit from Bob Bowman, the founding president of FEBC and his wife Elinor.

It was one of their first visits outside of the 'American World' to our northeast. But here in independent Singapore and Malaya the Bowmans seemed to enjoy the efficiency and cleanliness, as well as the friendliness of local people, and their warmth was reciprocated by the Christians. I drove them up into my old stamping grounds in Malaya, and at Teluk Anson Bob Bowman regaled the evening congregation in St Luke's Church with a rendering of the hymn *No One Ever Cared for Me Like Jesus* – accompanying himself on the pedal organ. We drove on to Ipoh and Penang, which gave us similar welcomes. This was the first time that the Bowmans had experienced such warm fellowship within main-line churches.

With some difficulty, we secured seats in a plane for the Bowmans from Penang to Bangkok. Meanwhile I made my way back to Singapore, collecting Stephen Choo, my future 'best man' so he could experience Singapore and my church there.

Church-wise, as part of FEBC, I had to find our way around a complex, even baffling

Taking Dr Bob and Mrs Elinor Bowman (Founders of FEBC) up-country into Malaya. The Singapore Studio's Fiat 600 car gave endless trouble through overheating. Bob's subsequent tales of this trip became more embellished with each telling! (From a badly-faded colour slide.)

scene. A single Council of Churches for both Malaya and Singapore[2] had been formed by the expatriate heads of the historic denominations. However, by the time I got there about half of Singapore's churches (mostly newer arrivals) had refused to join. The World Council was stressing a goal of structural unity of all churches; this struck fear into the smaller denominations who were usually very supportive of us, especially of our broadcasts to China. So while respecting the Council's member-churches – many of whose members also supported us – we sought the fellowship and support of *all* of the many churches who would welcome us in both Singapore and Malaya. The local Council of Churches had

---

2   This Council went out of existence in Singapore. The current National Council of Churches of Singapore (NCCS) has almost every one of the Republic's Christian groupings and organisations in membership, and has no goal of 'one super church.'

also secured a monopoly of all religious radio time on Radio Singapore. (Later on, I was able to moderate this regime.)

However, the churches really started to get to know each other in 1964. With some involvement of FEBC, a group of self-appointed evangelists from across Asia (with strongest representation from the Philippines and India) decided to hold their 'Asian Evangelists' Conference', to be followed by rallies in the National Theatre – the Asian Evangelists' Crusade[3]; Nothing in Singapore on this scale had ever been done before without a good deal of Western input. The Filipinos and Indians knew much more about evangelism than did the Singaporeans, but the Filipinos were impressed with the tidiness of Singapore, and its lack of slums or squatters – or corruption! They were especially struck by the extensive low-cost housing estates. They thought that the British had done it, but in fact almost all of Singapore's housing projects were initiated *after* independence.

Not long before the Crusade I had taken a carload of young people from the Church of the Good Shepherd to the beach to swim and enjoy a picnic. Unbeknown to me, rioting had broken out in part of the city and the whole island was put under curfew. I was fortunate to be able to gain a curfew pass when I showed the Indian police inspector my Letter of Authority as a worker in broadcasting. He seemed quite sympathetic and may have had some contact with the Christian faith.

Notwithstanding these ethnic riots and the curfew which had closed down the city's life for a few days, Singaporeans from virtually every kind of church and from none at all poured into the vast National Theatre for the Asian Evangelists' Crusade. The bus company even ran extra buses to transport the attenders home.

The Council of Churches looked on uncomprehendingly, having refused its official stamp of approval because the organisers did not work through what the Council considered to be their own proper channels. Nevertheless the Asian Evangelists' rallies, though held between two periods of curfew, closed with the exhilarating feeling that 'we've never done this before and it has been a God-blessed success.' We at FEBC were involved with the Crusade's communications but with the Crusade

---

3   At this point 'Crusade' was not a sensitive term; no one connected it with the crusades fought in the Holy Land centuries ago.

over, it was now 'back to the studio' with the constant need to keep the equipment running and seek support from churches far and near.

One weekday per week I took off to explore Singapore and visit Sandes Soldiers' Home, which I had known since Army days. There I could laze in their lounge or swim in the pool before lunch!

Wealthy Chinese Christians were usually older Chinese-speaking men and women, and they tended to bestow their largesse on those missions who ministered to scattered Chinese. These warriors of the faith also sympathised with our broadcast ministry to China, and often opened their wallets to us. I was glad that however poor my grasp of Chinese, I had made some progress and was seen to have tried! But I was discovering that it was the English-speaking churches (though ethnically Chinese) who eventually became the most generous to rise to our particular challenge. Remarkably, month by month there seemed to be *just* enough money to pay our rent and staff, and to keep the equipment going.

On my weekly day off I often explored the countryside on the island or in rural Malaya.

Almost half of the money seemed to go on rent. For months we scoured Singapore to see if we could find a property of our own and a way to buy it. There was nothing within our reach or anywhere near it, though we certainly prayed a lot. FEBC indicated that a small monthly subsidy was a possibility if we could finance a suitable property with a local loan. We also leased a small part of our floorspace to the new staff-worker of the Fellowship of Evangelical Students, Chua Wee Hian ('Freddie'). Freddie's brief was to preside over the huge growth of student Christian groups in both Singapore and Malaya. Their visits to our building were a fertile source of support and interest in our broadcasting.

Our studio's landlord in Tanglin Rd was Kian Gwan Co., a large Indonesian-Chinese business house. Unexpectedly I was visited by the manager and it seemed that they wanted their property back – would we be willing to terminate our two-year lease? If so Kian Gwan would let us off our responsibility to restore our unit to its original condition. (We had done considerable alterations to build the studio.) I was faced with a dilemma – we could stick with the lease and face the expense at the end, or we could take Kian Guan's offer, but then where would we go now? More doubt, more uncertainty, more sense of inexperience with handling property. However, God knew, and as we prayed the answer came.

One of our Singapore Board Members noticed that the government-owned Singapore Housing Board was offering some ground floor shops below a nine-floor block of flats. The building was located up a hill at the end of a cul-de-sac – meaning there was very easy parking. So our studio's new home became 338 Jalan Minyak – the building is still there. The rent was less than at Tanglin and it served us well.

We engaged a contractor, and I spent many days in working clothes until we finished up with a small but soundproofed studio.

Our team remained small: a Chinese lady broadcaster named Mrs Lee Sew Fun, plus the many part-time volunteers who came in once or twice a week. When our first operator resigned we took on David Wong, a youth fellowship member at the Church of the Good Shepherd. David was an energetic and able young man, ready for almost any task, and was enrolled at Singapore's Polytechnic for a course in Electronics. He was like a breath of fresh air and fell into the studio routine immediately. Later as a degreed engineer, he and I became fellow-workers together in Seychelles.

But I was due for a year's furlough and Dale Golding offered to leave FEBC Manila and serve in Singapore for a year to lead our studio again. I made my way down to the *Fairstar*, sailing to the UK and was farewelled by the studio staff and many of the youth members from the Church of the Good Shepherd. Over a year later I was welcomed back by Dale and the staff. The Jalan Minyak studio was serving us well; nevertheless, we really did need a place of our own where we would be free from constant dependence upon landlords and monthly rentals.

During my first furlough Ruth and I had started to correspond a little and even to swap small tapes. She came down to Singapore for a medical appointment on the day I landed, but more of that in the next chapter!

Out of the blue, Mr Goh Ewe Kheng, a Christian businessman friend contacted us; he was planning the redevelopment of a dilapidated old property, and indicated he would like to offer us a spacious unit in his proposed block of flats. We looked at the price and thanked Mr

While/started with the Singapore studio, Ruth was helping to plant a
new church in Triang, Pahang State, Malaya, seen here (centre) with
some of the church ladies.

Goh, and suggested he advertise for a suitable buyer. He did, but no
one bought it!

A week or two later I had to fly to Bangkok. I was about to walk
through the glass departure gate when I felt a hand on my shoulder. It was
our businessman friend Mr Goh. Would we like the unit? I explained how
ideal it would be but we had no money – his reply was that we could have
the unit, and pay him at leisure.

My OMF background made me cautious of anything suggestive of
debt. So we decided to follow Gideon (the story is in Judges, chapter
6) and put out a fleece: we told everyone on our mailing list of the
opportunity, and asked for either a straight capital gift, or an interest-
free long loan, or a promise of cash. I thought that would be the end of
the matter. But something like 20 percent of the money came in quickly.
Nothing succeeds like success, or more accurately, as Hudson Taylor had
declared, 'God's work done in God's way will never lack supply.'

Excitedly we watched the property grow, and moved in to 130-S
Sophia Road, now freeholders in our own right[4]. Re-installing the studio
at the new site was a big job, and David Wong and I spent many late hours
getting the recording gear connected up ready to re-start programming.
We were able to incorporate many lessons from the two previous studios
into the new installation. It seemed good – no outside noises came in, the
acoustics were excellent and the air-conditioning was truly silent; three
essentials for a good studio.

---

4   The Singapore studio has moved several times since then and the work carries on today.

For many decades the sole radio voice within the country, the government-owned Radio Singapore, had aired an edited church service programme on Sunday evenings, rotating round the Council-affiliated churches. The co-ordinator was Michael Counsell, a fellow Anglican clergyman, and when he left Singapore he proposed me for the task and I accepted, unopposed. Slowly I was able to open up the roster for the half-hour Sunday broadcasts to unaffiliated groups. The Brethren and Baptist churches joined in, as well as some para-church organisations such as Scripture Union and Youth for Christ. Most jumped at the opportunity to broadcast though a few saw it as a chore – even to the point of backing-out at the last moment. I would then have to find someone a bit more visionary to fill the gap! These broadcasts were effective and after every programme I received appreciative comments. There was no need to 'build an audience'; anyone listening to the lone English-language channel heard us without choice!

An interesting side-line of that job was an invitation to join the Mass Communications Committee of the Council of Churches. Thus I became the Bishop's nominee to the Committee on behalf of the Anglican Church.

But ah! The Council was distantly affiliated to the World Council of Churches. In Singapore, one of the smaller denominations had affiliated itself with the self-styled International Council of **Christian** Churches (ICCC), a tiny but vociferous body based in the USA with very little following elsewhere. It proactively fought the WCC with its militant pronouncements.

Up in Malaya, my friend John Hewlett, also an OMF missionary and the Anglican Vicar of Taiping, had been elected to chair the town's inter-church fellowship. In some way or other, it was also found to hold a very distant and tenuous link with the World Council.

Enter the presumptuously named Singapore Council of **Christian** Churches. Their chairman, whom we knew quite well, wrote to OMF on un-headed paper on behalf of his 'Council'. The tone was formal but firm: 'OMF must ensure that Hewlett and Huntley vacate their respective posts with the Taiping Churches and the Mass Communications Committee', 'or else! …'

John Hewlett and I were both contacted by Ernie, a kindly Director of OMF who was most happy that both of us were involved in key tasks and he saw these committees as contributing to the church's overall mission. OMF desired to serve alongside *all* churches, and did not wish to be seen to take instructions from one small group. But as an American, Ernie was only too aware of the adverse publicity which the ICCC could raise in the USA against OMF if they got hold of our story. We managed a compromise; John and I had only a few months left to remain in office anyhow. Ernie wrote an eirenic reply and we heard no more.

Another activity stemmed from discovering how valuable a language laboratory was in learning a language. After seeing a circuit for one I decided I could build it – and did. I used this for a while when I was welcomed to teach a class in Phonetics at the Singapore Bible College. Though all the students spoke quite good English, many had problems with pronunciation, and even more so when as intending missionaries themselves, they tackled another language.

In Sarawak, the Borneo Evangelical Mission (BEM) had planted a wide self-governing network of churches in North Borneo and radio seemed an ideal means of Christian teaching and even evangelism, and there was space for a studio by the BEM's airstrip at Lawas, Sarawak. Somehow I rustled up some money for flights to visit Lawas and I enjoyed a few days' hospitality with the BEM personnel. The compound was quite modern – apart from aviation there was a radio telephone with some of the outlying mission centres and jungle airstrips, there was also a sizeable generator. Nevertheless the Sarawakian Church leaders (as well as the expat missionaries) were also excited about the possibilities of broadcasting; and short wave listening (such as FEBC's) was the only kind they had at that time anyway.

My ticket took me on to Tawau at the extreme north-eastern tip of Sabah, to monitor our radio transmissions from the Philippines, and assess their viability for northern Borneo. Thus in due course, the keen-ness of the Sarawak church leaders bore fruit and a studio was built that continues today. Back in Singapore we noticed the start of a gradual change. As the neighbouring Malaysian Government's control was extended to Borneo, missionary visas were gradually cancelled, and the BEM was merged into OMF. The former BEM's studio thus became the only one ever directly operated by any part of OMF.

On the FEBC scene, each year the various Directors – one per country – would meet in the Philippines or elsewhere for a Director's Conference. One conference was held near Tokyo. En route there Lauw Kim Guan (already designated as my successor) and I were able to make a stopover in Okinawa, about to revert to Japan, and one of FEBC's major transmitting sites to mainland China. In retrospect we see how the Lord had indeed given us excellent transmitting sites in Asia, even though so few governments allowed this kind of activity.

The efficiency of Japan struck us immediately. Their airports were free from the tiresome queues at check-in and immigration, and there were no declarations to be filled in. Indeed, one barely stopped walking from the plane door to the Greeting Area. The cities were tidy and everything was spotlessly clean, if sometimes cramped and crowded. Our hotel seemed helpful and friendly and offered Japanese and 'English' menus – the latter were written in French. In the hotel, Kim Guan and I wanted to rinse out some clothes; and in a local shop where no one spoke English there were packets with a picture showing clean linen pegged out in the breeze. It did not lather… it proved to be starch! Overall, our time in Tokyo was most refreshing and we learnt a lot.

Occasionally we wondered if the Singapore government would ever let us operate our own local station for Singapore itself. We did wonder about setting something up in Riau – the Indonesian island-province within sight of Singapore. But much more recently, our vision came about. Transport links to Riau became fast and frequent; FEBC-Singapore now rents a long daily time-slot from a Riau station. It is heard clearly on the FM band in Singapore and southern Malaysia.

Back to 1971. The time came for our furlough, and our original vision for a Singaporean Director was approaching fulfilment. Mr Lauw Kim Guan, our board chairman was a well-known leader in the Brethren and in other churches. Though only upper-middle-aged, under the Singapore Civil Service rules he was eligible for retirement, and with the support of his family and church he became our new Director. No further Western expatriate has ever been needed there. At our farewell meal I was presented with a Favre Leuba automatic Swiss Watch – which I still possess. Then Ruth and I, together with Jill and Andrew, were on our way to our second furloughs but our first one together!

Singapore
– Family

When we OMF missionaries arrived newly in Singapore for orientation, there was much elder-brotherly advice about marriage and opposite-sex relationships. We were reminded that the local culture demanded extreme circumspection. Indeed, the usual advice was to encourage candidates to apply as singles and only to consider marriage after the couple of years of language-study in Asia.

Lady applicants were reminded that because there were so many single lady missionaries and so few bachelors, the chances of meeting a suitor were slim. However as regards to bachelors, the comment from most ladies was 'give them a couple of years and they won't be bachelors any more!' My first four years with OMF were coming to a close and my furlough in Britain was due.

It was 1965 – four years after my arrival in Asia. Was I still an *eligible* bachelor? It seemed the case because one fellow missionary spoke to me on holiday in Cameron Highlands[1], and offered to pave the way for me to get to know a gifted lady missionary serving only a hundred miles or so distant. Though I knew the lady slightly, I had never thought of her as a life-partner. A few months later, however, she married a very fine young man working near her.

But I had started a very occasional correspondence with Ruth, and our paths had crossed once or twice when she came to Singapore on business or for activities. One evening we went out for a Chinese snack near the Jalan Minyak studio, where we were unlikely to meet anyone else from OMF! On another occasion, I went up to Malaya with my successor at the studio, Lauw Kim Guan, and visited the small town of Triang, Pahang State. Ruth was leading the Sunday afternoon English service as we tried

---

1   *Cameron Highlands* – a cool hill station in Malaysia where OMF owns a vacation bungalow.

to slip quietly into the little church there. Margaret Dyke, the senior missionary at Triang invited us to stay for a tasty meal and later (I learnt about this afterwards!) suggested to Ruth that I might make a suitable lifetime partner for her.

I had just been made Deacon shortly before departure. I spent a term in St Peter's Hall, part of Singapore's Trinity College to prepare for ordination as a Priest in the Anglican Church – and Ruth sent me a special greeting.

The Ordination Service in Singapore Cathedral was a longish ceremony starting with a figure-of-eight sung processional litany around the aisles. Bishop Kenneth Sansbury, the last expatriate Bishop of Singapore, presided and administered the ordination vows. That night in College Compline[2] I got a firm dig in the ribs from my fellow ordinand (now Canon) James Wong, as I was the only priest present and therefore pronounced the 'absolution' for my first time. Presiding at my first Communion the next morning went smoothly – if nervously.

Two ordinands (in white) with Bishop Kenneth Sansbury (centre), Archdeacon Chelliah (left) and John Savarimuthu, Chaplain and later Bishop of Malaya (right).

With only a few days to go, I packed for the journey home; this time I was put aboard the *Fairstar*, a beautiful modern Italian liner returning half-empty from an emigrant trip to Australia. Charles Hillier (serving in Thailand until his untimely death in a motorcycle accident) was my

---

2   *Compline* – a liturgical service said or sung before retiring for the night.

cabin-mate. This swift vessel ran non-stop to Aden where Charles made contact with some of his former schoolmates then serving with the Red Sea Mission Team; they dressed Arab-style, but since it was still British territory, Christian ministries carried on freely.

Then Southampton again – it was July (my birthday), but still grey and chilly. I had been given luggage for other missionaries so there were about 10 trunks to be cleared through customs and loaded on the boat-train to Waterloo where my mother met me. I made my bachelor pad as a base at the OMF's UK headquarters and guest-home for the year's furlough.

Furlough passed quickly – mainly because of the heavy speaking programme which home assignment missionaries were then expected to undertake[3]. In the summer of 1966, I had another month at sea – this time with a complimentary upgrade to the all-first-class P&O *Cathay*.

Arriving back in Singapore, I moved into the OMF Guest House in Cluny Road. After lunch Ruth drove up in her car – she had come for her periodical back treatment! We had not shared our interest with anyone as yet but as I went out to help Ruth with her luggage, our Director, Arnold Lea observed us from his office – he phoned Denis Lane, his assistant on the floor below to say 'did you see what I saw?' He later told me how pleased he was to see it! Sometimes we went out together to a restaurant, and one of these occasions, Ruth noticed that the young waitresses kept peering out from the kitchen, seemingly at us. They were indeed! Two of them were members at the

Our Engagement-day picture.

Church of the Good Shepherd. So the news there was out!

There was much amusement about Ruth's medical trips to Singapore, not to mention my visit to her up-country church for 'homework'. Courting couples had to be careful about local norms. A

---

3   It was quite normal to be confronted with over 50 engagements spread across the whole of the UK to be undertaken during a year's furlough. In this case a Lambretta scooter was providentially available and I used this for almost all my OMF engagements.

Our Wedding: (Background) Ruth's mother – Beryl Davies, Rowland Butler; (Front)Stephen Choo, David, Ruth, Barbara Johnson; (Flower Girls) Christine Lane, Lee Fong Chee.

few evenings later I proposed to Ruth in the grounds of the mosque on Island View Road[4]. The next day we made our engagement known to the OMF directors and staff. Alfred and Rosie Yeo took us to a goldsmith to get rings made, and our engagement photo taken, and we booked long distance phone calls to both our homes for the afternoon. (These then cost over £3 for three minutes!)

Meanwhile I was taking the FEBC recording studio management back from Dale and Belvah Golding; the death of their school-age son from encephalitis illustrates the possible costs of mission service, even today. Our wedding was on 21 January 1967 in the Church of the Good Shepherd, Queenstown, where I had been serving almost since the inception of the English-language service. Ruth's mother flew in from Melbourne for the occasion and Rowland Butler, an OMF Director who knew Ruth's family acted as the bride's father. The Ellisons acted as my 'parents for the day'. The Vicar, Canon Lau Teik Oon, and OMF's Chris Ellison[5] who pioneered the English ministry there officiated at the wedding. The young people acted as stewards and the choir prepared a surprise anthem for us. My Best Man was Stephen Choo,

---

4   This was a British military area and the mosque was provided for their Malay soldiers, but it was also a quiet uncrowded place with a breath-taking view across to Sumatra. In retirement we tried to locate the mosque, but it had been moved elsewhere when the entire Island View Estate was redeveloped for Singapore University.

5   Chris Ellison died in 2005 aged 100.

whom I had spent time with in Teluk Anson; he became a gifted school teacher and on retirement a businessman. The Wedding Breakfast was held at Cluny Road where we crowded into the old dining room because of a torrential downpour; thus we could not enjoy having the meal in the garden. Afterwards we drove off for our honeymoon up into Malaya[6], stopping off at Kluang, Port Dickson and the cooler climate of Maxwell's Hill.

Just over a year after our wedding, Jill was born at Kandang Kerbau[7] Hospital, Singapore, and Andrew joined us 21 months later. So having left the UK single – where someone had commented that I was not the marrying type (!) – I was to be welcomed back to Croydon four years later with a wife and two children.

For Ruth, her artistic gifts were in demand: book covers, cards and the like were needed for OMF Publishers in Kuala Lumpur and in Hong Kong, as well as occasional jobs, such as an illuminated Bible text for the OMF's centenary.

The studio job in Singapore now involved a

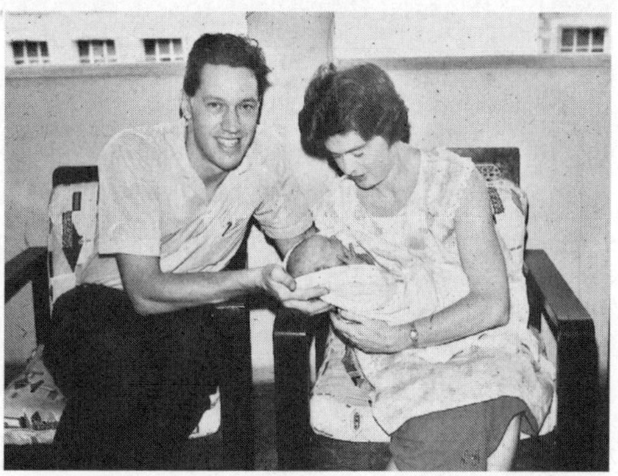

Jill was born in Kandang Kerbau Hospital, Singapore.

fare-paid visit to FEBC's annual Directors' Conference at their major station in the Philippines. For this, my first Conference, we rustled up enough money for Ruth to join me as a kind of honeymoon extension! Hong Kong was an intermediate stop where FEBC and OMF friends welcomed us; we enjoyed an excursion to a small hillock near the China border where we could look out over the high security fences to the rice paddies and canals in then-closed China[8].

The Manila gathering was a great opportunity for cross-fertilisation of ideas with other leaders and gaining insight into the extent of Christian

---

6   now West Malaysia

7   *Kandang Kerbau* means Buffalo Stable.

8   China was then a closed country; the same view today would be completely urban.

Ruth's original text deteriorated in the climate and she drew a fresh one recently. This now hangs in the air-conditioned office of the Guest Home Hostess.

broadcasting right across Asia[9]. We all put on suits and ties for the group photo – it was felt that the American home constituency would not understand casual dress at a business gathering! On the way back from Manila we stopped-off at Sibu in Sarawak to help a Methodist recording studio with whom we had struck up a relationship. Trevor, the Director and his wife had an uphill task but we were at least able to offer him fellowship and some technical assistance, and to encourage him in making local radio programmes.

There was time off too! Once every year or so we made a family trip to the OMF Bungalow in Cameron Highlands. This was a long drive usually involving a night stop en route, but worth it for the cool and restful location in the mountains. From the Bungalow, we could walk to the 6666ft (2020 metres) summit of Gunong Brinchang, the highest point in the country. Close by was the OMF's boarding primary school and we were able to introduce our children to it before they were of entry age. They loved what they saw and happily looked forward to their own starting there.

Our first married tour of service was drawing to a close. Before leaving Singapore, we handed over the studio to Lauw Kim Guan, the former Board Chairman. En route home, separately from Ruth, I took a ship to Seychelles where FEBA radio (based in the UK) had just started broadcasting to India, and spent a month working on the various sites.

A proper Seychelles airport was under construction – a factor in starting broadcasting there – and was ready for initial air trials. A small eight-seater plane service from Kenya had already started a weekly flight. One day we were primed about a much larger visitor; an RAF Hercules would arrive from Singapore. We duly assembled along the edge of the future runway and the plane landed without difficulty. There were no particular security arrangements. The crew climbed out and chatted with

---

9   FEBC's long distance broadcasting equipment in Manila was then the world's most powerful non-government broadcasting system.

us sightseers for half an hour or so and then the plane took off, executed a circle over the bay and returned to Singapore.

A further week at sea took me to Mombasa in Kenya where I rode a taxi to Scott Theological College near Nairobi. Desmond Hales (a classmate from LBC) extended hospitality to me with visits to the city, and to see the flamingos on Lake Naivasha. Missionary service there was much the same as that in Malaya; but African missionary work had already brought a much higher proportion of the population into the churches than was the case in Malaya. We passed through the Africa Inland Mission's Kijabe, at that time probably the world's largest mission station, with residences, schools and hospitals, plus its own post office and railway station. Then a charter flight took me back to London – and Ruth.

Ruth on the other hand waited a few weeks more in Singapore and then flew to Britain with toddler Jill and baby Andrew. They had to transit in Bangkok; Jill still recalls looking down from the hotel window to the garden below inhabited by realistic-looking crocodiles – but which never moved!

We spent eight months in Croydon, often visiting relations in North Wales as well as many shorter journeys. More divine provision came in the form of an affordable Morris Minor car, though our deputation programme for OMF was much lighter this time.

I had been able to enrol in an Educational Television course at the Centre for Educational Development Overseas (CEDO) aimed mainly at those in developing countries (which most in Southeast Asia were still considered to be). It was a thorough course and assumed that each participant was interested in some kind of teaching that television could help.

My first project was to present the entire Bible on a panorama of still pictures. I was grateful for Ruth's artistic gift in preparing them on orange card, with black and white paint to give the best shading on the then standard black-and-white TV pictures. The entire panorama was about a foot high and about 16 feet long; so I took it to London in sections and two fellow trainees slid the panorama slowly along blackboard easel pegs, passing it in front of the camera, while a third was the commentator from a script which I had prepared.

Because Christianity was taught in most UK schools by law, a religious subject was no problem to CEDO especially as most of the

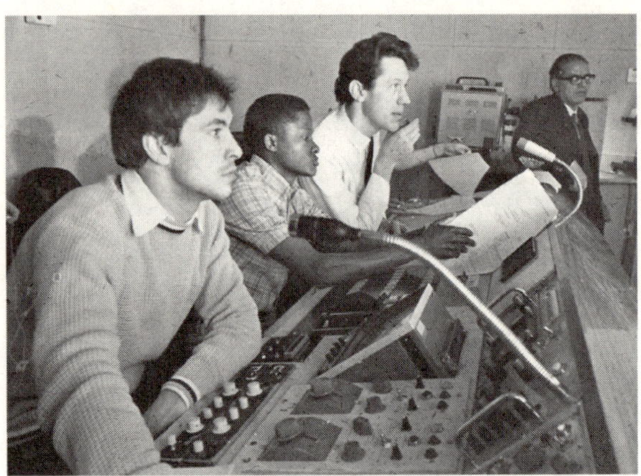

Making an educational TV Programme at CEDO. The team making my 'programme' in the gloom of the control room at CEDO, London, Autumn 1971. The two fellow-trainees on the left came from Egypt and Uganda.

trainers were experienced UK schoolteachers, and the overseas students – even the Muslims – had no problem about a Christian subject. The presentation was very well-received, but there was then no medium by which I could keep a usable video copy.

So, without any computerisation, I planned to explain the use of various types of microphones in use. I created an animated drawing of each type of microphone showing how sound moves the sensitive parts, and the various advantages of each type. Elements of the picture to be added later were covered up at first and then revealed at the right point by the withdrawal of a 'sliding hiding' card. This experience and knowledge became useful later, when I was able to help develop a Christian video-teaching project in Thailand.

For our time in the UK, Emmanuel Church invited me to be an honorary Curate. This included preaching my own valedictory sermon on the final Sunday before returning overseas. I did not think it had been a particularly effective sermon at the time, but many years later I gathered that one member had had his call to the Ministry confirmed while another first received a ministerial call.

We experienced a white Christmas (rare in London), and for Ruth, new to the UK, it was a Christmas Card scene as we walked up to the snow-covered church with warm lighting showing from inside. After the Christmas season, my mother came to look after the children so that Ruth and I could accept an invitation to Amsterdam. My visit was 'business' –

to the giant Philips electronic works at Eindhoven to prospect for future studio equipment. We took a cabin on the night boat across the North Sea. It happened to be our wedding anniversary, and on the boat-train from London a chatty waiter asked us what we would like so he could cook it specially! For a nightcap at the ship's cafeteria, the attendant took two small bottles of drinking chocolate from a rack, unscrewed the tops and put them in a small 'cupboard' after which he filled our glasses with steaming hot drink. It was our first encounter with a microwave oven!

Our next stop was Australia, but there would be intermediate stops on the way.

Australia and Indonesia

FEBC had expressed pleasure with our work in Singapore, we had built up a very economical operation, finding most of the funding locally. So during our first married furlough in the UK, FEBC invited us to route our return to Asia via their HQ in California, and we worked this in with a visit to Ruth's home in Melbourne, Australia.

Thus in late 1972, we flew across from London to Philadelphia with Jill (almost five) and Andrew (three) where Audrey Jackson, Jill's Godmother welcomed us to American soil. Based in the CIM[1] Guest Home we passed a busy week there speaking at meetings and taking up invitations to attend missionary presentations and displays in some large churches. The once-familiar Automat restaurants had changed with inflation; the antique coin-operated pigeon holes for the food could not accept the much higher prices and a cafeteria system had arrived.

While a few of the American OMF missionaries come from the traditional historic denominations, we found that the majority are sent by totally independent but well-attended congregations where plenty of families are in evidence and they enjoy excellent biblical teaching – there really was no counterpart in Britain or Australasia, and very few even in Canada.

Calvary Independent Church in nearby Lancaster funds a wide panel of around 60 related missionaries worldwide. Located outside town, it was the focus of a network of church-run social activities and of course a vast car-park. The (Canadian) minister invited me to give a brief report about our work overseas; there are few places anywhere in the Western world now where a church could be filled for seven days of world mission teaching and preaching.

---

1   CIM – the old title was still in use in some circles, especially in North America where abbreviations of some other societies were similar to 'OMF.'

We briefly stopped in Chicago with excursions to Wheaton College – a university, one of the USA's many missiological power-houses. We were invited to chat with several young people who manifested an interest in overseas ministry. In North America missionary service was still the subject of great interest – and challenge.

The next stop was California, and we enjoyed looking out over the Grand Canyon as we glided over its plateaus and abrupt depths. When we started to lose height over the outer suburbs of Los Angeles we gazed down bemused by the fantastic freeway network – so many wide roads, up to 10 lanes – and all filled with speeding cars. This was indeed the world capital of motordom, and one might think, the motorist's heaven. School children could start learning to drive at 14½ – accompanied, of course. Petrol then cost under 30¢ per gallon and most cars seated six passengers. There were few bus lines, and those that there were mostly stuck to main roads and hourly intervals; we were told that only the very young, very old and ethnic minorities used them! The famous American yellow school bus catered for most journeys of the young when not chauffeured by their parents. In Californian cities, almost all shopping was done in sizeable indoor malls or outdoor squares.

The California stopover was quite an excitement as a large car was loaned to us. In addition, our family were treated to several tours, and given a free day in Disneyland. There in Whittier, California we met Basil and Betty Costerisan, missionaries with another society, Overseas Crusades. They had a wide experience of Indonesia and good language; moreover, they had an interest in starting a recording studio under FEBC in Jakarta. Would we join them?

It was an all-night flight on to Melbourne (with a stop at Fiji) and a warm welcome from Ruth's family. It was my first visit to Australia and its distinctive culture. I had had excellent impressions of Australian visitors to the UK, though there is always much to learn in a new country. Our house in the suburbs was well equipped though chilly by UK standards; there was no insulation, little heating and very few electric points to plug heaters in. The house boasted a modern bathroom but, as in most older Australia homes, the flush toilet was located on a verandah *outside* the back door!

At that time Australia was emerging as a nation of major importance in the Far East and was anxious to project a distinctively Australian image. It seemed as if Australia was still 'importing' immigrants from the

UK for a £10 fare. There is no doubt that for a young family Australia has a lot to offer. Most young couples there pay off their mortgage by their early thirties, and more than once we would wrestle with this possibility in our later missionary career.

FEBC confirmed their invitation to us to serve in Indonesia, and moreover to buy a new Holden car in Australia, use it, and ship it to Jakarta when we left. Ruth and I visited Sydney for some mission-related meetings and found time to explore the famous bridge and harbour. The deputation (speaking in churches on behalf of the OMF) load in Australia was quite undemanding. We joined a small Anglican Church and enrolled Jill in their week-time kindergarten which she loved. The Vicar at that time was David Binns who gave us a warm welcome. He later pioneered a rewarding ministry among drug addicts in Adelaide where we met him on another furlough.

It was now clear that our next stop would be Jakarta, where we would have a lot to do with small radio stations. I enrolled in a radio theory course with the Wireless Institute of Australia leading to the government exam for becoming a ham operator. I rang the government office and was amazed that I had passed the whole test. Although I still hold a ham licence, I have never used it to become an operator.

After much difficulty in getting clear definitions from FEBC and from OMF as to exactly how we should plan our return to Asia, the car went off to Jakarta and our boxes were sent to Singapore with us to follow. Due to a strike we were re-routed via Canberra, where our luggage had been unloaded, then Sydney, where baggage-less, we were given a free night in a hotel but without the things we needed for our toddlers. At last we were driven to the airport for a Singapore flight and arrived there utterly exhausted!

There were some weeks to pass in temporary housing before the Indonesian visa could be finalised. For the OMF-Jakarta team, broadcasting was well aside from OMF's mainstream activities; churchplanting and teaching has always been their first objective. Nevertheless with FEBC's high profile broadcasts, OMF was happy for a few of their personnel to be loaned to radio ministry.

I spent much of the waiting time back in the Singapore studio assembling Heathkit electronic test gear from kit-form for using in the Jakarta studio, while Ruth looked after the children.

Indonesian visas always involved a long delay. Ruth, Andrew, David and Jill were Indonesian waiters for two months' stopover in Singapore.

Finally we boarded a plane for Jakarta ready for work in a totally new environment. We arrived with a great deal of luggage, including two large suitcases full of the Heathkit electronic gear for the studio. With two small children officials whisked us to the front of the immigration queue and our heavy baggage sailed through customs – unopened – with the same expeditiousness.

However, from well-organised Singapore where we knew just where we could buy anything or which office to go to for formalities, we were in for some culture shock. Even though we had already obtained a visa, and registered it on arrival at the airport, there seemed to be endless visits to offices, form-filling, fingerprinting, cards, immigration identity papers and so on. Finally we needed to register with the Local Community office and again with the Street Warden – who fortunately was our next-door neighbour and was most helpful.

We were welcomed at All Saints Church, the Anglican congregation in Jakarta where I was to officiate almost weekly. Most of these overseas English language churches are very much family-oriented affairs, so Ruth – as in most places – was active in the children's activities. She was able to bring experienced leadership to rejuvenate the Sunday School, and also took an active part in the women's activities. Many of the wives arrived with no knowledge of the local language, and the church ladies took some of them out shopping and helped them to find their way around a town where little English was spoken.

Jill and Andrew loved the play schools and we were all overjoyed at the arrival of Lynette a few months before we were due to leave Indonesia. She was born on the last day of Ramadan, the Muslim fast, when all domestic help has the week off. I had locked up the house as best I could, turned on the radio, and contrary to the usual wisdom left our home empty while I dropped Andrew off with friends and rushed to the hospital. Jill had by now started at the OMF's primary boarding school, Chefoo in Malaysia, so I sent off a telegram to tell her the news, with similar messages to Ruth's and my parents. The Dorm Auntie read it out to Jill and she responded 'Are you sure it's a little sister, not a brother? I've already got one of those!'

Indonesia had passed through a silent but bloody revolution in which conservative forces of General Su*hart*o had taken over the country from what was generally considered to have been a pro-Communist but self-styled 'non-aligned' leadership under Su*karn*o. Meanwhile the country's new leaders under Suharto's early reign still found that they enjoyed much sympathy from the population and especially from students – who were encouraged to go on the air with small home-made radio transmitters. Licenses were given to them on the nod, so they just built the equipment and started broadcasting.

We discovered that local radio receivers at that time used the so-called 'Tropical Band' rather than the common FM and Medium waves ('spots on the dial') familiar to most of us elsewhere. One of the properties of that band is that a very basic, low power transmitter, using just the power of a good sized light-bulb, could cover the area of a sizeable city. This was an ideal situation for do-it-yourself broadcasters such as those who sought our programmes! Was this just an irrelevant technicality, or was it God's provision for that time?

A number of Christian groups had grabbed this opportunity of using the radio waves to present and teach their faith. Such freedom is the more remarkable because Indonesian law allowed only the single government channel to use the air waves at all. Moreover the largest religious sector of the population was Islamic.

Through OMF's good offices an inter-church body had earlier invited me to Jakarta to hold a series of seminars on the subject. As we visited the many small stations, it became clear that there was a wide-open window of opportunity for FEBC. Firstly, they could make and supply more professional-style programmes to these stations. Secondly, we could answer the many requests for basic training in broadcasting and technical problems. Thirdly, it would supplement FEBC's short-wave transmissions from Manila, which reached out on a wider basis across the whole archipelago.

During our time in Australia we had been shown two ex-military transmitters which we were instructed to buy and ship to Jakarta. FEBC's counterpart in Australia funded the whole project. It seemed that there were two main open doors: 1) rebuilding the two transmitters for use in local stations, and 2) developing our studio productions to suit the scores of small, programme-hungry local stations. Remember that the Indonesian archipelago is larger than the USA and around four times as populous!

Basil and Betty Costerisan had moved to Jakarta to direct FEBC's operations, to feel the way and to shape up the future ministries. Basil was very good at getting things done, and a studio was already constructed and in operation. Basil had assembled an able production team and our programmes were put on offer to any stations that would air them – in fact about 90 did. We mailed the programmes on tape cassettes and were never charged for any airtime.

Meanwhile Jill started at an excellent English kindergarten[2]. It stood her in good stead until age six when she went to Chefoo School in Malaya. Andrew soon became old enough to attend a pre-school run by a gifted American lady teacher, who seemed to bring out the best in the little ones.

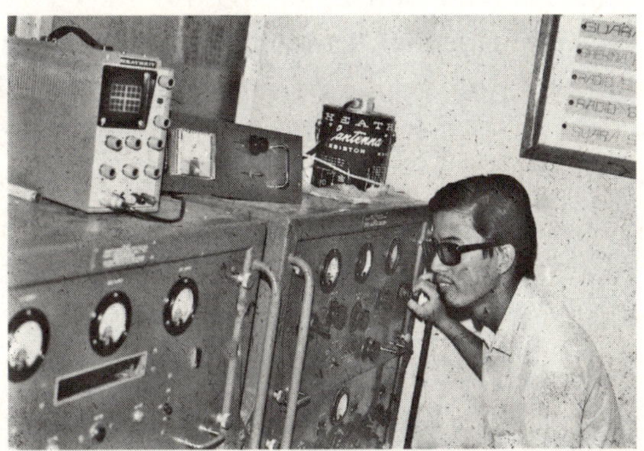

Prof Samuel Tirtamihardja tuning up the Australian transmitters before placing them with radio stations in Java.

Then the two Australian transmitters arrived. We knew enough to see what needed doing, but Samuel, the engineer, and I needed someone with actual experience to stand by us as we worked. God had indeed prepared… in the person of Captain August Jaxell, a US Air Force officer on detachment to the American Embassy in Jakarta. With perfect confidence

---

2   This school later grew to become the British School in Jakarta.

he led us step by step through the rebuild, and then helped us to test the two transmitters before we placed them. One went to a large Indonesian Chinese Church in Jakarta, and the other one went to the opposite end of Java – to Radio Ardjuno in Surabaya.

Yunus, our programme manager updating a board showing which programmes were being aired on which of over 80 local radio station across Indonesia.

Sometimes studio work had to stop because during the dry season – when Jakarta's hydro electric plant ran out of water, and power was cut off. Our ration was 16 hours 'on' then 16 hours 'off'. This gave us effectively alternate days and alternate nights with electricity. We got familiar with pump-up kerosene lamps, plus the occasional luxury of bottled gas lighting and cooking. The ordinary humble oil lamp with a wick and glass chimney came back into its own, and we discovered that these are surprisingly efficient.

Word of our activities got around and we were approached about a station in Bandung. Friends in another mission considered buying the station and going on-air to back up their Bandung Christian Book Shop. August Jaxell and I decided on a day trip by train to look the 'station' over; we found that it belonged to two high-school brothers who had built and operated it, but had also run up a sizeable debt in doing so. They wanted the debt of about £170 paid, and the mission could have the equipment, which is what happened.

There were visits to other parts of Java: to Surabaya and Malang in the East of the island of Java to help studios there, and to Pekanbaru in Sumatra (where All Saints Church Jakarta took its turn supplying a 'chaplain' every few months to minister to English-speaking Christians).

My mother spent a few weeks with us, travelling via Singapore on a cheap flight. Like us she found it somewhat different from glittering and clean Singapore, but enjoyed being with her family! We managed one rail excursion together to Bandung and its nearby volcano; sulphurous steam sputtered from cracks in the ground, with nuggets of bright yellow sulphur lying everywhere.

Other vacation breaks enabled us to enjoy a few days away from crowded Jakarta. By this time Jill was by now boarding at Chefoo School, so we took Andrew to the seaside with its simple lamp-lit rooms and tasty grilled fish.

Though Indonesia is the world's largest Muslim country, it also has many mature and active Christian churches which have enjoyed the Bible in their own respective languages since early in the 1900s. Thus as our second year drew towards its close, it became clear that Indonesian management could easily run the FEBC studio under our excellent Jakarta-based board of Indonesians. Basil had done the foundation work and was now busy helping other organisations to start, so he was rarely at his desk. By the way, in mission situations this is by no means unusual!

We were invited to serve the remaining two years back in Manila. And so after two years in Java, we were farewelled. We took a short vacation in Cameron Highlands, where Andrew was invited to spend a couple of lessons at Chefoo with Jill. In this way, he was better prepared to join her a year or two later.

A great shock came when Basil unexpectedly passed away just after our departure.

The Indonesian engineer with whom I had worked on the transmitters, Sam, became Director shortly after that and is still there today. Under Sam's leadership they operate several FM transmitters across Indonesia as well as supplying programmes to other stations. The FEBC ministries have been 100 percent Indonesian-staffed ever since our departure.

And so Manila beckoned us a second time.

Manila Again!

Our plane touched down at Manila Airport when 1974 was only a few days old, some 11 years after I had completed my orientation there. FEBC had asked us to live on their flagship station to help train the Filipino staff in aspects of broadcasting operation. On our first day we were taken aback when a slight earth tremor rocked the parked cars, reminding us that we had come to an earthquake-prone land.

But we were in for a culture shock comparable to that experienced in Indonesia. There had just been a radical and sudden change; the Philippine Government was passing laws designed to place Filipinos in executive positions in all foreign organisations. The FEBC leadership decided that at one stroke, every expatriate department-head should change places with his Filipino number-two. This was implemented from the Station Manager down to expatriate section-heads. The intention was

The main office and studio building of Christian Radio City Manila. A similar building housed transmitters.

praiseworthy, but this unplanned, ad-hoc move proved to be a disastrous example of how *not* to indigenise!

Few of the new local section-chiefs had had any proper training for leadership. Moreover it was strongly counter-cultural for a local to teach his own acquired abilities to the staff subordinate to him; many thought the Westerners were mad to assume that they might do just that. Quite a few frankly told us so!

The culture also condoned what in many countries would be regarded as outright nepotism; managers found it almost impossible to refuse a subordinate's request to fit a son or nephew, goddaughter or cousin however distant, into a job. Decision-making, which had been quite expeditious, now became a tedious and long-drawn-out process. Fortunately, our decade-and-a-half in Asia had already familiarised us with much local culture and we were able to work well with the staff, while not condoning certain practices. Reassuringly, after we left two years later, several of them wrote us warm and friendly letters.

We had the three children to look after. Jill went to Chefoo School in Malaysia, flying back twice a year. Andrew started at Faith Academy – a school in Manila for missionaries' children – and Lynette was still a toddler at home. Ruth was busy as a full-time mother and housewife, but she helped with children's activities on the radio station where several other families, Asian and Western, were housed.

It became clear that we would need a vehicle. Then Ray, a missionary due for retirement, offered us his newish car for a modest sum. It was a Mitsubishi Minica, a very small four-seat station wagon with a petrol-oil two-stroke 360cc engine, and its simple design meant that I could carry out most maintenance tasks myself.

Apart from the crowded City streets, motoring was pleasant. On my earlier visits to the Philippines, encounters with the police with 'invented' traffic offences were common. But now President Marcos – for all his many faults – ordered that the police should always be helpful to motorists, and during our two years' stay there we found them to be so.

My job description was 'Production and Quality-Control Supervisor'. It was one of those jobs that you could make anything or nothing of! I updated broadcasting manuals, held some seminars on scriptwriting, and designed a basic oscilloscope to monitor the efficiency of transmitters. Another more important task was to hold upgrading courses for junior Filipino technicians. They were warm and friendly people and good learners, but some felt that the station had been operating for 30 years and that they could not see why they *now* needed to study mind-bending theory; were not the expatriates always handy to solve complex engineering problems when they arose?

There was another culture problem, perhaps a remnant of the philosophy from local animistic backgrounds – roughly, things will always happen so why try to forestall them? – by, for example, preventive maintenance! A transmitter fault could put the station off the air but technicians would not worry. They felt that listeners could resume listening the next day – or the day after that! As citizens of a former American Colony, many bright young Filipinos sought study in the USA or other Western countries where they were introduced to forward-thinking and sophisticated management planning. Their homeside compatriots often regarded them as *coconuts* – brown outside but white inside!

On some Sundays I officiated in services at St Stephen's Chinese Anglican Church while Ruth often helped with a children's Sunday School on the station. In the American school vacation tradition, some of the station's parents decided to run a Daily Vacation Bible School, or DVBS, an excellent institution. Each morning the children would enjoy activities, usually concluding with some Christian teaching. The American mothers were amazed that such skills could be found in someone who had never even *been* to the USA (actually she had). Parents and children were impressed when Ruth produced programmes and achievement badges for the DVBS activity. FEBC seemed to us far more able at teaching spiritual issues than at instructing their technicians!

In our second sweltering-hot season I was asked to spend time on a new transmitter project at the western coast site of Iba, a couple of hours' drive north from Manila. Construction had started at Iba on FEBC's giant medium-wave transmitter for beaming into the then-closed land of China; and these transmissions would be received there on the cheapest receivers locally available. The long hours of work at Iba were enjoyable though dehydrating. I drank about five litre-bottles of water each day, plus mugs of coffee at meals. Even at night it was hot and oppressive until relief came with a brief cooler period in the small hours. Experienced radio missionaries erected six 200-foot tall masts while my job was mainly installing components in a switch-house at the centre of the array. The entire installation focussed a radio beam on Shanghai, but it could be 'swung' to cover Vietnam and certain other target-areas at suitable times of day.

We made sure that our local cook served meals fresh and hot, and she fed us with variations of squid: fried squid for breakfast and lunch, and squid soup in the evening. It was quite tasty – rather like fishy bacon – but we rejoiced when one of the engineers decided to bring his family to Iba and his wife became our cook. From then on we enjoyed choice American cooking complete with the traditional multi-egg breakfasts – we needed that!

Another interesting experience was on the island of Jolo (pronounced *Ho-lo*), at the south-western tip of the Philippines. The area had been the object of Islamist insurrection and much of Jolo city had been burned down. I waited at Zamboanga airport for my onward flight to Jolo, but discovered the plane had been skyjacked, so I was then transferred to an elderly Dakota aircraft. That night I was reminded of World War II and the anti-aircraft fire during German raids; the Philippine army was shelling the jungle, trying to flush the rebels towards their soldiers.

One night, behind locked doors we examined a faulty transmitter. We diagnosed a string of faulty components, each of low cost, however FEBC eschewed holding much in the way of spares as they tended to have 'disappeared' when needed. A telegram was despatched to Manila to order the parts. I returned to the airport to find a technician was hammering away at the Dakota's engine, but it got me back to Zamboanga and I relaxed with a tea-tray on my lap for the longer BAC 1-11 flight back to Manila – and home.

After my having met each of the six provincial stations' staff, FEBC decided to assemble the six respective technicians in Manila for some in-house training. We spent time on lectures, discussions, visits, homework – and even a swim. Each evening they joined us in our home for late-night refreshments – a human touch to what was probably a tough study-programme for them. Though each had gained a government Radio Operator licence, few had really grasped *how* a circuit works. When quite elementary technical problems arose, they called for an engineer to fly down from Manila to sort it out. Now our job was to get them to grasp *why* the various components were, *where* they were in the circuits, and

At the Iba Transmitter site – hot work loading granite chips on the truck. Here I shovel granite gravel in 1m² loads. It was hard work on the Iba station site. We took turns with each load!

what to do when a fault developed. In those pre-calculator days we taught them to master a locally available circular slide-rule.

One of my most unusual assignments came without warning. Insurgents had killed an Australian tourist with a bullet through the head. This was a major catastrophe for the government; they had just invested in an elaborate and costly tourist promotion in Australia. So the Philippine Government ordered a no-expense-spared funeral and flew the family in from Sydney. But there was a problem: who would conduct the funeral? The family were Anglicans whereas most Filipinos were Roman Catholics and the officials were unfamiliar with anything else. Enter a remarkable character within FEBC – Hann Brown. Hann was a self-appointed 'liaison officer' of FEBC to the Presidential Palace; he 'volunteered' me to officiate at the burial. Hann drove me to the cemetery chapel, where we filed past the costly black and gold coffin. The lid was off it but a glass panel remained to view the deceased. I took the usual Prayer Book service with a brief sermon and the family seemed pleased. I also wrote to Sydney to ensure that they were afforded bereavement follow-up by their local parish.

FEBC's own missionary engineers erected six masts to beam across the sea (in distance) to China. Frank Matias, Chief Engineer in Philippines, checks the wires.

Our little car took us everywhere, including a longer family trip up to the OMF vacation house in the cool of mile-high Baguio City, a resort well endued with children's playgrounds and hiking routes. One morning we were warned that a typhoon was approaching; after lunch rain began, followed by increasingly high winds. The rain gained intensity and lashed the windows like torrential rain on the windows of a fast train. One of our windows was a poor fit and I attempted to open it a little in order to slam it closed, but the storm caught the window and ripped it from its hinges. With much difficulty I was able to get it back at least enough to prevent flooding. An hour later the

The family shortly before leaving Manila: Ruth, Lynette, David, Jill and Andrew.

storm subsided and all was sunny and peaceful again.

Time in the Philippines was running out. We were looking forward to furlough in Australia and then in Britain. We farewelled our many Filipino friends, and were glad to slip away quietly from the radio station on a public holiday. We felt we had given what we could give to the warm Manila team, and they were appreciative – and welcoming on my many later visits to the station.

We reached Melbourne just in time for a hot-as-Philippines Christmas. Jill and Andrew were able to attend the local school – great experiences for both. Meeting me at the airport after one of my interstate trips, Ruth told me that Auntie Doily[1], back in North Wales, had passed away.

But for us, what was next?

---

1   *Doily* – Aunt Dorothy, my mother's sister, had passed away.

ECCE!

ECCE is the Latin word for 'behold!'

Whereas OMF's orientation is mainly towards personal evangelism and churchplanting, Michael Griffiths (General Director of OMF in the 1970s) had chivvied his fellow Directors into working much more through mass communications. But Mike's own missionary service had been in Japan, where little penetrates the privacy of the family household except for television.

Though he knew it would be expensive, Michael proposed a grand inter-mission consortium to be called *Encouraging Contemporary Communications Enterprises* – ECCE for short. With a view to our helping in this field we were assigned to Hong Kong to work under Dr Ted Marr, an experienced Chinese film producer and communicator.

But first, we enjoyed time in North America as a whole family en route from Croydon, England back to Asia. After our Valedictory Service from Emmanuel, we landed in Toronto where we were driven along snow-verged streets to the warm-welcoming, snug OMF Guest House. The trolleybuses outside stirred the slush and Lynette, having never seen overhead collector-poles before, wondered if they were 'crane-buses'.

Our hosts arranged for Jill and Andrew to join their own children at a local primary school, where one assignment was to present their family tree; so one evening we all sat round the table and tried to remember as much of our ancestries as possible, and to chart them.

The OMF leader, Gordon, and I took a side trip to promote OMF, the longest of which was to Canada's eastern provinces. I had my first experience of a dome-topped railway car and we sped across the snowscape to the bustling French-speaking city of Montreal. Our hosts, a student group at McGill University, escorted us via Montreal's Paris-style 'Metro'. Entering a shopping mall we moved into a vast atrium which stretched up to the top floor and down to the sub-basement where the Metro station crossed it.

Quebec City was the next destination. The ethos of the City was more intensely francophone, so there were very few English-language communities – or churches, but we enjoyed speaking engagements there for a week. Because of an accident, our train left Quebec on a different line, but this alternative route had no station at all! We climbed aboard the train from the trackside as best we could. Our accommodation for the night was in soft and comfortable bunks on the night train to Halifax.

By breakfast time (a full American breakfast, of course!) we were in a near monochrome wilderness – white snow was everywhere broken only by the dark greenish-black conifer trees. It was saddening to reflect that far away almost identical countryside hosted the oppressive Russian 'gulag archipelago'[1].

There was a heavy speaking-and-meeting programme in Halifax and Saint John, and a group at the Old Stone Church at Saint John became our prayer and financial supporters for the rest of our missionary career.

After Toronto our next call was Chicago, where we were reintroduced to Wheaton College whence OMF recruited many of their missionaries – prospective ones to chat with on this occasion! Then we flew on to Los Angeles, circling over the iced-up Lake Michigan en route, till once again the outer Los Angeles freeways came into view.

There was one FEBC car available for our use, though I had to fly up to Portland, Oregon to collect it, enjoying a half-way night stop with some FEBC friends near San Francisco. Apart from the various speaking engagements, Chinese friends took us to Disneyland (our second time) and to Knotts Berry Farm; both theme parks were great family experiences. On a spare half day we took the children kite-flying on a dry riverbed.

Then came the long flight by China Airlines back to Hong Kong; OMF placed us temporarily in the Tsimshatsui YMCA, where taking meals we could look out on the Star Ferry terminal and the buses leaving for every part of Kowloon. Could there really be destinations called Tse

---

1   *Gulag Archipelago* is a film about the chain of prison (*gulag*) 'islands' across Russia.

Wan Shan and Ngau Tau Kok? Well certainly buses went there and we were to get to know both quite well!

At St Andrew's Church, Kowloon, Ruth was soon involved in various ladies' activities and found a niche leading the children's Sunday school, and there were plenty of age-group activities for our children as well.

Ted Marr decided to return home to the USA, and I was left to see what else could be done for ECCE. The most obvious sphere to develop was the then-new home entertainment and education medium of videocassettes, already in use in Hong Kong schools[2]. A local Chinese group was interested. One of their members, Anthony Leung, had creditably produced a full-length 8mm movie, *City of Fools*.

Michael Griffiths had been the locomotive of the ECCE Concept, and he expected it to keep running while he went along many other widely variant tracks! So I was alone without much lead but it became clear that Hong Kong was bursting with talent – in scriptwriting and production.

However moving along with our approach to video, the main achievements were not in Hong Kong but in Thailand – and here we linked up again with FEBC in Bangkok. The Director there was keen for me to visit and explain how we might start producing short Thai videos on health, education, and teaching the Christian message. As outlets for the programmes, OMF's three hospitals warmed immediately to this

We lived in a ninth floor flat the Meifoo Sun Chuen complex Jill, David, Lynette, Andrew and Ruth.

as did one or two other similar institutions.

FEBC Bangkok had already received some basic but ideal video recording gear, so it was mainly a matter of teaching the Thai staff to

---

2   Videocassettes were to be the principal medium till DVDs surpassed them.

Hong Kong Airport: Jill is off to Chefoo School in Malaysia. Andrew, David, Lynette, Jill, Ruth.

use it, and the Thais' natural gift for art and acting simply took off. My next task was to help the Christian hospitals choose monitor screens and equipment to replay the tapes throughout the various wards and patient areas.

I had earlier been to the extreme south with Udomsak, our technician, a friendly and helpful Thai Chinese who was studying electronics at university. We had taken some portable video players to trial-run a couple of our early productions on a real southern audience – including many Muslims. One of our shorter health programmes warned of the danger of eye disease through faecal contamination – a real problem in a land with so many waterways. Some of the visuals drawn were very matter-of-fact, indeed quite earthy! But the audience appeared to understand them perfectly and nodded in appreciation of the message conveyed. The rail journey back took most of a day and a night, in a comfortable two-bunk cabin with Udomsak. We killed the time as he asked me to teach him some English slang! Since then I have made many journeys south with Thai fellow-workers, and enjoyed them all – and they in turn expressed appreciation for the eye-opening experience.

Michael Griffiths – keen as ever to make ECCE work – sent me across North America to the UK, then to Holland and Germany to garner financial support and prayer-partners. Success in North America was limited; it is hard to fund-raise in the USA unless you have a headquarters on American soil. Moreover as an OMFer in a faith mission I felt somewhat inhibited to make direct appeals myself. But in Germany, the local OMF Home Director introduced me to a church-related body in Stuttgart which donated a very substantial sum, enabling the whole of the hospital video project to go ahead. Sadly a missionary in India heard about this and, much to my embarrassment, endeavoured to block the remittance; but fortunately the draft had left the German bank, enabling the whole of the hospital video project to go ahead.

Many people are unaware that so much of Hong Kong is still countryside and of course, mountainous. Nette, Jill, Ruth, Andrew and David rest during a country hike.

We started video-equipping at Manorom Christian Hospital, a couple of hours' drive north of Bangkok. Some years earlier I had helped install a sound system and now video was to be added. It was a hot, steamy task as wires had to be run and secured, monitor screens fixed on walls and explanations made to the Thai teams. We all perspired freely but in those days short trousers on men were not acceptable, even off-duty, so we needed to make good use of their daily laundry!

After installing the gear in Manorom Hospital, George from FEBC and I journeyed south again by rail to Saiburi. The road to the south was unpredictable and our gear was too bulky and heavy to go by plane. So we enjoyed the Thai night express train again, a comfortable and cool way of travelling with excellent food en route.

The pleasant journey concluded as the next morning our train drew into our destination near Saiburi. When the round of hot, sweaty wiring and installation had been completed, we returned to Central Thailand and at OMF's third hospital at Nongbua, we incorporated all the video-playing equipment into a single wheel-around cabinet.

Now the Thai Video Venture was all in local hands. Back in Hong Kong, ECCE was adopted by local leadership (merging into the Christian Drama Association), and our next furlough was approaching.

Another possibility was presenting itself. I had wondered if it would be possible to advance from my London University BA to a higher level. On our way through California I had met with Dr Arthur Glasser, Dean of the Fuller School of World Mission[3] in Pasadena, who I had known from his days in OMF. He was much more encouraging. He explained that they were not especially interested in degree *grades* obtained many years ago; Rather they were concerned about what the potential student had done in the

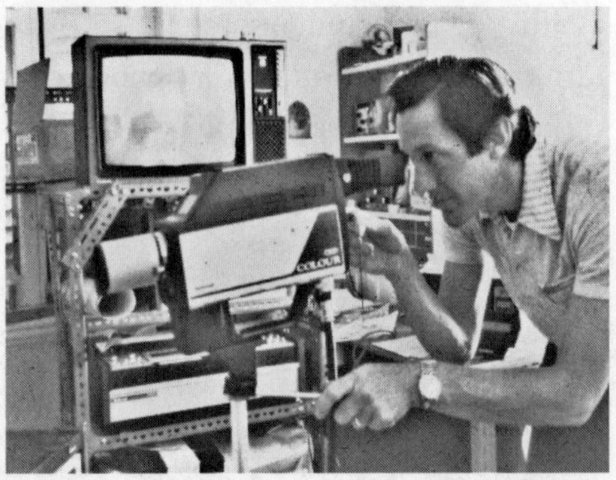

David with ECCE video camera equipment.

meantime. (In my case I had had 20 years' service in Asia under my belt, plus knowledge of two languages, and had produced several small books related to Christian broadcasting). So Fuller ruled that this would enable me to proceed with an M.Th degree – usually a year full time, but by taking courses while overseas it could be completed with only a single term's residence at Pasadena.

I was able to work part time on these studies while in Hong Kong. I listened to recordings of lectures in Fuller – often Ruth joined me in the evenings – and I completed the taxing assignments. Finally I passed three stimulating months on Fuller's Pasadena campus, thus completing an M.Th (Hons) in missions. There was little emphasis on swotting for exams but much more on discussion of varying ideas, experiences and concepts – brain-bending at first!

My M.Th thesis was titled *Video and Missions* and as well as theory, I drew extensively on experience from Thailand. My mentor, the late Revd Dr Paul Hiebert, was a veteran missionary from India and he encouraged my thesis as something very relevant to the Asian scene.

Long-term Fuller resident students who welcomed me were Angus and Carol Chu from Hong Kong. They went out of their way to make me feel at home and often had me to meals in their flat. We were to meet them later as they passed through Seychelles and even later serving in Kenya, and do the same!

During the last month or so in Hong Kong we had been able to finalise arrangements for our children's schooling on return to the UK. Jill had a place in Archbishop Tenison's School, Croydon, a church school

---

3   Now Fuller School of Intercultural Studies.

within the government system, so there were no fees to pay. Lynette was admitted to St Peters Junior School, adjacent to our home church. Andrew gained a free place at Whitgift, a public (i.e. private) day school, and this provision came about in a most remarkable way.

Fearing their high fees I nevertheless collected a Whitgift prospectus and entrance exam forms. On my way out I noticed the Christian Union notice board, and glancing over it out of curiosity I heard a voice behind me saying, 'Can I help you?' It was David Raeburn, the Headmaster. I told him my story and his reply was: 'Well… first get your son through the entrance exam and we'll be able to help you with the finance.' Andrew duly was awarded as a 100 percent bursary under a scheme crafted by Prime Minister Thatcher… the literature mentioned that some grantees were the children of impecunious parents such as dustmen, bus conductors and clergy!

But before reaching England and school, we passed some winter months (northern summer) in Australia, near to Ruth's family in the suburb of Box Hill North. This time I flew up to Sydney for speaking engagements and the entire family came up on the train to join me for a few days. It was a great experience to take the children to the glorious scenery of the Blue Mountains and the Three Sisters Rocks, to hear the bell-birds sing en route, and of course to cross the spectacular Harbour Bridge on foot. We toured the Opera House and then ate fish and chips at the harbour-side cafeteria; and noticed a small sign on the till *No refund will be given for food taken by seagulls*. When we sat down we realised that seagulls were diving at our plates trying to carry off a morsel, or more. Hardly surprising as many diners were waving chips in the air to attract them!

Back in England, it started with misty weather moving into a very hot summer followed by an unusually snow-bound winter, but early in the piece I was able to finalise my own application for Australian citizenship. Ruth had already acquired UK nationality, so now the whole family were dual citizens.

And as ever we were unsure just what the next step would be…

Seychelles

Back in my earliest days of orientation at FEBC's Manila station in 1962-3, the search was on for a better transmitting site to beam our programmes into India. We already had good listenership in *southern* India, but the complexities of radio transmission made reception *west*wards from Manila worse as one sought to swing the beam *north*wards from Sri Lanka up through the Indian subcontinent. The obvious answer to reaching the whole of India was a transmitting site to its south, in the Indian Ocean. Moreover a sea water path is better for radio waves than one with intermediate land. Thus started my own involvement in the search.

John Wheatley made tentative enquiries of the Maldives, Sri Lanka, and the US-leased but British-owned Island of Diego Garcia, but he drew a blank in them all. But by that time a much better location became available. Though it enjoyed almost no air service and only infrequent sea access, Seychelles was the obvious possibility. At that time it was still a British Colony. John finally secured a sea passage and even got as far as an audience with the Governor. The proposal document contained references from obviously reputable personages such as the Archbishop of Sydney. The Governor seemed impressed. Work had started on a Seychelles airport and electricity would be available.

There was the precedent that the British had never licensed a private radio station[1], let alone a missionary one. In the UK the Far East Broadcasting Association (FEBA Radio) had been set up to support FEBC's transmitting operations in the Far East; now the desire was that FEBA should take responsibility for developing and operating an entirely

---

1   There had been small private stations in some of the remoter colonies, and commercial television had already come to Britain.

new station. The American end of FEBC was keen on this though they had never run an overseas station far from an American military base. So they were reassured when John reported that indeed, Uncle Sam's air force operated a satellite-tracking[2] facility in Seychelles!

The Christian constituency in Britain knew little about radio as a Christian *missionary* venture; Although to the average Briton 'Christian broadcasting' meant the BBC's weekly church service, the response in prayer and financial support from the UK for the proposed Seychelles station was surprisingly good. Indeed by 1969 the famous off-shore aerials started to rise from the shallows, one kilometre out to sea. Back in England 'Crusaders' started a *Meet a Metre* fundraising plan for their classes – to raise at least one metre of mast each. By 1969 basic transmissions were on the air and over a decade later, there was a ready invitation to serve first as Programme Controller, then as Station Director for FEBA's fully operating Seychelles station.

We needed to find somewhere for our teenagers to be if we accepted. The Mowll family in Croydon offered hospitality to Jill and Andrew, while Lynette could attend Chefoo School in Malaya, joining us in Seychelles twice a year. Fortunately Jill and Andrew were able to visit us twice yearly too. We never knew for sure beforehand whence funding would come from, but it always did. So our three children must have been among the most 'flown' school kids in the world!

At last we boarded Air France's cramped and foodless flight in 'vacation class' (an ultra austere aerial 'steerage class') to Seychelles and David Wong, my former co-worker in Singapore, now a graduate radio engineer was among those to meet us. Seychelles, by then a Republic, was a mixture of creation's natural beauty – and a developing brand of extreme socialism, which stopped short of Communism. We were left free to carry on, except that there was an annual £1000 visa cost per working adult, plus a very high licence fee.

Socialism was a selective term, and we had to adapt to its omnipresence; in some ways the one-party government were quite capitalist, if only because their biggest income was from foreigners and the nation desperately

---

2   Mozambique, now a Commonwealth Member, had been caught in the political terrorism involved with ending apartheid in South Africa, and the US Air Force facility has now returned there, having left Seychelles.

needed investment in hotels, air links, etc. On the other hand, no one was allowed to arrange, say, a football match – this was the prerogative of the Party-run Community Centres. Churches were free to carry-on in their own buildings but house-meetings attracted suspicion. Scouting had been supplanted by the Party's Young Pioneers with their Cuban-style red scarves. In fact both Cuba and Russia supplied small items of aid plus a number of scholarships, while the North Koreans provided a Presidential Guard and instructed Seychellois troops in the dark arts of 'interrogation'. All of this was balanced by Seychelles' substantial relationship with Britain and the Commonwealth, plus the American satellite tracking station!

Nevertheless it was a site ideal for transmitting to India, Pakistan, the Gulf, East Africa and even to Madagascar. The topography allowed a single multi-tower array of transmitting wires out at sea on the reef, to beam to all of these. The beam could be 'swung' anti-clockwise, so that the optimum (i.e. evening and early morning) listening times followed the time zones starting at the east and moving westwards.

FEBA allotted us a spacious three-bedroom bungalow with a mountain view one way and a sea view at the end of a valley the other. This was to be our home for four years, and we enjoyed receiving many guests from around the world.

Because our transmissions were to distant places, we missed the immediacy of that direct contact with our audience which we had enjoyed in Jakarta and Manila. Nevertheless there was no doubting the effectiveness of our station – each year it generated 120,000 letters from India alone, far more than all other transmitting centres put together across FEBA and FEBC's worldwide network.

As I was an ordained Anglican minister, Bishop French Chang-Him of Seychelles kindly licensed me to officiate. In this capacity I took various services and filled-in as needed in the island's half-dozen Anglican churches.

Bishop French was anxious to encourage Seychellois vocations and FEBA felt they should be encouragers to him, even if indirectly. French saw that when sending young men overseas for ordination many went and did not return, while others returned but went into business. Bishop French realised that there had to be a theological college right there in Seychelles, and one of the expatriate clergy couples, Revd Charles James and his wife seemed ideal people to be College Wardens. Various visiting lecturers (including myself) complemented Charles' one-man faculty and our student body of just half a dozen were deeply committed men[3], each with a clear sense of call. However this merely started the theological ball rolling. 'Why', asked many Seychellois Christians, 'cannot *we* have some Bible training too?' So a kind of part-time weekend theological college was formed; missionaries took a strong part, and of course Bishop French himself. We held 'training days', often at the beach-side Vicarage of Charles James and these grew in popularity. We had inaugurated the first-ever systematic Bible-training in the young republic!

Sharing Bishop French's vision for the seminary and other matters about the church led to many pleasant times on French's veranda chatting, praying and sipping fresh passion fruit juice. He seemed to be a firm and sure rock, anchored in prayer during a time of uncertainty in Seychelles.

In fact improvement in relations with the socialist rulers led to mutual respect. In due course the churches were invited to send clergy or lay persons to take worship or Christian instruction in the National Youth Service (NYS) Camps, a kind of boarding school system and the only secondary education schools permitted for Seychellois. Much later when I took my successor to see a government official, he commented that "in the National Youth Service we need input from, for example, some Christian priests."

To some, the NYS seemed very much like left-wing indoctrination of youth, since the camps were located in remote parts of the island, but President Rene of the Seychelles had realised that the youth *needed* the disciplined frame work of study and work together in a somewhat military-style camp regime. This was new to the socially stratified Seychellois and helped to give them an identity and a sense of self respect. After completion of the NYS, all of those who sat for and passed a UK-sponsored School Certificate could move on to a basic tertiary education – a remarkable achievement for a small and young nation with little in the way of intrinsic riches.

Another milestone affecting us – for better or for worse – was the introduction of 'denominational Christianity' to Seychelles. Hitherto the

---

3   This was some years before women were ordained in the Anglican Church.

population were about 12 percent Anglican and the rest[4] were assumed to be Roman Catholics, with much nominalism in both. Nevertheless we in FEBA were able to contribute and to remain friendly with all.

A Seychellois lady who had been living in Nairobi decided to bring back the inspiration of the church she had attended there – and mild Pentecostalism was born on the island. The RC Bishop was openly antagonistic, but the application to the government for a visa to bring a missionary minister to teach them was granted. (Possibly, some said – to put the RC Bishop in his place!) And so the Revd and Mrs Eli Chiarelli arrived from the Pentecostal Assemblies of Canada. It was a breath of fresh air to have this new movement around, though shortly after that, during a broadcast service the RC Bishop made clear his displeasure at the arrival of Pentecostals, then warned his flock that the Anglican clergy too were only laymen masquerading as priests. Many Seychellois Christians came and asked our advice, and as foreigners there only by courtesy, we had to be very careful.

Heading-up FEBA had other interesting sidelines, and as it was one of the larger organisations in Seychelles I, as the 'number one' of a major local entity, enjoyed occasional invitations to the British Embassy – a privilege normally reserved in a larger place for bank heads and business tycoons! Many present hoped, as the liquor flowed, to meet contacts to favour their own agendas. So my conversation was mainly with those who were neither power brokers nor politicians. Nevertheless I was once introduced to the Soviet Ambassador, an ex-KGB man. We shook hands – his was cold and clammy and his expressionless stare much the same.

At one function, we were introduced to the Chinese Ambassador, very much the gentleman and his wife; they had a 20-year-old son in university back in China. He appeared to understand our Christian objectives. At that time China was just starting to open up its sealed frontiers and churches had recommenced normal function. We had heard that educated, thinking Chinese were interested in the Christian faith and that many had sought baptism. We wondered if the Ambassador perhaps was just old enough to have had some contact with the Christian faith before the Communist takeover. Since he obviously knew who we were and what

---

4   Apart from tiny gatherings of Adventists or Eastern faiths.

we were doing I thought that there would be no harm in inviting him to visit our station. So His Excellency arrived in a chauffeured car along with a Chinese minibus full of his staff. After refreshments we gave them a conducted tour including that of our newsroom. Teleprinters were clacking away with the world's news items and they asked whether we produced anything in Chinese. They were appreciative guests and we never had cause to regret our openness towards them. A few weeks later I took our daughter Jill down to the Chinese Embassy. She was writing-up a high-school project on China and the Ambassador's wife, a motherly lady, loaded her up with

All in high school now! – taken during a brief working trip back to the UK. Andrew, David, Lynette, Ruth, Jill.

quality literature. At that point in time, for an OMFer to relate to such a senior Chinese official was indeed a God-given privilege!

Four years passed quickly and we oversaw small developments in the station, but little major change. The programming was mostly pre-recorded in the target areas and mailed to Seychelles on cassette tapes well ahead of airing time. The news programmes were a great attraction to listeners and in Seychelles we had on-site experienced journalists; in retrospect I believe a superior news production resulted, but am inclined to feel that for a 'mission' radio station, the *rip n' read* newscasting as in Manila gave a wider coverage with much less labour or expense.

On our weekly days off, we usually made our way to one of the more remote hotels where we could enjoy a full breakfast, a swim, and time in the sun! Sometimes I left Ruth water-colouring and hiked in the hills. After a day in the office, some evenings I took a leisurely jog up to a reservoir, or down to sea-level from our 600 feet high compound. Our agreed four year term was extended slightly to accommodate FEBA's personnel needs. There had been talk of our returning to Seychelles after furlough, but OMF had been pressing us by long distance phone calls from Singapore to take on a job there. We did not feel able to drop out of FEBA when they had been so generous to us and were actually asking us to extend our tour there. But the voice over the phone continued, "David, with your experience in this field, if we don't get you now we'll have you next time."

Thus did our four and a half years in Seychelles draw to a close, and with all the usual farewells and send-off meals, we flew to London via Singapore and Australia.

We had no idea where our next job would be.

Uncertainty!

We duly left from Seychelles for furlough, starting with another visit to Ruth's family and friends in Australia. Stu Devenish was pioneering promotion for OMF in Victoria and Tasmania, he found it an uphill task as for years OMF-Australia had relied on a decreasing circle of old-established, but ageing supporters, almost all Baptist or similar. As time passed these churches took on younger ministers, and the OMF interest had started to wane – pressed by the Australian Baptist Union which was instructing its member-churches to confine their missionary support to their own Society. However there were bright spots as I worked with Stu. He was a young and visionary man; we organised *Ministers' Breakfasts* in Ballarat and Hobart. These were well received, but we sadly lacked the necessary help in follow-up – always a problem in mission deputation.

Our time in Melbourne drew to a close, and we farewelled Ruth's family and flew to the UK. Thus we found ourselves back in Croydon in late 1987. Emmanuel Church once again found us a comfortable house and Gordon Kuhrt, the Vicar, welcomed us to be fully involved in the ministry of the Parish.

By now Jill was working her way round Australia with a cousin as a 'gap year' project. Andrew was in Form V1 at Whitgift School and was accepted for Oxford University. Lynette was boarding at Dean Close School in Gloucester, a wonderful place with a real Christian environment along with a number of other

During our home-assignment in the UK, Andrew became School Captain at Whitgift School, Croydon.

ex-Chefoo OMF kids. Dan Harding-Young was Chaplain at Dean Close, and shared with us that a major link in his call to the ministry had been our valedictory service in 1972 – well over a decade and a half before.

Alas, OMF had an abrupt change of policy; close after an explicit assurance that *no* change in schooling support would be made, they decided that they could no longer cover the cost of private education for Lynette. A full explanation has never been given, but in no other OMF homeland did the OMF pay private school fees. Though annual fees were about 2½ times our total combined annual income, remarkably God provided – from varied sources – enough for us to pay each bill for the remaining six years!

As regards further overseas service, OMF seemed to have forgotten their unambiguous invitation. Thus for some months we wondered what the future would hold – should we stay at home? England? Or Australia? It was our longest and most difficult period of uncertainty during our entire time with OMF. Should I take-on a church? Or at least a mature curacy?

God's guidance can be both negative and positive. What at first seemed a positive answer was a job as 'International Secretary' with a growing Anglican Mission Society; but at the interviews, one of the council members asked me how I thought I would get along with the boss. I thought this was a surprising question to be asked; it appeared to infer at least one council-member's doubts about him. I did not get the job, it seemed I was 'too oriented to the Far East' whereas this mission was more interested in Africa[1]. That evening when I got home to Ruth, a long-time friend, Joyce Muddiman, had come to tea; she said she had been praying about my interview, and that although her lips were sealed, she was relieved that I had *not* got the job! So this time the guidance was negative, but also positive – to look elsewhere!

Ruth's mother passed away in Melbourne, and Ruth could only be 'present' at the funeral by a telephoned tape recording. We toyed with the possibility of visiting Australia before any further service back to Asia. Our return to OMF was far from finalised; however we now all held Australian passports, and David Penman, the Archbishop of Melbourne,

---

1   This mission has since sent personnel to serve in Indo-China with the Diocese of Singapore.

had indicated we'd be warmly welcome if I would take on a church there. We wondered… but made no definite approach.

Only a few weeks later did a small envelope with a Thai stamp on it appear. It was from Alan Bennett and his wife Averil, veteran missionaries from New Zealand serving in Thailand. Alan had already forged many links with FEBC's Bangkok studio, and we had worked together in ECCE. Would we consider at least two years – maybe more – in Bangkok? If so, he would 'fix it' with the OMF Directors in Singapore.

And he did!

The seal was set when the OMF's Australian Federal Director, David Hayman, invited us to spend six further months in Melbourne, Ruth's original home, helping with OMF's deputation. His office would pay our fares, Ruth could have family time, and accommodation was available. A long wait was necessary for the Thai visa so we would have time on our hands anyway. This seemed another divine provision, confirmed when a member of Emmanuel congregation handed us an envelope – a cheque for £500 for our travel! And thus in late 1988 we left Heathrow for the long ride down-under.

Fortunately we'd been invited to break the very long journey at Bangkok for a few days to preview our future sphere of service and to meet some of the people we'd be working with. Our OMF hosts were most kind and welcoming. We stayed in an air-conditioned guest-house and were taken for a swim at a club pool! Behind this was the hand of OMF's Thailand Director, Ian Murray, a warm-hearted Scot who I had met before in Glasgow. All of this encouraged us as did our future boss as Director of FEBC-Thailand. We felt more comfortable with the prospect of serving in Thailand!

On to Melbourne where Stu Devenish with his young family had accepted leadership of OMF in Victoria, and they made us welcome and comfortable for our stay. It was to be a very full programme and there were to be visits around Australia as well as speaking engagements in the Melbourne area.

Deputation again gave us some interesting visits; notably one to the North. Our long itinerary by Queensland Rail was an experience punctuated with frequent signal-stops on the single-line track. Breakfast after a long night-run was served as the sun rose on the Great Divide and the ghost-gum trees gleamed white against the blue sky. By day we were entertained in the Club Car with a James Bond film and as the

evening meal was served dusk started to cover Mount Bartle Frere –
Queensland's highest. Deputation ministry was quite heavy, with almost
daily appointments in Rockhampton, Townsville and Cairns.

Our OMF team leader suggested a visit to Cooktown, accessible in a
small eight-seater aircraft, and there we could sense the real tropical bush
of Crocodile Dundee! Venomous snakes slithered away as one walked
along pathways – it was inadvisable to stray far. Our task was to make an
OMF presentation in two of Cooktown's churches. We were well received
but by 10 am drunken Aborigines stretched themselves out in the shade of
churches and other buildings. It was the day of the annual re-enactment of
Captain Cook's first landing, and the Aborigines announced they would
have nothing to do with the celebrations. (A decade or so before, a law
forbidding the sale of alcohol to aborigines had been repealed in the name
of human rights. Missionaries to the Aborigines require a special sense
of call to a people with millennia of culture so distinct from any other.)

Happier was another trip to escort other OMFers to the off-shore
Great Barrier Reef with its incredible marine gardens, the giant clams
and brilliantly coloured fish. We were privileged to see so much of God's
design, usually only observed on a screen! At the nearby crocodile farm a
handler with a large plastic rake kept a huge leviathan at a distance and we
were awestruck with the instant power as it leapt and snapped a chicken
and rolled over several times in the 'death roll' – whereby middling to
large animals – and humans – can be overturned and pulled into the water.
Crocs are probably the most powerful land animals in creation today.

Back in Melbourne I was occupied with some editorial work and
production of the Australian edition of OMF's *The Millions*. Then news
came that our Thai visa had been granted and that we could make travel
arrangements to move to Bangkok shortly.

At last the next step was clear.

Thailand

My first impressions of Thailand were as a young national service soldier in 1952, but were distant and by proxy from Singapore, mostly romanticised by their attractively priced artifacts.

Nine years later in 1961, when I was heading for North Malaya, those assigned to Thailand got to work on the Thai alphabet, sounds and culture to ready themselves for service in Thailand as pioneer church-planters. Large swathes of the country were totally unevangelised – some of the provincial towns had no known Christian residents, let alone a church, which is still the case in much of the country today.

Thailand OMFers found it an unresponsive ministry. Reception of the Christian message was slow due to the tightly integrated religio-cultural system. Every aspect of national life was knit together: the monarchy, the religion, education, modes of employment, family relationships, farming, the military, the Civil Service and so on. After a decade or so, response to the Gospel became more evident and actually accelerated, with baptism figures rising exponentially. Nevertheless today Thai Christians in total account for under one percent of the population. My own visits to Thailand (from Manila and Hong Kong) were during that earlier, discouraging period.

Now our faces were set to serve in this Kingdom ourselves, with its joys and difficulties.

From Melbourne OMF's Thailand leader, Ian Murray, met us at Bangkok airport along with representatives of the Board of FEBC Thailand, some of the studio staff were with them – complete with Thai welcome-garlands to put round our necks! They all helped us settle in.

A crowded all-Thailand OMF conference was scheduled at Pattaya, a seaside resort, so we were included as part of our induction. Despite the bus not being air-conditioned and making our way through a pall of dirty brown smog for most of the journey, the conference was a great opportunity to meet so many new co-workers. Ian was one of the few leaders who did *not* pack his annual gathering with meetings, but wanted the missionaries to have spare half-days and evenings to mix and meet their friends.

Language study came next. We really wondered whether in the second half of our fifties, we could assimilate another tongue but found that with excellent teachers and language laboratories, we could! We mastered enough Thai for shopping and I developed this to cover the studio tasks – and what to order in restaurants. The Thai spend a great deal of time eating; economical, tasty and clean food is the norm, whether in a downtown shopping arcade or a rural thatched eating shop.

As soon as Ruth and I had completed the basic language course. I started at the FEBC Office, located in a new building. The studios had been built but not acousticised nor equipped nor wired, and supervising the necessary work took me over a year, especially as there were very few experienced studio-builders. The Thai leadership was welcoming and easy to work with – one might even say *fun!* We spent many sweltering days going round hardware and electronic shops on the studio motorbike – great for my waistline!

Ruth and I visited most English churches in Bangkok but finally settled on Christ Church. Monty Morris, a lively person then heading the church, was delighted to discover that Ruth had Sunday School teacher-

Our Thai FEBC radio team on the roof of our building. An FM broadcasting transmitter is now located there too.

training experience and skills, and the number of young people soon climbed from eight to 80! I was licensed as an honorary Curate and took services or preached as needed. Christ Church became deeply involved with the Karen refugees, a very large tribal group, who seek safety from the political situation in Burma (Myanmar)[1]. The refugees still live in camps along the Thai side of the boundary river. A high proportion of them are Christians, but the situation means they can have little or no communication or fellowship with their fellow Christians in Burma's capital city.

As a preacher at a Karen Ordination in the jungle refugee camp. Behind David (seated) is the former Bishop of Willochra, Australia, who came on behalf the Bishops of Burma who were separated from the Karen by the political situation.

So it was decided that since one of their number in the camp was presented for ordination, we should hold the ordination service there. A retired bishop from Adelaide was asked by the Archbishop of Burma to officiate and I was asked to preach. English was still a major language in Burma so only minimal interpretation into Karen was needed. We started in the early morning from Bangkok, and finished with a motorised long-boat ride to the camp. The service went well and we slept the night in a large and well-appointed wooden home before starting the trip back.

Ruth made further visits to teach the Bible and household skills to the Karen ladies. Later, while we were on furlough, our daughter Jill spent some weeks with the Karen, working on an English-teaching syllabus – which she later wrote up as part of a M.Phil degree at Cambridge. Sadly, she contracted a very nasty attack of dengue, a mosquito-borne disease, with the possibility that it was the feared – and much more serious – haemorrhagic fever in which the skin itself bleeds. So she had to make her way back to Bangkok carried in an improvised sling-stretcher several miles through jungle, and so she arrived at the OMF Guest Home in

---

1   As I write the Burma situation seems to be taking a turn for the better.

Bangkok in a sick and exhausted state. The Hostess was a qualified nurse and found her a bed in her own flat for a few days until she had recovered sufficiently.

During our time there Ruth needed a hip replacement and a friend arranged this at the prestigious Chulalongkorn Hospital. She was well-looked after, but Thai hospitals assume that a relation of each patient will be there most of the time to attend to non-medical needs, and some basic bed or couch is provided for them. Some of the ladies at Christ Church Bangkok undertook nights with Ruth, while I visited twice daily.

Time flew by. Jill, Andrew and Nette variously dropped out of the sky – sometimes expected, sometimes not, and occasionally with some school or college mates. The latter seemed to enjoy sleeping on our carpet or on a thin Thai mat, and it was a great joy to have them as our guests. Andrew made a couple of trips to Taiwan for a practicum in his Chinese studies at Oxford. Lynette was still in school so we were better forewarned about her coming. One night our bedside phone rang at about 2 am; Lynette had been awarded a substantial bursary towards her school fees and in the excitement, forgetting all about time zones, rang us straight away with the good news.

Our term in Thailand drew to a close and the future was less than clear, once again. Our Thai Director had made advanced plans to

All teenagers now: Jill, Lynette and Andrew joined Ruth and David for a vacation at the OMF vacation house on the sea coast south of Bangkok.

spend a year or two with his family in Australia to study for a PhD. He farewelled us at the airport and we assumed that his year in Australia would roughly coincide with our furlough and that we would not be required there again. And at the same time FEBC had invited Dale and Belvah Golding – who we had twice succeeded in Singapore – to fill-in in Thailand, and they were well-received by the Thai team.

It was 1991 and again we made our way to Australia to be with Ruth's family, and to do a little more deputation for OMF. Then back to the UK where Emmanuel Church found us a comfortable and spacious house to live in. The Vicar, James Jones (later Bishop of Hull, then Liverpool) absorbed us into the parish's ministry and the usual preaching and taking of services, funerals, weddings and the like. James was welcoming, and was not in the least threatened by the fact that we were much older than him. He often dropped into our home for a light lunch and was keen to involve us in the parish's ministry and overseas mission promotion.

An interesting diversion was a Japanese couple who wanted their marriage to be blessed in church. They had very little grasp of the Christian faith – and not too much of English either! James Jones decided that since we had served in Asia, I should look after this delightful couple's requirements and officiate at the blessing.

However this did not answer the question as to what we *should* do! James Jones invited us to stay on for an extra three months working at Emmanuel – and even had Emmanuel Church pay our full OMF support in recognition of that, thus exemplifying his gift of involving everyone possible in his ministry.

There still remained some uncertainty for us; Dale contracted a nasty ulcer and started to make definite noises about returning to the USA. Then a clear invitation for us to return to Thailand came, and notice was quite short. If we failed to be back on Thai soil by one year after our previous departure, a much more complicated visa application would be needed.

We flew to Bangkok and Dale was at the airport to welcome us. By this time our former Thai Director appeared to be taking root in Australia. Nevertheless he assured us that he looked forward to returning to head up FEBC Thailand, and the Board even put aside a sum of money towards his resettlement. It was with this background that we had been invited back to Bangkok and to direct FEBC for up to two years by which time it was assumed that the former (or some other) Thai leader would be available. After that we would have little in the way of years to serve OMF before retirement.

But I faced a dilemma. After a few weeks in Bangkok it became clear that our anticipated Director wanted *much* longer in Australia. Of course he was warmly welcome to return, but meanwhile – as had been agreed beforehand – he must leave the operation to the Board and the current Director in Bangkok. We would have looked forward to his returning for he had always been extremely kind to us.

I faced another problem. Someone in Bangkok had put together a Thailand Christian Directory and FEBC had had some small input into that, but it was far from accurate. So our former Director had the idea of producing a much better one – this he did with considerable success and business acumen. He had the studio staff working late at night on preparation and paste-ups, and his natural enthusiasm carried them with him. However the downside was that the staff felt it was fine for *once* – and so was the small honorarium they received – but they did not look forward to a second edition. Moreover the preparation and unfinished distribution was taking over much of my FEBC team for weeks at a time, something the Board had explicitly forbidden before the project was first given the go-ahead.

Our former leader's commendable vision now took a step forward. From Australia he proposed that the Directory be at the centre – or at least well within the mainstream – of future operations, and that various other Christian ministries be spun off it – and off FEBC. These would have included things like Christian pre-marital counselling, sex education for teenagers and other worthy objectives which were indeed badly needed in Thailand.

I was caught between admiration for his vision, and by my earlier experience of problems with FEBC Directors who intertwined miscellaneous activities with FEBC's operations, premises and/or staff – not to mention mixing-in the funding of these with the money FEBC had remitted solely for their broadcasting ministry.

The down-to-earth fact was that our Bangkok studio was supported by FEBC in Canada for Christian radio programming and for nothing else. There was no budget for ancillary ministries, however worthy in themselves, and even for the radio ministry there was as yet almost no funding from local sources. Local gifts would barely have kept the office stocked with coffee-creamer!

The solution came in an unexpected way: a long letter came from Queensland indicating, among many other issues, that if the Bangkok FEBC Board did not agree with his proposals, he would not be sorry, nor shocked, nor upset, nor disappointed, but would not come back to FEBC!

We called a special Board Meeting (with a mainly Thai membership) – it was one of the few that enjoyed not merely a quorum but full attendance, and the unanimous decision was that we should view his letter as his resignation.

Nevertheless we took off our hats to such an able Thai leader. He had been an encouragement to many, he had helped some of the staff get on the 'housing ladder' when property was still cheap, and he was a born pastor – albeit sometimes offering employment to his pastoral basket cases! But down under in Australia he had landed a good job, his family loved it in Queensland, the two boys were doing well at school and he was active in an Austral-Asian church. We were all sure he'd be happier there.

There were a few other wrinkles to this story, but the net result was that I still had over a year to run as Director, and so I carried on.

Meanwhile in Bangkok, with a weather-eye open for a potential Thai Director, we saw a steady consolidation of the broadcasting ministry and upgrading of the production staff. A drama series started bringing in a notable increase in listeners' mail – which latter was our main indicator of how many people heard our broadcasts.

Taking a complete break from FEBC and broadcasting, our usual vacation spot was the OMF's seaside bungalow at Prajuabkirikan, a few hours south of Bangkok, a peaceful and comfortable guest house with all meals and laundry provided – no work to do whatsoever and lots of open country to hike and drive around.

After the pressures in Bangkok we enjoyed an exciting trip to visit Andrew, then working in Taiwan with the Jardine Organisation. Since he was single and did not have to bring a wife or children out to see him, Jardine subsidised our fare instead. He drove us for a sightseeing treat: an overnight stay in a nice hotel overlooking Sun Moon Lake. He had learnt how to order delicious food at roadside cafes – all piping hot and so welcome on a chilly day. En route back to Taibei we toured the Mountain Tribal Village – they supplied us with a wheelchair for Ruth, who had only recently recovered from the hip operation. The uphill part was an authoritative reconstruction of hill dwellers' life and it was interesting to meet tribespeople in their hillside villages and slate-slab housing. Lower down, the rest of the property formed an entertaining theme park. It was more of a fun-fair with miniatures of world sights: the Grand Canyon and a 'British Royal Train'! A musical fountain played the *Halleluya Chorus* and on the final note sprayed the audience!

I visited various other parts of Thailand in connection with the broadcasting task. I usually took with me one or two of most promising senior staff, partly for company but also to see how Thai personnel would take to a different part of the country; Thailand's regions differ culture-wise quite radically one from the other. For our next Director we needed a Thai who could and would handle visits across Thailand and who could also handle English language correspondence. Some idea of broadcasting, or at least an interest in it would be essential too.

It became clear that we were fast running out of time. We had served over three years heading up the studio and looked like reaching four, when our retirement date would be reached. Each six months or so, the Board had invited us to remain 'for a bit longer'. So now the search for a person to take over leadership of the FEBC recording studio from me became pressing.

We advertised in the Christian press, but no one with the background and abilities we needed came forward. Finally after Ruth and I had prayed about it, we informed the Board that we would definitely leave around late 1997. Still no Thai person appeared ready to take the job on. Then Ruth suggested, 'What about Georgina?' Now Georgina Stott was an Australian missionary, a member of WEC International. She spoke Thai like a Thai, and had served many years heading a studio in Chiengmai, North Thailand. She was currently working in a book ministry nearby and the future of this was uncertain. We sounded her out with positive results, and her mission society was happy for her to retain her visa and be loaned to FEBC.

The announcement of Georgina as our successor went without question or comment from the staff, though we were sure that it was news to all of them. There was a considerable turnover of staff in the offing, because a few of the longer-serving and therefore higher paid staff – but not necessarily the most productive – decided to move and this gave

Georgina a much cheaper payroll as well as freedom to choose her own new team.

And so we handed over to a successor with more programming experience than I had had. As I write, she is in her 14th year there, and has served far longer than any of other of the successive Thailand FEBC Directors. Recently she started local broadcasting from a transmitter on the studio rooftop. Our one disappointment was that unlike most of our previous spheres of service, we did not leave by handling over to a local person. This looks like being Georgina's privilege!

Every year or so FEBC calls a Director's Conference; those I attended were a bit like a Church of England assembly! The deliberations had no binding authority but it was a good opportunity to talk with other Directors, to swap experiences and to air possibilities and share visions. At one of these the Chairman of FEBC-Australia asked if Ruth and I would be willing to work with them for a period.

Now with our retirement finally fixed, the Australian FEBC board invited us to do six months or so of FEBC promotion based in Melbourne, thus giving us plenty of time with Ruth's family. FEBC-Australia were generous in paying our rent and supplying a car – virtually essential in Australia, and also paying our travel over and above OMF's basic provision. FEBC would fly us out to Australia and back to the UK. 'Back to the UK' was to include a stopover in Saigon, Vietnam, where Andrew had moved – still under the Jardine organisation.

Andrew introduced us to Cu Chi, the underground quarters of the former Vietcong during the long stretched-out war, first against the French and then the Americans. A museum demonstrated the gory booby traps which the Vietcong had laid for the Americans. Disused hangars and rusting US military equipment lay here and there around the cities, but rebuilding and modernising the infrastructure were evident everywhere. Everyone seemed to be working hard. The Christian Church was re-starting after hostilities and would shortly regain legal status. Millions of bicycles and motor bikes packed the streets – one wonders what it may be like if and when those riders all drive four-wheelers! Andrew lived outside the centre, in a quiet estate with a swimming pool and a motherly servant to cook for us all.

And so on to the UK, having gained an insight into the Vietnam War, and the present life in that country. We paused again briefly in

Bangkok; this final week or so in Thailand gave us a rest and a change with the sun and sea at Prajuabkirikan. What a great kindness it was of OMF to supply this full-board 'rest and recreation centre' for their members! There remained the flight back to England in the comfort of Eva Air's premium economy cabin.

In six more months, nominally assigned to deputation for OMF, we would be retired and did not have to wonder where our next OMF country would be.

Indeed we doubted if we would ever return to Asia.

But here again we were quite wrong!

Retirement

It was 1997. Lynette, our younger daughter, along with Tony Sharpe, a long-time friend and supporter welcomed us at Heathrow from Bangkok. The first six months would be 'retirement home assignment' which meant we would undertake speaking engagements on behalf of OMF.

By now all our children were independent but often came to stay with us. When, a little later, Andrew and his wife LinhDan returned to live in London, we were all in the same area together long-term for the first time in 27 years!

It is never easy to locate an affordable rented house for missionaries on furlough, but eventually Emmanuel discovered that the Vicarage of St Francis Church, Monks Hill was available. It was tucked away in the far end of a small Council Estate[1] on the edge of South Croydon. Moreover Emmanuel was offering us assistance with purchasing a house in South Croydon so that we could be nearby and assist in the Parish as we had done on our several former furloughs. So it came that we embarked on the purchase of our small semi-detached house on the Monks Hill Estate.

Four years earlier at Emmanuel, we had enjoyed a supportive working relationship with the Vicar, James Jones (now Bishop of Liverpool). However by the time we returned for retirement, a new Vicar had been appointed and hesitantly welcomed us. He had been weeding out as many over 50s as possible from active service in the church; he added that he approved of missionaries in principle but felt that the mission *societies* had 'lost their way'. He opined that teaching in church from overseas mission personnel would not be well received by the congregation. It is sadly true

---

1   Council Estates were built by local government as low cost housing for rent to working families, but under Margaret Thatcher they were sold off to the occupants. For them it was to be the investment chance of a lifetime – considering the value that they would attain.

that some mission speakers are less than inspiring to listen to, but on the other hand others get invited merely as a free 'pulpit-fill' for the minister who is not particularly interested in their mission!

Furthermore, many mission sending agencies have rarely taken the challenge to address future clergy at their training colleges. Thus many ordinands entering busy church life see overseas missions as a 'niche' activity for those already interested, but not as something vital to the individual and corporate life of the congregation. In fact once we had retired, the tally of Emmanuel couples or singles serving overseas had fallen to nil. None had been valedicted for almost two decades, although three were to start overseas ministries shortly after. I came across an Emmanuel commemorative publication a few decades old, and was interested to see that seven of the 20 pages were to do with Emmanuel's dozen or so overseas mission partners. We have far to go to catch up with the past!

In other ways, however, the Vicar at Emmanuel was quite welcoming. He invited me to be a co-ordinator for a cluster of his newly established housegroups, a job which I continued for nearly a decade. He was also supportive of our first post-retirement sortie, backing us financially – a three-month assignment back in Hong Kong.

Two avenues for further ordained service opened up: the first was a small branch-church, St Francis, next door to the Monks Hill Vicarage. In due course it became apparent that its mother-church did not have the strength or interest to give the lead that St Francis needed. I started to negotiate for Emmanuel to render some assistance, in particular in the realm of youth ministry – almost no teenagers attended our St Francis' activities. The then-Vicar of Emmanuel came for a visit enthusiastically, but was not so keen when he discovered that overall ministry could involve relating with St Francis leaders, including some who were far from young. But there was a bright side; St Francis was paying its way, and under Ruth's leadership the Sunday School (*Kidz Hour*) grew and we urgently needed more separate rooms. Emmanuel offered us a portable 'cabin' which became surplus following the completion of an extension project of their own. This eventually found its way to St Francis via high cranes and a wide low-loader vehicle. Though we had done most of the negotiation, the actual job took place while we were in Cambodia[2].

---

2   See later chapter.

The Bishop was approached and I was invited to become a licensed priest at St Francis as soon as a proper minister-in-charge could be found. However, the person selected for the job did not welcome retired personnel officiating at services either!

I had been involved with St Francis' Fabric, Grounds and Equipment Team. There was always something to do – call a plumber, change electrical wiring, install a second projector screen, as well as endlessly adding and changing locks and their scores of keys! Other activities started up: we welcomed 'Dr Bike' – which repairs bicycles and teaches youngsters to ride; there were various projects for slow-learners using our Hall. We joined with local churches in taking turns to run a weekly 'Floating Shelter' for homeless people. My job was usually the major dish-washing task!

Various gifts, and also a local council grant enabled us to decide on another cabin; on a huge vehicle a tall crane lifted it onto its four prepared blocks. Almost the entire neighbourhood turned out to see its installation! This gave us two more rooms. We also added, for good measure, a basic shed for 'Dr Bike'.

A number of Christian families from West Africa have moved in locally, adding a lot to church life. They have reintroduced the Mothers' Union – with a decidedly positive Nigerian flavour.

A new Vicar at Emmanuel, Trevor, was very positive and he and the church put much effort into getting St Francis back onto its feet. As I write, there has been an inter-regnum, and a new couple, Revd Peter Wyatt and his wife Michelle and children have occupied the Vicarage and now lead the church with a stress on working through prayer and strong relational ministries. Peter's experience with top teenagers and working-age men make him an ideal team leader.

The second avenue of post-retirement service to open up was at St Mary Magdalene Church in nearby Addiscombe. Earlier I had enjoyed a warm relationship with Richard Williams, the Vicar. It was clear we held similar views on most things and he was positive towards overseas missions – especially to OMF – and also to me! So it was a privilege to be invited to share in their ministry – leading, preaching or presiding, even at very short notice.

Richard is a visionary person, warm and outgoing. Even when I pointed out to him my age (a problem to some clergy) he responded

David and Richard visit Banpot Church, Central Thailand, which ran its own town-community radio station, seen here with the duty announcer.

that he was anxious to involve *all* ages. St Mary's is a growing church and the youngest and oldest worship together for part or all of the main service. Richard has seen several of his members enter the Ministry, and the church supports half a dozen missionaries. In a new Sunday service, 'The Informal', I sometimes taught or led the Communion service for a lively group of top teens, twenties and thirties – as well as a sprinkling of much older folk. This has been a great opportunity for a teaching ministry in Sunday sermons, and also at our one-time three months of weekly teaching at Addiscombe School of Theology.

Richard and I spent a week together on a trip to Bangkok – to the once-in-three-years Missions Round Table of the vast Diocese of Singapore. For him it was a life-changing experience, especially when we went 'up country' to see some of OMF's church planting ventures. (One of them runs its own radio station.) He was also impressed with the spiritual outlook of the missionaries. After nine years in Addiscombe, Richard was chosen from a wide canvas of applicants for the Parish of Cranbrook in Kent. He is certainly the man for the job, backed by a fine family. He has maintained interest in our links with East Asia and I have been able to introduce him to some of the Bishops visiting from Singapore-Malaysia.

I enjoy a Bishop's Licence called *Permission to Officiate* (PTO) which allows me to accept invitations to help any church in the Diocese –

including most of Greater London south of the Thames. This gives me freedom to accept invitations, so whether I am welcomed as part of a team depends very much upon the disposition of the Minister in charge.

Though most of our work is at St Francis, we still belong to Emmanuel, where there remain most of those Croydonians who have prayed for us during our years overseas. Interestingly, not only older folk, but also the top-teenage group and their parents have most readily enrolled as our prayer-partners. There are about 40 of them in all. The current Vicar gave me a job description involving teaching in the Parish about overseas missions and intercultural issues, and he kindly supports the cost of my attendance at occasional Clergy retreats and the like.

Our up-country hosts were Alan and Averil Bennett, veteran church-planters in Thailand. We enjoy a riverside evening meal together. (Left to right: Alan, David, Averil and Richard Williams.)

Emmanuel has supported us in prayer and finance on five post-retirement sorties to Singapore, as well as to Hong Kong, Cambodia, Kenya, Thailand and Malaysia as we shall see in the following chapters.

So overseas service did not end on retirement; it was just that the future remained hidden!

Five Directions

Hong Kong

Early in 2000, a feature of our retirement which we could never have foreseen popped up. Out of the blue we received an e-mail from Alfred Yeo, my former room-mate in College. Would we be willing to serve Transworld Radio (TWR) in their Hong Kong studio for three months while there was no Director, and to 'hold the fort' while planning was made for the future? The Vicar of Emmanuel was encouraging and his Missionary Committee gave us a generous gift towards expenses while TWR paid the rest.

While wondering whether to accept, we were honoured by a visit from Dave Tucker, a senior person in TWR. Dave took the trouble to make a day trip by train from Swansea (200 miles away) to prepare us for Hong Kong.

Politically Hong Kong had become part of China in 1997, but many local Chinese told us that they felt little change since the British had left. There had however been much more building and also reclamation from the sea since we had lived there 19 years before, but it was still an easy place to get around and to get things done, and the transport was even better than we had known it.

We revisited St Andrew's Church, now full of young graduates who had returned from study in the English-speaking world; but several faces we had known previously were still there. During our stay Ruth had a small involvement with a ladies' group that she had known when we lived in Hong Kong.

The two-floor TWR studios had been built into the top area of a 10-floor factory block. It was a professional-standard job with excellent soundproofing and acoustics, and a keen and dedicated team of about a dozen producers and follow-up staff, all of them Chinese. Most of the programmes were aired over TWR's short-wave station in Guam, and were aimed at the Chinese Mainland. The staff also visited China, often taking CD recordings of their broadcasts to distribute as they travelled. There was much to learn from them.

The whole TWR team made us most welcome. The team were all busy making programmes in various Chinese languages, or supporting the programmers. The broadcasts were well thought out, and very acceptable to the stations that broadcast them. However, many programmes comprised just the fairly basic format of music and preaching. Helping them to add variety, we worked through some simple drama scripts before they themselves produced mini-dramas; this exercise they greatly enjoyed. My main task was to report on any possibilities for the future, but my feeling – which I freely shared with the staff – was that they were doing a good job, though there was room for some more advanced training for some of the programmers.

Having had experience of moving studios before – and the difficulties involved – I warned them at a Board meeting against quitting the present excellent, well-built installation, especially as the mortgage payments had only a year or two more to run.

Alfred and Rosie Yeo decided to hold their '40 Years of Ministry' celebration in Singapore and invited us (complete with ticket!) to fly across from Hong Kong for the banquet. The pleasant extra interlude, back in old stamping grounds, was enjoyable, especially as we had never envisaged returning to Asia at all.

We had no idea there could be further overseas service until one day when Ruth answered the telephone. It was a call from Transworld Radio. Would we be willing to do another three-month fill-in, in Phnom Penh, Cambodia, while their normal studio managers took a well-earned furlough?

Cambodia

This was a bit more daunting. It was 2002 and the murderous Khmer Rouge were still in evidence though the capital city of Phnom Penh was quite safe. We consulted several people with a good knowledge of the situation and it seemed right to go. This time there would also be lecturing in an adjacent Bible College for both Ruth and me. Ruth was reassured, for during my working hours in Hong Kong, there had been little for her to do. Only then did we grasp that the TWR leaders in Cambodia were Rose-Ellen and Dan Blosser, who we had known years before in Hong Kong. They wrote to say we'd be living in their well-appointed flat with aircon and use of a vehicle, and there would also be a Cambodian lady who would come daily for domestic chores and cooking. I was catapulted into the modern age by having to carry a mobile phone and a laptop computer to and from daily work!

The Cambodian staff were a fine, hard-working team with a vision for the Gospel. Again, the content of the broadcasts seemed to be simple music and preaching, though some were translated from sponsored Western productions. However, there was no problem getting them aired on the many local stations. We invited them to tackle simple dramas and they showed themselves to be creative in ideas which, of course, fitted the local scene. The studio backed up its ministry by visiting various provincial towns to meet responding listeners or supporting churches. Most listener response came by mobile phone and e-mail, there being only a very limited postal system.

I was made very welcome both in the studio and as a part-time teacher in the adjacent Bible College. While Ruth worked through some of the Epistles, I tackled the books of Deuteronomy and Joshua. Few of the students could afford books, so the College invested in 'class sets' to enable each student in one class to borrow the relevant text for the subject they were studying. It was reassuring to see such a large number of aspiring teachers and preachers for the future Cambodian church.

Most people who come to Cambodia aim to visit Angkor Wat, a cluster of huge, ancient temples covering a zone about 20 kilometres across. They are indeed a wonder of the world and the remaining product of a lost civilisation. However we decided instead to join a staff member on a trip towards the coast. He made various stops, mostly at small emerging churches and at each he explained what TWR-Cambodia was broadcasting. He handed out programme schedules and also sold quite nice all-band radio receivers at a cost-price of a mere five dollars each, complete with batteries. After a seaside meal in a rustic restaurant, we started the long, slow, bumpy ride back. At one point we had to negotiate a metre-wide gap in the centre of a river bridge! Driving was tiring and darkness fell as we thankfully approached Phnom Penh.

Lunch with students at Phnom Penh Bible College – Ruth at end of table.

I drove the minivan daily to the studio, usually starting around 7am. The roads were very crowded, and some were full of deep potholes and pools of mud. One day on a minor road I came up against a motor-cyclist riding in the opposite direction carrying 15-foot bamboos across his saddle. Most of the traffic drove on the right-hand side of the road, French style, but a small minority used the other side, especially just before attempting a left turn.

The Chinese government had gifted new traffic-lights for one of Phnom Penh's main boulevards. These are surmounted with large count-down numerals above the signals themselves, to indicate how many sec-onds there are before the next phase. The tendency is that with only a second to go on the 'red', many drivers shoot forward without waiting for the 'amber', let alone the actual 'green' to appear. I remain ambivalent as to whether this feature of traffic signals is conducive to safety, or the reverse!

Once while waiting at one of these signals a policeman came up to me and demanded $40[1] for some traffic offence which I never re-ally understood. This would have been a substantial prize for him as a constable was only paid $150 per month. He threatened pris-on and waved his gun. I realised from experiences in Thailand that some haggling would help. I got the price down to $20.

During the time in Phnom Penh an e-mail arrived from Angus and Carol Chu. I had got to know the Chu's quite well

In Cambodia, as in many Asian countries, it is common for a whole family to travel on a motor scooter.

---

1   Cambodia uses US Dollars for most transactions, but local currency for smaller amounts (or change) below $1.

from time at Fuller Seminary in California. They had come to Fuller from Hong Kong and we were then working in that territory. Angus and I would spend time together – sometimes late at night – working through some of the lecture material. He was tackling advanced missiology which can involve some rather arcane and specialised English[2]. The Chu's were considering service with OMF in Asia but they became involved with the Africa Inland Mission (AIM), hence their call to Kenya.

Now Angus was Principal of Eldama Ravine Bible College in Kenya, which he had built up almost from scratch. They were looking two years ahead to their own return to the USA, and realised that there would be a three month gap during which they would be unable to give time to teaching. Would we fill that gap? This was such a radical departure from anything we had done before that we had to think about how to reply!

On the return journey from Cambodia we took a few days' vacation at OMF's holiday home by the sea in Thailand; then had time in Melbourne with Ruth's relations and friends. Jill and Jonathan, Andrew and LinhDan and Nette all joined us while we were 'down under'. Jonathan arranged for us all to go to the Boxing Day Ashes Cricket Match at the famous Melbourne Cricket Ground – the English put up a good performance (for once) against the sports-mad, and well-trained Australians but they still did not win!

The journey home to the UK took us across three continents.

Kenya

Preparing for Kenya proved to be a challenge. Where Transworld Radio had picked up all our travel expenses and accommodation in Hong Kong and Phnom Penh, the Africa Inland Mission (now **AIM**-International) required us to provide all of our own travel and living expenses plus our share of *their* own overheads. Also, we short-termers had to undergo a fairly comprehensive medical assessment. Altogether, we would need

---

2   Unlike Singapore Chinese, whose education attaches great importance to fluent English, and among whom English is spoken in many homes and all schools, most Hong Kong Chinese learn English as a foreign language and use Cantonese Chinese at home. It is also used in most schools, and all business with other Chinese. Standard Chinese Mandarin is, however, fast becoming the main language.

almost £5000 for a three-month stay for the two of us, though a longer term would have cost proportionately less.

Emmanuel Church was in an inter-regnum but the Curate and the Treasurer of the Missionary Committee were encouraging, and so we took the plunge. All the money came in and we left with a full list of prayer partners of all ages from Emmanuel, from St Francis and from St Mary Magdalene.

We visited Julian and Rachel Jackson, former Emmanuel missionaries with AIM, to gain some advice for our prospective visit to the Africa Inland Church (AIC) – planted by the AIM. It has the largest number of *churches* of any denomination in Kenya, though the Anglicans have slightly more *members* than the AIC. The AIM churches are baptistic in their views on baptism but are governed more or less along Presbyterian lines – with the addition of a Bishop! Almost all their ministers are the product of their own Bible and Theological colleges, which makes them somewhat inward-looking with little understanding of other Christians.

The UK Director of AIM explained to us that while the Christian Gospel has taken root very widely across East Africa (in the case of Kenya some 75 percent of the population are said to be in church on Sundays), yet the *depth* of the churches tends to be quite shallow. The key to the future therefore rests with good training for the emerging leaders, biblically, theologically and practically. We were privileged to have a very small part in this task.

On arrival in Nairobi we realised that Africa was very different from Asia. I had seen Mayfield, the AIM's Nairobi Guest Home, almost 40 years before – separated from the road by just a low hedge. Now the AIM's driver paused the minivan outside for doors to open in a 10-foot high sheet-steel wall around the property. We were warned never to be on foot outside after dark. Many cars in the compound had their registration numbers painted in large letters on both sides and the roof as a deterrent to theft. Once inside, Mayfield was welcoming and comfortable and the food had an African flavour to it.

Outside, Nairobi seemed to be ill-kempt and dusty. Roads and sidewalks were potholed and many of the city's parks were overgrown. The local bus company had disappeared, giving way mainly to cramped 14-seat minibuses. Most of the railway had been closed to passenger traffic for some years, due to unrepaired rolling stock and track. I walked through the dilapidated and grimy central railway station with few trains or passengers, the very antithesis of Singapore or Hong Kong.

On Sunday we attended a service at Nairobi Cathedral – some 2000 normally attended the English service. As we waited, an equally large congregation for Swahili-speaking worship processed out dancing and clapping.

A day or two later Angus and Carol picked us up in their Land Rover for the four-hour drive to Eldama Ravine, a pleasant rural market town located on green and fertile land.

The Chu's were the epitome of kindness and for the first few days fed us delicious Chinese food in their own home. We were allotted a pleasant staff house – quite well appointed with modern sanitation and hot water, but with very basic cooking arrangements and furniture – and at first we had only a picnic cool-box as a 'fridge.' We made this an issue for prayer, especially as the single-burner electric stove never really seemed to get hot enough.

Then a week or two after arrival we received offers of loans of proper beds plus a fridge, a microwave oven, and some armchairs and curtains. We bought a Japanese bottled gas stove with two burners and a grill, simplifying our cooking and enhancing our comfort, and we could invite guests in for meals. Ruth soon devised a microwave-cooked chocolate sponge cake which was devoured appreciatively by the Americans!

A kerosene wick lamp covered the all-too-frequent power cuts (a reminder of Jakarta 31 years beforehand) and our minimal e-mail traffic was handled through a mobile phone adaptor to our laptop computer. They were taken outside the house at first because the phone masts were quite distant; fortunately, there were no lions in Eldama!

Almost on arrival, Ruth and I were plunged into heavy

In Angus and Carol Chu's family home at Eldama Ravine. (Front) David, Ruth, Carol and Tryphena. (Rear) Angus, Nathan and Stephen.

teaching programmes. The students had all served as junior 'pastors' for at least two years after completing their basic Bible College course, so they had had considerable experience. They were now embarking on a further two-year course leading to formal 'ordination.'

Spiritually they were very high calibre, but their education and general knowledge were sketchy indeed. In any encounter with Christians of other denominations they felt out of their depth. Although the government went to great lengths to stress that all Kenyans were a single nation, tribal loyalties remain as both a strength and as a threat to social integration.

'Theological English' was a problem for some of our students; they found education based on books – even on the Bible – difficult. Coming from a tribal background meant that tradition, precedent and age governed everything, and their college training had largely been memory-based. They would study say, a Bible book and then be given a written exam. There was little learning by bouncing-around of ideas, nor discussion among them of varied viewpoints, as one might expect in a theological college elsewhere.

An interesting task arose when Angus asked me to teach them a course entitled *How to Write a Research Paper*. This was a new concept to all of them; instead of answering exam questions from memory they were asked to research something that could be given back as new knowledge for the library.

I sent a few students to local churches to find out what other denominations thought about their respective topics; I had forewarned the Anglican Vicar who warmly welcomed those who approached him. Sadly, other students told me it was contrary to their custom and ethos to make such visits.

I suggested that it would be good if they took the initiative with a 'ministers' fraternal' for their town or village, to have fellowship with other pastors, and to pray for each other's needs as well as to consider any local problems. As with the 'research', the students seemed out of their depth at the very idea. It seems that they were unsure of their own theology, thus they could not confidently distinguish the orthodox from the cults. Apart from this insular ethos, they also expressed a fear that a 'ministers' fraternal' could be an opportunity for the other pastors to steal their sheep!

Finally 14 hand-written research papers were ready – no typewriters or computers were available. I checked the scripts to remove ambivalent grammar and unclear sentences, and looked through their brief bibliographies. One of the least academically-able students chose the most adventurous subject: *Female Circumcision,* an illegal practice in Kenya and forbidden by the churches, but commonly performed in most tribes nonetheless. *Cliterodectomy* is an extremely painful process and it can lead onto disease, often to HIV, and cause subsequent problems with intercourse, conception and birth. For this reason I encouraged him because few Kenyan Christians are willing to stand up and be heard on this issue.

The Academic Dean was pleased with the results. The students were permitted to keep their A4 manuscripts and we placed A5 size photocopies in the library for future reference.

I felt that the stress on exams was unsuitable for experienced pastors. So as an alternative, at the start of a lesson I would set short quizzes on the previous session, and for homework I invited the students to suggest ways in which the Bible passage (or other issue) under study could be applied in their own tribal setting. They gave some interesting answers but, even more importantly, it primed the class to engage in useful (if unaccustomed) discussion.

One pre-arranged Sunday evening, we had a 'live' phone call to the Evening Service of Emmanuel Church, back in England. The necessary circuits had been installed by Robert Burch, who had served in Seychelles with us. After exchanging the Africa greeting *Jambo!* we told our home church about our progress in teaching, and received an encouraging 'live' prayer back from the minister.

At half-term, Angus treated us to a few nights on an island in a lake. The ride from the College was hot, dusty and rough. Our destination was a tourist 'safari camp' in which the 'front room' of each chalet was a tent, but a brick ensuite bathroom was behind each. We enjoyed full board, a swimming pool, and then a boat ride to observe fish-catching eagles, crocodiles, hippopotami and exotic trees and wildlife.

One Sunday at Eldama, the Anglican vicar invited me to preach, and we duly arrived at St Swithun's Church. I was invited to baptise three infants and a youth, and to assist with Holy Communion.

There were several churches in Eldama Ravine – the Africa Inland

Church (which had just completed a large and prominent edifice), Presbyterian and Salvation Army churches, plus many informal house-type ones. One of the latter assembled in a sort of cow-house, while another met in a tent sewn up from maize sacks. Yet others consisted just of a pole with a loudspeaker horn on top and a battery amplifier below. The Town Council were considering a by-law to eliminate this ubiquitous, if rarely intelligible, noise.

Sometimes we attended the Eldama Africa Inland Church on Sundays, and once I was invited to preach. It was well attended by about 250 people, but when Holy Communion started towards the end of the service, about 200 took advantage of the short interval and left. One explanation for this was that a high proportion of Kenyans, even Christians, carry charms on their persons, or use them at home. Conscious of this being unscriptural, they desisted from Holy Communion rather than giving up their occult practices.

Towards the end of our time in Eldama, an American Chinese couple, Tim and Christine suggested a visit to the Nakuru Game Park. We piled into their 4x4 for an early start, though not quite early enough to see the lions. Nevertheless it took several hours to drive around the area, passing a herd of giraffes – two of which appeared to be fighting with their long necks. There were rhinos busily eating grass, and thousands of flamingos standing in the lakes. This gave us some idea of the animal life of East Africa, which is less obvious now as more land is being absorbed into the populated area. The spectacular in nature is always a reminder of our God of creation!

The term drew to a close and soon we were on our own way back to Nairobi. There was one more experience in store for us at an intermediate stop.

The AIM's Rift Academy at Kijabe is a high school for missionaries' children. Run mainly on American lines, there is a GCSE stream for British and Commonwealth students. A High School Graduation was due, a very important rite of passage for American families. Earlier on the Chu's two sons, Nathan and Stephen had done well there and now their young sister Tryphena was about to graduate; Angus had obtained guest-tickets for all of us. The programme was a typical academic occasion; the graduands wore gowns and mortar boards plus a 'year scarf' which they would keep as a memento of the occasion.

Most of the prize-winners were already aware of their awards, but we were thrilled to hear the announcement for one particular award which had been kept for the occasion: 'for the student who has showed the most courtesy, loyalty and helpfulness' – Tryphena Chu!

Angus treated his family plus us missionary teachers at Carnivore, a Nairobi restaurant which serves all kinds of barbecued wild game meat. Emu was rather nice but the crocodile flesh was somewhat rubbery. Some meats – such as elephant – were forbidden as they came from protected species but we were assured that although they were not on the menu, waiters could sometimes be persuaded to produce them!

And so to our plane home, we were soon aboard for an airline evening meal and then to doze our way to London. Jill and Jonathan welcomed us at Heathrow.

We were to find that Africa had indeed changed us!

China

Both Ruth and Andrew suggested that I might like to join him on one of his business trips to China – neither of us had yet entered the Peoples Republic. Ruth felt she could not manage the travel but was happy for Andrew to take me. We entered a rather unusual way – via Vietnam and the Red River Valley aboard the Victoria Express, sponsored by our hotel near the border.

Our first journey actually inside China was aboard a night bus fitted-out with quite comfortable bunks. Every couple of hours or so the bus made a toilet stop – some were quite modern and spotless, others just unisex situations with planks over pits. However it was a good way to make a long journey and we arrived in good time in Kunming, south-west China.

Andrew worked out our programme, mostly well-known sights such as Lijiang – a traditional Chinese city but developed as a tourist resort, mostly for Chinese people themselves. The Chinese government encourages their people to travel and learn about their own land. Xian is noted for the Terracotta Army and the tomb of the Emperor Qin Shi Huang Di – he 'abolished' earlier history, and unified China. He is often regarded as the founder of the nation – which is what he wanted to be!

Nearby is the 'Tiger Leaping Gorge' where reputedly a man was pursued by a tiger but managed to jump across a gorge over a rocky constriction in the river!

Pingyao is the last remaining fully-walled Chinese city where we stayed in a traditional Chinese inn – no longer were fires kindled under beds because central heating had been installed! Our stay in Pingyao included a Sunday and we worshipped at the Chinese Protestant Church, originally founded in the 1930s by the China Inland Mission. We were made very welcome and invited to lunch.

Beijing is the capital city and rich in history, notable the formerly 'Forbidden' City which is now one vast museum of history and early scientific development. That evening we tasted true Beijing Duck, although you can guess the name of the burger chain who also sold us 'McDuck!' Of course we could not miss ascending the nearby Great Wall. Many people walk up on foot but I was quite glad of a bubble-car lift which eases much of the ascent. Militarily the Wall was not a success – having been built at enormous cost to keep out the very people who predominate in China today.

Our final stage was an overnight train to Shanghai – quite luxurious with a twin-bunk ensuite cabin and a delicious Chinese evening meal

Shanghai. Just inside the former front garden entrance gate of the former China Inland Mission headquarters and guest home. The original building is straight ahead; those on the sides were added after the government appropriated the building.

on board. The train averaged 75mph and landed us in Shanghai for breakfast. Our first visit was to see if we could find the former China Inland Mission building at 1531 Xinzha Road. It was indeed still there! An extra storey had been added plus an external shaft for a lift, but the former front garden had been completely built over. It is now a hospital for children, and with Andrew's fluent Chinese we found no problem looking around inside! China impresses one; the cities are sparkling, modern, clean and well-equipped. From the air one can see remote rural villages with no roads nor power lines, but modernity is fast approaching these outlying centres.

Andrew remained in China on business but as I dozed on the plane back to London, I realised this was the trip of a lifetime!

Europe

Though these trips seem unrelated to missionary work, it is doubtful if we would have made them had we not been missionaries! We view them as a seamless part of our learning, as well as family interludes and gifts from God between assignments.

Our children had facilitated a short visit for us to Rome. Historic cities were a delight, especially to Ruth who saw great opportunities to explore history and gain scenes for later paintings. We noticed that the magnificent cathedrals in Europe – including St Peter's Basilica in Rome – rarely or never charge for admission even though they are beautifully maintained. (This is in contrast to England's gloomy buildings where a substantial admission charge, up to £16 per person, applies). We also viewed the Vatican Museum though sadly the missiology section was closed. Visiting the Coliseum we paused in front of a large timber cross to remember the Christians and others who had been sacrificed there to entertain the crowds. In some cases 'entertain' was not always the right term, because attendance by all citizens could also be compulsory!

Our younger daughter Lynette was working in Brussels for a year or so, and invited us to see this quaint city that is less modernised than most Western capitals. She suggested a trip to a nearby museum exhibition on the Congo and King Leopold, so we boarded a tram meandering through woodland to Louvain. In recent years Belgium has afforded Congo considerable aid and assistance. Moreover under Belgian rule, a strong missionary movement planted small though strong and expanding churches.

Andrew's engagement was an occasion for celebration. His wife to be, LinhDan Pham is French, of Vietnamese origin. The engagement party was held in her family's home in The Hague, Holland where we enjoyed warm weather and sightseeing with sumptuous food and hospitality, not to mention a lake cruise within the famous reclaimed area. (For the rest see the chapter 'Three Weddings' at the end of the book!)

Jill was working for a while in Dublin and invited us there for a few days – giving us an experience of the friendly delights of the Emerald Isle. We explored the Viking history and the arrival of the Christian faith in Ireland. Taking the traditional lunch at Bewlays Coffee House, we arrived about 12.45 and the waitress warned us that the menu would change at 1 pm so it was too late to take orders from the current one. However, she added, the 1 pm menu would be the same one as that in our hands. We were indeed in Ireland!

Then we celebrated several family anniversaries together with the children. For one notable gathering my cousin Mary and also Ruth's brother and sister-in-law – visiting from Australia – all joined us; we took over a small guesthouse in the Dordogne region of France, noted for its verdant river valleys and gastronomically for its duck cuisine.

Nearby was the Chateau Milande, former home of the entertainer Josephine Baker, a black American who made a fortune in French cabaret. She then put her energies into bringing up orphan children whom she boarded at the chateau. During German occupation she evidently entertained German officers and, remarkably, was given permission to visit Spain for her performances. But she is also credited with helping downed RAF aircrew to escape to Spain. She was not a businesswoman, however, and financial problems saw the end of her philanthropic enterprises. But there remains a museum of Josephine: notably photos of her with the orphans from all over the world, and her skirt of bananas worn on stage – when she wore anything more than an ostrich feather!

On another occasion Ruth and I responded to a newspaper offer of a cheap day-trip to Lille; it meant a 5 am start from Croydon, so it was a long day. In Lille a multilingual bus tour gave us a bird's eye view of this historic city, followed by walks through the oldest part, and then a visit to the museum. It was a tiring but interesting day!

A year or two later, while attending a technical exhibition at London's Earls Court I chatted with one of the stallholders. He invited me to drop a card into a goldfish bowl on his desk – there might be a prize. We do not take part on lotteries but I duly complied even though we didn't expect any result. A few days later a phone call advised me that we had been given two first-class return tickets on Eurostar!

Finding dates when Andrew and LinhDan's flat in Paris would be vacant, we claimed the tickets and were able to fill in some of the sights we hadn't managed before. We took a day to see Monet's Garden, with the curved bridge over the lily pond usually featured in guide books. It was a pleasant though sweltering day, but we got lots of photos to take home for Ruth's art work. Unexpectedly Andrew and LinhDan came to Paris too. After attending St Michael's English Church, they wanted to treat us to a trip to the Palace of Versailles but the entry queues were very long. So we settled for exploring the gardens.

That evening LinhDan's parents invited us to a delicious home meal in their suburban house. Their residence was built out over a steep descent with a breath-taking view across Paris to the Eiffel Tour and hilltop Sacré Coeur Cathedral.

Another gift from our children was a visit to Venice – much to Ruth's delight with so much art and history. Here we are standing on Salute Island looking across to the Bell Tower and (right of centre) the Doges' Palace.

On our final night Andrew and LinhDan's family had decided to celebrate Ruth's birthday. We made our way to the nearby Gare de Lyon, the station for trains to Lyons and southern France. We strolled along a shopping arcade below but were not led to the fast food or cheap chain cafés. We mounted some ornate stairs to the Train Bleu, one of Paris' most famous restaurants. We enjoyed a sumptuous meal with superb service under ornate French revival arches and murals of places served by the former Paris, Lyons and Mediterranean Railway Co.

But these short trips were mostly family affairs. Revisiting Asia would be another story!

Study?
– and Singapore

Back in 1981 at Fuller School of Intercultural Studies[1], I had taken the M.Th course with a view to continuing to a Doctorate in Missiology (D.Miss). During our time in Seychelles, we learnt that Fuller was no longer offering doctorates via distance-learning. I did however get as far as a research paper on Christianity in the Seychelles, and though it was never submitted as an dissertation, a few locally bound copies were well-received by the Seychelles churches.

On retirement it seemed worthwhile looking again. All the theological Colleges in the London area were dubious about helping me with a D.Miss. Moreover, most said they lacked a staff member qualified to mentor at this level of missiology.

Then I noticed an advertisement for Trinity College, Newburgh, Indiana which offered doctoral level studies, mostly by distance learning. Next I visited John Warwick Montgomery, a colourful human rights lawyer based in London who was Trinity's academic officer in the UK. He looked at my Seychelles thesis and encouraged me to research with Trinity.

I checked with Liverpool University that the accreditation was what it appeared to be. All appeared to be well at Liverpool, even to the extent that if the arrangement with Trinity were ever to terminate (which it has done), Liverpool's accreditation would stand. So I started on the theology subjects prescribed as course work, and took a number of Trinity's seminars held in London. Then came the thesis[2]. I asked if OMF would be happy for me to research the topic, *The Withdrawal of the China Inland Mission from China and their Redeployment in East Asia*. I would need to spend time in their archives in Singapore, which I learnt were yet

---

1   Then *Fuller School of World Mission*.

2   In the UK – but sometimes *dissertation* in the USA

to be sorted fully. I volunteered to help sort them out, and my request-and-offer were accepted with encouragement. I also spent long hours at London University's School of Oriental and African Languages, who hold the CIM archives in the UK; and at the OMF's UK headquarters in Kent.

When I reached Singapore I was given a free run of the archive room. Much indexing remained to be done and I was jetlagged for some time, so I rose early and spent the time ploughing through the old files in the basement. Later I put together an almost step-by-step account of the CIM's reincarnation from China into East Asia.

Going through old files I found the solution to a number of questions which never seemed to have been answered when I was a young missionary. Why, for example, had the CIM never recruited personnel of non-Caucasian ethnicity[3]? The main answer was that very few, if any, had applied hitherto. There were also unresolved racial issues in North America. However the main point so far as Asians were concerned, was that CIM wanted to *avoid* at all costs being seen to **employ** nationals, generating an employer-employee relationship[4]; but rather to work with them as equals, shoulder to shoulder.

At the time of the CIM's withdrawal from China in the early 1950s, two pivotal conferences were held, one near Melbourne, Australia, and the other in Bournemouth, England. The minutes of the latter were never published. The secrecy was occasioned by a full transcript of the events leading to the resignation of Bishop Frank Houghton, the then General Director who had been a sick man. He had stepped down under some pressure, but continued a ministry in a large UK parish, and in full fellowship as a continuing supporter of (and writer for) the CIM.

However there need have been no secrecy because the American version of *China's Millions* included quite a full report of the matter! It seems that across the Atlantic, much of CIM's support came from independent 'Bible' churches who had questioned the CIM's having an Anglican Bishop as their 'supremo'. (Incidentally none of the participants of those conferences, nor anyone else involved, is still alive today.)

---

3   As from the Centenary in 1964, OMF formulated a policy to accept suitable candidates of *any* ethnic group and any country, so long as, like the current membership, they were ready to cross to another.

4   This had become an issue in China with the 'employee' becoming seen by his fellow countrymen as a 'rice Christian.'

As for the thesis, the final finishing touches were completed a year or two later while Ruth and I were in Cambodia. Trinity's rules allow the 'viva' (the live interview) to be held by e-mail instead of a conference telephone call. So with the 'viva' behind me I sent the finished article to Newburgh by courier knowing that it had already been passed – indeed by God's grace at 'high distinction' level. About 65 copies of the thesis have been accepted by academic institutions across the world, including the Universities of London, Oxford, Cambridge, Birmingham, Yale, Hong Kong and even a couple in China. Most of the missiological and intercultural institutions in North America, the UK, Australia and the Far East also hold copies.

The formal British Graduation was held at Canterbury Christ Church University, followed by Evensong in the Cathedral and a meal. Ruth, Jill, Andrew and cousin Mary supported me, and only Nette was prevented from joining us by a longstanding business engagement.

As a result of my research in the OMF's Singapore archives, I was invited back again to frame-up a long-term plan for the archives' future, and each time it was good to meet several more friends whom I had hardly met since my earlier years in Singapore.

One day William – a GP friend from back in my early days – invited me to join the Singapore Adventure Society's night hike along part of the Island's northeast coast. I had known this area as estuarial swamp, but now several dozen of us hiked along a huge empty shrub-studded reclamation with the southern Malaysian coast visible across the straits. Most of these modern 'adventurers' were well-educated young professionals with a strong sense of ecology and liveable development. Many were William's fellow-Christians.

With Ruth at doctoral Graduation in the Chapel of Canterbury Christ Church University, followed by Evensong in Canterbury Cathedral.

Singapore's FEBA studio has grown enormously and to our surprise they invited Ruth and me to a 45-years' celebration, which included subsidised fares from the UK, and a Chinese dinner with over 1000 present in the magnificent Suntec Conference Centre.

During those two brief weeks we found almost every meal was booked by old acquaintances who welcomed us; again, we had to 'eat our way out' of Singapore! We stayed at the OMF Guest Home and chatting there with the new Director of Missionary research, Dr Warren Beattie, I received a further invitation to come and serve in Singapore.

This next archive visit I found that we had accrued enough air miles for me to upgrade to business class on the flights – what a pleasant change, with the rarefied atmosphere and quiet in the departure lounge, and the flat-bed spaciousness of the seating and a wide choice of food on board.

Warren and I worked through the boxes in the basement for several days and finally decided that about 60 percent of the stuff could go to the recycler. The next decision needed to be made: *who* would index all this material – probably a year's work for an experienced librarian or indexer – if one could be found. In addition there was much valuable report-material and forgotten theses to be bound in hard covers, and an even larger pile of back-numbers of missiological journals to go to the binder.

It was interesting to fit in a circular trip via Bangkok to Cambodia. I touched base with Christ Church, Bangkok whose Karen refugee ministry we support, and also rode up to Nakhon Sawan where Alan and Averil Bennett were based. Alan took me to see a small-town church which was operating its own radio station. This church used their broadcasts to get to know the community, share local news and interviews, as well as to explain what sort of people Christians are and what they believe. OMF entered Thailand in 1955, working only in unchurched areas. Now it is thrilling to learn that there are some 24,000 Christians in those same areas!

In Cambodia I was given hospitality with Dan and Rose-Ellen Blosser of Transworld Radio; Phnom Penh had improved since my last visit, the swampy pot-holed road that I had driven the 4WD over twice a day is now a level tarmac highway. Restaurants are more numerous and good value. China has given liberal aid to Cambodia for hospitals and transport.

But Cambodia remains constrained by inefficient bureaucracy, with poor or non-existent legal institutions. On arrival at the airport one first has to queue for a visa and pay 20 US dollars. If you can't produce a photo they will take one for you – for a further fee. Having got the visa you then move on a couple of yards to the immigration desks. Here as well as stamping your passport they... *take your photo*! Nevertheless, as with Indonesia years ago, the remarkable thing about Cambodia is how much one *can* get done! Moreover, the high rate of church growth[5] shows the importance of having a high grade of theological and Biblical education available to train the future Christian leadership.

Returning to Singapore there was little time left, but when meeting new OMF workers – of which a group had just arrived – there are usually those who want a word of encouragement, or first-hand comments about the country of their interest. It is a privilege to sit and chat informally and encourage them – and in this case with a half day's relaxation on Sentosa Island. We enjoyed the pleasant sandy beaches for swimming, then an evening's 'film'. In fact it was a Hollywood fairy tale projected onto multiple 'screens' of water fine-sprayed up from a pier. Part of the story included explosions and fire, with flames shooting up making most un-Singaporean black smoke!

So for the time being I completed the archive tasks as best as could be done. Warren drove me to the airport and in business class there, all one has to do is sit in an armchair while an official handles your check-in, passport and baggage! After that it's a shower, refreshments, newspapers and snoozing till the plane leaves, and I finally farewelled Singapore.

Or so I thought!

---

5   Said to be something like 30 percent per year over the last 10 years – but from a tiny base.

Three Weddings

We had first met LinhDan when our son **Andrew** invited us to a sponsored charity dinner in Ho Chi Minh City (formerly known as Saigon). At that point we were still working in Bangkok and he had only recently met her in Vietnam.

When Andrew announced his engagement to LinhDan, to be celebrated at her parents' home in The Hague, we had already retired to the UK. Though her entire family enjoyed French nationality, LinhDan's father based his architectural studio in The Hague. But LinhDan's actual home was in Paris, so the wedding was at the International Church in Paris. Les and Dorothy, Ruth's brother and sister-in-law joined us from Australia.

Actually we had four wedding functions on one day: registration at the Mayor's Office is compulsory in France, and there was a Vietnamese family ceremony as well as the formal service in the Paris International Church. Finally came the evening reception. We gathered on the top floor of the Louvre Department Store under a glass dome designed by Eiffel – whose famous Tower we also ascended.

Andrew's fluent Chinese (from an honours degree at Oxford) gives him plenty of opportunities to return to Asia on business, sometimes stopping-off in Ho Chi Minh to visit LinhDan's relations. Later on her parents moved back to Paris, but Andrew and LinhDan now live in Central London.

Andrew and LinhDan at the International Church in Paris.

Jill had gained an M.Phil degree in anthropology at Cambridge, having written up her thesis after her few months' service among the Burma-Karen refugees in western Thailand. She works for an American consultancy company with a large UK operation, where she met Jonathan Rose, a former officer in the Royal Navy. It soon became clear that an engagement was very definitely pending, and Jonathan took me to a delicious Thai meal in the London's Lancaster Hotel to make the traditional request for our daughter's hand!

In the process of collecting materials for the wedding, Jonathan and Jill both visited several other Asian places where either or both had been before. They were far overweight for the flight home – but they told the Thai Airways check-in lady that it was all for their wedding and she let it all through! Asia does not always see that 'rules are rules' in the same way as Westerners do.

Jill, having thought much about a location for the wedding, remembered our very long connection with Ashburnham Church in East Sussex. Before he passed away, John Bickersteth who had inherited the stately home and grounds, and developed the Ashburnham Christian Trust, had supported and prayed for us overseas for many years and had often invited us for visits and holidays in the beautiful grounds.

Thus the new Vicar of Ashburnham, Steven Talbot, led the celebration in the ancient church – adjacent to the former stately home. It was a sunny and breezy day, an ideal day in the English countryside and it was my privilege to preach. Jill and Jonathan were anxious to invite all their friends to a reception, original in style, but also to avoid any whiff of ostentation.

Tables were set up in a rented marquee a few miles from Ashburnham, in the grounds of a ruined abbey. The tables were not numbered but were identified by a place connected with Jill and/or Jonathan. Ours was 'Singapore' where Jill was born. Then the fruits of the Thailand visit began to appear. Thai glass bowls on each table contained floating tea lights. The 'place mats' were copied from assembled cuttings from the *Financial Times* newspaper, plus a crossword made up of places-names connected with the two of them.

Thai baskets served as the 'dishes' for the main course of fish and chips – freshly fried from a friend's mobile kitchen parked adjacently. Small Vietnamese lacquer boxes served the sweet: chocolate truffles made by Jonathan. Again Ruth's brother and sister-in-law came over from Melbourne to support us together with their son and daughter-in-law.

As I write Jill and Jonathan have presented us with Alex, Evie and Gabriel. They live at Hammersmith, where they are active in St Paul's Church.

Lynette, our younger daughter completed a degree in English at Oxford, and found a job with the Home Office, some of the time living in Brussels. Finally she was accepted for a senior post in the office of a new Government watchdog, 'Offcom' – which regulates telecommunications, broadcasting frequencies, and related media, almost all of which have been privatised over the last couple of decades.

Jill and Jonathan on their Wedding Day at Ashburnham.

Then she met Chris Newman, who she recalled from days at Dean Close School in Gloucester, and was reintroduced to him by a mutual friend. She took us to a delicious dinner to meet his parents who live in a delightful re-developed cottage in Bisley (not the famous rifle range, but the Gloucestershire village).

For their wedding they chose the beautiful, ancient church whose parish includes Bisley. Again, as with Jill's wedding, we enjoyed a sunny but breezy day for the service. The reception and evening meal were held in yet another former stately home. An original touch: the wedding 'cake' was made up out of various cheeses, which were then cut up to complete the evening meal.

As with the two previous weddings, our Australian relations came across to join us for the wedding, and a short walking

Lynette and Chris signing the Marriage Register.

holiday; thus we took them to taste some of the lovely hiking country and spectacular views near us in Croydon.

So now our three children have truly 'flown the nest'. Nevertheless all are in the Greater London area, so we enjoy seeing plenty of each other.

As I write we have five grandchildren!

Winding Down

It was mid-2010. With so much travel behind us and our three grown children just as mobile, it did not seem strange to consider a further trip.

I had received a further tentative invitation to work short-term in Singapore on the OMF archives, so our children suggested that Ruth should go to Australia at the same time to visit her friends and relations. In fact, they encouraged us with contributions towards the cost.

So with a little more trepidation we booked tickets. The fares would obviously be considerable, but almost as soon as we made bookings, a very large gift arrived, seemingly confirming the way ahead. I left just as Autumn was showing its early signs in the English country side, and arrived in Singapore in late August.

Landing in Singapore was as easy as usual, with hardly a pause between the trolleys placed ready at the plane door, and the stewarded taxi rank. There are no crowds and almost no waiting – the government does not allow airlines or officials at Changi Airport to generate Heathrow-

Ruth (second right) in Australia with six of her contemporaries – all of them now grandmothers.

style queues. One Westerner commented favourably on the efficiency and the Singaporean response was 'Welcome to the First World!'

At OMF, my initial job was to check what was in each archive box and to make a rough list of contents, while Dr Steve Wolf, another volunteer developed the necessary software. Unlike the

In the new OMF archive room in Singapore. Note the school magazine from Chefoo (pre World War II) and also the silver Chefoo achievement shield – both recently discovered among the archives.

more recent documents, the 1950s papers had been sorted and indexed, and placed in proper acid-free archive folders and boxes. There was one index-card per file, which meant that a researcher could not easily locate material on specific subject unless he knew the single word entered on its card. The new computerised index allows a 'keyword search' of *any* word in that file's full title.

Dr Warren Beattie, then in charge of research and in-house education, was a most helpful and supportive boss to have. He also interspersed the long hours and paper-wading with staff trips out to afternoon tea or ice cream bars!

Another task was to sort out recent missiological magazines and get them bound. There is a surprisingly large number of these, and the OMF Research Library subscribes to most of them.

The OMF's own magazine *The Billions* (formerly *China's Millions*) is produced in several countries and in differing versions. We had to find out what was missing, and try to obtain duplicates so that we could complete this research facility too, where our back-numbers dated from 1875.

As before, I received invitations from old friends. Many came originally from the Church of the Good Shepherd, where I had served my Curacy. Then there was the ever-gracious Archbishop John Chew and his Director of Missions and Dean, Kuan Kim Seng, as well as OMF friends with whom we had served a long time before.

I was invited to the inauguration of a new church located on three floors of a commercial building in Singapore's Financial District. It seems to attract as many families as any suburban congregation, and after the evening service many of them retire together to a nearby food court. I was invited to join a group and was kept busy because an Indian lady, who, new to the Christian faith, quizzed me at length!

William, my GP friend took me on week-end hikes along the Telok Blangah Heights, with its breathtaking views across Singapore and outwards to Sumatra. It was there that I realised my former army camp had been razed and is now entirely covered by a new jungle nature reserve.

An interesting local visit was to meet the student body at Singapore's Discipleship Training Centre for Asian missionary-training.

A delicious Asian lunch with John and Alice Wong who we had known since our young days together. John is active in overseas missions from a Singapore Parish and Alice serves in the Cathedral Office – except when grandmotherly duties call!

Another invitation came: Would I come and help with the OMF archives in Kuala Lumpur? I felt right to accept this invitation as it was only for about a month's work, and the travel cost, via Singapore, was covered from various sources.

I booked a seat on the day train to Seremban from Singapore (over 55s can upgrade to first class for free). The main hall of Singapore station is a magnificent piece of architecture with soaring art-deco columns and ceramic scenes of the peninsular. It brought back memories of Army days when I had never foreseen missionary service. Fortunately it and the murals are to be preserved as a heritage building now that the Singapore rail terminal has moved to Woodlands, close to the causeway to Malaysia.

Seminari Teologi Malaysia (STM) at Seremban enjoys a hill-top site. Its purpose is to train ordinands and laypeople for the original 'big four' – Anglican, Methodist, Presbyterian and Lutheran churches; both the teaching faculty and student body now include members of other churches plus several from overseas. Mr Sakti, the archivist graciously gave me some spares of theses and articles from the early history of OMF in Malaya in the 1950s and 60s, 'pure gold' for our archives in Singapore.

Singapore appears to have abolished the itinerating food hawkers with their tasty wares, but they still abound in Malaysia and I enjoyed a delicious breakfast at one before continuing the short stage on to Kuala Lumpur – always known simply as 'KL'.

The OMF Centre in KL is down a quiet street off the busy Ampang Road, and for a month I worked in shirt and shorts in an outbuilding. Though there were some 50 large unsorted boxes, the valuable archives seemed to be few, so I spent most of my time 'slimming' files, keeping only matter likely to be of future research interest. Lots of paper went for recycling! There were the usual invitations from the staff to eating markets, and from former acquaintances, but more important was to induct a local volunteer, a qualified librarian, into indexing the files on a computer – certainly God's gift for that task.

Archive Meeting at Kuala Lumpur: (Left to right) Miss Yap Hian Mong – OMF Director for Malaysia; Miss Moly Mathews – librarian, helping to register OMF archives; Dr Tan Jin Huat – lecturer at STM.

Just outside KL lies Malaysia Bible Seminary (MBS), having moved from a row of urban shophouses to a spacious former resort among rural rubber trees. The property includes a swimming pool, tennis courts and a sizeable sports field. Apart from a large cohort of full-time students, the Dean has started a Christian study series in KL for high-level businessmen who face special problems in their Christian life. It is a similar ministry to that in London's at St Helens, Bishopsgate, and STM does the same.

Back in the pioneer New Village days of the 1960s, we had longed for a good residential theological/Bible college to become available with evening course branches in the main cities. Now Malaysia is well endowed with both.

I had time to visit my old friend Robin in Ipoh, and was impressed that Malaysian Christians see it as their calling to remain in Malaysia as Christians, and not to simply emigrate as do many of comparable education. A fast, brand-new Korean electric train whisked me back to KL in just one hour 57 minutes – against the usual time of over three hours. It held about 90 mph for long stretches of the ride, in spite of the narrow gauge (one metre) of the track.

Back in Singapore the days passed quickly with archive-sorting, correspondence and visits to the bookbinders. We had to keep library copies of all theses written *by* OMF members or *about* matters related to the Fellowship.

One of the most remarkable features about this stay in Singapore was that almost daily there seemed to be someone to have a serious conversation with. Some I could help, some helped me.

I put this down to the loyal cohort of prayer partners across the world, including many at Emmanuel Church, at St Francis, St Mary Magdalene and others – including many overseas. I also used taxis quite a bit, and found that seated in the front most of the drivers were quite happy to tell me about themselves and what they really thought. They always warmed up when I used a few words of my rusty Hokkien Chinese, but of course standard Mandarin is now taking over from these Chinese 'dialects.' All were pleased to be Singaporeans but many expressed opinions that differed appreciably from the official releases!

I was often asked how long I had been in Singapore, and when I told them it was just a few weeks, but that I had been there before several times, actually going back to 1952, they usually asked me what changes I had seen. It would be better to ask, "Is there anything you have seen that has *not* changed!" At the end of the journey, driving into the OMF property, the drivers often noticed the English and Chinese sign 'Trust in God' and asked what we do. As I paid the fare I explained briefly. One driver replied 'I am a Buddhist but I value people who help others' – and handed me the fare back. One sows, another waters!

In happy anticipation of another visit to Thailand, I embarked on a low-cost airline for Bangkok. My main task was to help Dr Tan Boon-Itt

Working through the text with Dr Tan Boon-Itt (centre) and his wife Mily. Dr Tan's book is based on a thesis introducing Christians to an understanding of Thai religion.

with some English-language writing based upon his Nottingham thesis. We had known the family since our days in Bangkok and I had drafted a possible 'easy English' version to explain Thai Buddhism and thinking to foreign visitors, especially to Christians.

Then followed an occasion which was indeed a milestone – the first-ever ordination to be held in Christ Church; I had served there as an honorary minister when the Thai congregation had started. Now the ordinand, Revd Pairote, serves as their assistant minister. The English service is 150 years old, and well attended by Anglophones from all over the world. Thailand is part of the Diocese of Singapore and they have some nine mission centres in the kingdom, where they are planting Thai churches. All the missionaries are Singaporeans but they warmly seek and welcome help from committed Westerners. They are wonderful people with whom to have fellowship.

Ruth joined me from Melbourne where she had had family time with friends and relations, and now we journeyed to the OMF vacation facility on the rural seaside. We rode the train about four hours south of Bangkok and duly arrived at 'The Pines' where we could read, swim, laze and stroll with no pressure at all.

Our final ride back to London was *subject to variation* – as the airlines put it. Qantas' A-380 Airbuses were grounded after an engine problem and the net result for us was a departure time of 0425! Fortunately we had booked a very late check-out from the Christian Guest House. We followed the night as it moved westwards, so quite a bit of sleep was possible.

Home at last – and no more plans for overseas trips. Back in the UK, we were soon involved with family and church, and we had told many people that we did not envisage much more globe-trotting, if any.

Ruth and I look back to the many and varied opportunities to serve God and to edify the Church in so many ways and so many places. We recall, and thankfully concur with, the two carved stones in the original CIM building in London[1]. The stones read:

Jehovah Jireh (*The Lord will provide*, Genesis 22:14)
Ebenezer (*Hitherto the Lord has provided*, 1 Samuel 7:12)

But rather than dwelling on the past (as older people are in danger of doing) we also take St Paul's words: **forgetting what is behind and straining to what is ahead, we press on towards the goal to win the prize for which God has called us heavenwards in Christ Jesus.**[2]

After the last visit to Asia, we really thought that it was to be 'the last'.

But then another e-mail arrived. Mark Leighton, OMF Field Leader in Thailand, asked if I would spend a month or so in Bangkok in early 2012 – on archives!

---

1   They are still there, but the building is now a Christian student hostel.

2   Philippians 3:13-14.

Another Title from Armour Publishing

Fulfilling Your God-Given Destiny
– Your Personal Destiny and the Destiny of Your Nation

Israel is God's time clock for the end-times. She is God's anointed and the apple of God's eye. To touch Israel is to touch the Lord's anointed. This book will reveal more about the role of Israel in fulfilling your personal destiny and the destiny of nations.

This book also presents the seven key dimensions of Singapore's destiny. Rev Dr John S H Tay shows how her people can powerfully move in the fullness of her calling, join in partnership with the Lord's anointed people Israel, and unlock the destinies of the Asia-Pacific nations around her.

ISBN 13	:	978-981-4305-92-1
ISBN 10	:	981-4305-92-8
Paperback	:	215 by 150 mm
No. of pages	:	152

Other Titles from Armour Publishing

Rohtang Pass
– A True Story of Faith, Friendship and Fortitude in the Himalayas

In June 1979, two young Indian doctors with a mission first stepped into a forsaken hospital in a dusty Himalayan town.

When four junior Singaporean doctors embarked on an arduous journey to visit them more than thirty years later, they had no clue that the holiday would unfold into an incredible story of provoking life lessons and miraculous escapes from various rural dangers. While facing the wrath of a formidable snowstorm, testimonies of love, faith and courage were born in the valleys surrounding a merciless mountain pass.

Rohtang Pass is the gripping true story of doctors, teachers, children and heroes of the Indian Himalayas.

ISBN 13 : 978-981-4305-93-8
ISBN 10 : 981-4305-93-6
Paperback : 229 by 152 mm
No. of pages : 184

Beyond Words

This biography of Paul and Nathalie Means is well woven around the many letters which dramatically bring to life their unrelenting work to make *Kunci Pelajaran* (the keys to reading) a reality. Share their struggles and their triumphs. Read about how Paul on his deathbed was still planning their next mission to Malaysia, and how Nathalie fulfils her promise to him.

ISBN 13   : 978-981-4222-92-1
ISBN 10   :   981-4222-92-5
Paperback   : 229 by 152 mm
No. of pages : 376

The Story of the Sengoi Mission

Hidden in the pockets of the Malayan highland jungles are a people who have lived in the hills for generations, perhaps centuries, and maybe even millennia. In 1930, an American family decided to befriend and help these people, known only to the outside world as the Sengoi. Extracted from the notes and journals of Paul B Means, this is the offi cial account of the Sengoi Methodist mission.

ISBN 13   : 978-981-4305-26-6
ISBN 10   :   981-4305-26-X
Paperback   : 210 by 148 mm
No. of pages : 168

ARMOUR Publishing Pte Ltd
www.armourpublishing.com
Telephone: +65 6276 9976 • Facsimile: +65 6276 7564
Email: enquiries@armourpublishing.com

OUR Publishing is a leading publisher committed to publishing books with a purpose – through compelling, creative, and enduring Christian and Christ-centred media contents and services.